BETTE

A BIOGRAPHY OF BETTE DAVIS

Charles Higham

NEW ENGLISH LIBRARY

First published in Great Britain in 1981 by New English Library

Copyright © 1981 by Charles Higham
Picture research/editorial consultant: Romey Fullerton

First NEL Paperback Edition December 1982
Reprinted September 1983
Reprinted June 1984

NEL Books are published by
New English Library,
Mill Road, Dunton Green,
Sevenoaks, Kent.
Editorial office: 47 Bedford Square,
London WC1B 3DP

Typeset by The Yale Press Ltd, London, SE25.
Printed and bound in Great Britain by
Cox & Wyman Ltd, Reading.

British Library Cataloguing in Publication Data

Higham, Charles, *1931–*
    Bette Davis.
    1. Davis, Bette, 1908–
    2. Moving-picture actors and actresses—United
States—Biography
    I. Title
    791.43′028′0924   PN2287.D32

ISBN 0-450-05509-4

BETTE

A BIOGRAPHY OF BETTE DAVIS

ACKNOWLEDGEMENTS

Illustrations 6 and 13 are reproduced by
courtesy of Keystone Press; illustration 9
(top) by courtesy of Popperfoto;
illustration 16 (bottom) by courtesy of
Rex Features.
All other illustrations are reproduced by
courtesy of Warner Brothers.

Author's Note

THE ACCOUNT of Miss Davis's court battles is drawn from public access court records of Los Angeles, Portland, Maine, and London.

I owe a special debt of gratitude to Dr Robert Knutson of the Department of Special Collections, Doheny Library, University of Southern California, who gave me access to the collection of Warner Bros. materials, which include day-to-day records of Bette Davis's motion pictures, minutes of all her conversations, a large selection of her letters to Hal Wallis and Jack Warner, her telegrams and medical reports on her condition. The Warner files gave a very clear picture of her brilliant but troubled career at the studio in the 1930s and the 1940s.

I am grateful to Dr Robert Gottlieb, of the Library of the University of Boston, whose collection of Bette Davis memorabilia deposited for public access by Ms. Davis herself, is remarkable. It includes reviews of her stage performances, juvenilia, baby books, numerous notations by her mother and Uncle Paul and impressive unpublished manuscripts by both, covering very fully the star's childhood, family background, and upbringing. The Massachusetts Historical Society has proved most helpful in illuminating Miss Davis's ancestral origins.

Robert Mundy conducted a number of interviews for the book. Others I conducted myself, many of them before the book was planned. Peter Lev did a fine job of research.

1

The following people, some of them sadly no longer living, provided reminiscences that formed much of the texture of this biography. Among them were Eva Le Gallienne, Joan Blondell, Martha Graham, George Cukor, Marlene Dietrich, Frank McHugh, Wallace Ford, Miriam Hopkins, Louis Calhern, Brooks Atkinson, Blanche Yurka, Marion Gering, Sam Goldwyn, Rouben Mamoulian, Joan Bennett, Ray Jones, Carl Laemmle, Jr, Reginald Denny, John Bowles, Doris Lloyd, C. J. Wood, Darryl F. Zanuck, George Brent, Hal B. Wallis, Pandro S. Berman, John Cromwell, Henry Blanke, Jack L. Warner, Gracie Fields, Sir Gerald Gardiner, Mrs Justin Dart, Irving Rapper, Edward G. Robinson, Olivia de Havilland, Robert Buckner, Jeffrey Lynn, Henry Fonda, William Wyler, William Dieterle, Geraldine Fitzgerald, Adela Rogers St. Johns, David Lewis, Sally Sage, Barbara O'Neill, Casey Robinson, Anna Sten, Mary Astor, William Keighley, Paul Mantz, Raoul Walsh, Paul Henreid, Max Steiner, Jules and Doris Stein, Herman Shumlin, Lenore Coffee, Janet Gaynor, Vincent Sherman, Minna Wallis, Julius Epstein, Curtis Bernhardt, Catherine Turney, Norma Boleslavsky, King Vidor, Anne Baxter, Milton Krasner, Val Guest, Douglas Fairbanks, Jr, Robert Krasker, Stuart Heisler, Natalie Wood, Charles G. Clarke, Henry Koster, Daniel Taradash, Richard Brooks, Ernest Borgnine, Geraldine Page, Paul Beeson, Sir Alec Guinness, Antony Asquith, Dame Daphne du Maurier, Norman Corwin, Sandford Dody, Gig Young, Frank Capra, Robert Aldrich, Christina Crawford, Allen Miner, Edward Dmytryk, Joseph Cotten, Violla Rubber, Jill Bennett, Roy Baker, Sheila Hancock, Jimmy Sangster, Sir Michael Redgrave, Robert Wagner, Gerd Oswald, Liv Ullmann, Curtis Harrington, and George Edwards.

Prologue: 1963

THE ROAD winds upwards, through resilient clusters of Algerian ivy, magnolia trees, pink and purple flamboyants. Here is a French château, there a British witch's cottage, and there again a building that looks like a small Gothic tomb. The vegetation has a surrealist absurdity: Canadian pencil pines framing a doorway that suggests eighteenth-century Brazil; palms, cut down to stumps and stuck in actual Italian renaissance pots. In one of these houses, recently, I found the parchment text of a Gregorian chant used as a lampshade.

We arrive at our destination. Don Prince, crew-cut movie publicity man, who once splashed naked in a fountain with Helen Morgan, and whose favourite phrase summarising Hollywood is 'They eat their young,' points out the house. Beyond a stern, black-painted iron gate, two jockeys, ornamental hitching posts made of plaster, all too realistically stand servile on the lawn, hands outstretched for non-existent reins. We might be in the south, in Margaret Mitchell territory – but the cottage itself is New England, primly cosy and formalised, with self-assured red bricks.

A woman runs out, full-breasted and wide-hipped in shirt and slacks, looking like a thousand midnights, arms tense at the sides, hair tossed about in dyed red bangs. Of course, it couldn't be anyone else. The voice, commanding, snappy, with a ferocious emphasis on final consonants, seems, like so many voices, far younger than

3

its owner's face. The energy is all in the movements and gestures.

It is nice that, unlike most stars, she doesn't wait at the top of a regal staircase, to descend only when the guest has been kept waiting long enough. It is as though she is herself a quarter of a century ago in *The Great Lie,* running out to greet George Brent as he flies back after some South American mission to the bride he had left behind.

She vigorously pumps my hand; her grip is as tight as a boxer's. 'Come indoors, for God's sake!' she snaps, cheerfully commanding rather than asking, grinning and grabbing my arm. She looks me up and down. I suddenly realise something about her I seldom saw after her earliest pictures on the screen: she is very feminine and very sexual; she has the expert anthropometric gaze of a Mae West, Bette Davis is No Angel nor am I. Clearly, we're going to get along.

As we approach the front door, she says, 'You know, this is the first time I've had an Australian writer in my house!' British to my bootheels, I've never thought my sixteen years in Australia qualified me as an Australian, but never mind: the description gives me novelty value in her eyes, and provides her with an opening line in which she can surprise herself. 'An Australian novel – isn't this a strange coincidence? – arrived in the mail less than an hour ago. *Naked Under Capricorn,* by Olaf Ruhen. Thank *God* I don't have to answer the title description. There's nobody *left* who would be able to *stand* the sight of me in that condition. Instead, they want me to play a *missionary*. That's more like it. I'll be dressed from head to toe in grey felt. No, that can't be right. In all that heat, surrounded by flies?' She is now in the grip of a fantasy. '*What do they wear in Australia to keep off the flies?*' 'A hat with corks dangling from it,' I reply. 'Oh!' she exclaims. 'How wonderful! You mean, flies can't stand corks?'

4

I assure her they cannot. I also inform her from my encyclopaedic knowledge of such subjects that it is the slow but certain movement of the cork that alarms even the boldest flies. Then I make a mistake. I add, 'And talking of flies, George Kaufman once told Marlene Dietrich to do up hers.' Miss Davis is not amused.

'Can you see me as a missionary in a cork-lined hat?' she asks, not waiting for an answer, assuming it is in the affirmative. She has created for herself, out of a dull Bel Air afternoon, a little drama: the lawn has become a soundstage and on it she weaves, like a lonely child in a playroom, a fantasy of Australia: a young reporter, a book unexpectedly delivered to her door, a question addressed to herself for a likely audience of two.

Now I understand the secret of her screen personality. At best, she could take the most banal scripts, limp lines, flaccid leading men, and by the sheer force of talent, imagination and wit and will she assumed the correct manners and at the same time, triumphantly, remained herself.

And who is that self? Looking for clues, I enter the house. What I had taken to be a front door turns out instead to be a back door. We walk in through the kitchen. It is spanking clean: neat and organised as a kitchen in a department store, with everything, from huge blue dishes to brass cooking implements to glass jars of biscuits set out so conscientiously that they might be for sale. A strange couple materialises. The woman is the more striking of the pair. She is thin, pale, excessively nervous, dressed in a sad range of greys, whose eyes seem incorrectly aligned, the portions of her face oddly ill-matched, but who at one time may have been almost pretty. She is a figure in a jigsaw puzzle that isn't quite complete. The man is dressed almost like a servant, with black coat and striped trousers with pegged bottoms over black patent-leather shoes. Both husband and wife (for that, transparently, they are) look conscientiously miser-

5

able. Their smiles are fifth carbon copies of real smiles.

Now we are in the living-room. It exudes an atmosphere of Hollywood-New England snugness. It looks as though it was put together by a set designer for one of Bette Davis's pictures. A round mahogany table, polished to a fault, boasts a dumb waiter that, demanding to be spun, offers salt, pepper, nutmeg, and a half-dozen other spices and condiments. On a wall, a picture of the star in pastels dressed in somebody's idea of an ante-bellum lace gown as Jezebel is hanging in a gilt frame. Most stars order wooden books to match the wallpaper. Hers are real and have been read. They are for the most part novels of thirties vintage. The covers are designed to look like parchment, with heavy red and black classical lettering and pictures of the hero and heroine framed against Gothic sunsets. There are stained page tops, rare in our austere age, heavy-stitched bindings that would defy a wrestler to tear them apart, thick luxurious pages, reliable lending library names like Bromfield, Ferber, Marquand, Frances Parkinson Keyes. And, nearby, prints of hunting or fishing scenes, family pictures in silver frames, and a photograph of a girl with distracted, haunted eyes: probably the star's tragically backward adopted daughter.

I notice in one frame a handsome, clean-cut all-American boy with hair as bleached as a gull's wing: surely her son, Michael. A heavy-breasted, rather sombre girl – her daughter, Barbara. Only the latest of her four husbands is on display: the actor Gary Merrill, whose short-lived career reached its brief zenith in *All About Eve*. Later on, he will run a lighthouse. He looks craggy, rugged, strong, thick black hairs sprouting from his chest through an open lumber shirt.

Without asking us what we want, the star fixes us giant Scotches with small chasers and, with a bold characteristic gesture, strong as a lumberjack's, she strikes a large wooden match under the table. Her legs in slacks are spread wide. She lights a cigarette, sucking in her cheeks, but not inhaling. Now I know how, after a zillion cigarettes in a lifetime, she hasn't so much as a smoker's cough. I decide she is an even better actress off screen than on. She looks at me very hard, in the eyes, challenging me not to like her. No other actress could manage to seem as threatening and welcoming at the same time. It is an adroit and disturbing contradiction. She snaps, sharply, 'Shoot!' Yet I – not she – is facing this particular firing squad.

I ask how she feels about being alive today. I expect her to say, I even script the lines in my head, 'What a *mess!* The world today is a *dump!* God! How I hate the way things turned out! This country's *hell!* If only the Roosevelts were alive to tell us what to do! Maybe we should all go out and populate Patagonia.' Instead, she stubs out her third cigarette and astonishes me by saying, 'Life's too easy now. America's a *paradise* for young people! An *ice cream world!* Boys and girls "do it" to each other when they feel like it, they have the *pill!* Food is instant and frozen so what does a man need with a *wife?*'

I move her away from the contemporary scene to a discussion of her mother, known to all Show Biz as Ruthie. Bette lights up yet another cigarette, holding it between her thumb and forefinger and swigging away at another almost neat Scotch; clearly, the cigarette and the liquor are props in both senses.

'Ruthie!' Unexpectedly, she rises, and paces about the room, like the heroine of *The Letter* talking about a murder. 'Oh my *God!* How I miss her! I owe *everything* to her. People call her the typical show business mother. But she *wasn't.* She overprotected me and coddled me rather than pushing me out in the spotlight. It was *I* and *I alone* who decided to be a star. *She,* it is true, wanted to be an actress. But *she* never would have made it. *I* had to be the monster for both of us. I knew from the beginning

I was good and I also knew how to act the poor, woebegone little *wren*. Nobody knew what I was up to. They all thought, "She's impossible. She has two left feet and she wouldn't say 'boo' to a goose." How wrong they were! I would have said "boo" to a *bison!*'

I don't have the courage to mention that she is being excessively kind to Ruthie: a show-biz tyrannosaurus who ate her young, who drained Bette of her money, and lived in a house many times larger than Bette's own. While Bette lived on the wrong side of the tracks on Franklin Avenue, in Hollywood, her mother luxuriated in Beverly Hills. Bette continues: 'Why don't you ask me about Father?' A vision floats into my mind like a pale bubble: a white, bulbous forehead, ruminative blue eyes, prim and proper spectacles and a mouth like a scar. A patent lawyer to the soles of his tight Boston shoes, he was a cold fish by any hook. But once again, Bette is loyal: 'He walked out on us when I was nine. All I could think of saying was, "Now we can go on picnics again and have a baby sister." I ate my words later on and missed him like *hell*. He was a *brain*. He was *tremendously* proud of my career even though he thought I was *mad* to undertake it. He came backstage one night when I was on Broadway. I *ached* for his words of praise. But he was far too reticent to do anything except express admiration for everybody in the cast except me. I wanted to shake him and say, "I was good, too!" But I loved him dearly, just the same, and his death was a terrible shock to me.' As she says these words, she looks up at herself in the *Jezebel* portrait, and I recall that Harlow Morell Davis died when she was in the middle of making that picture.

I take a plunge. What about her husbands? She screams. 'My *God!* You reporters nowadays want to know *everything*, don't you? Aren't you going to ask me about my pickshahs?' (Oddly, she rhymes the word with rickshaws.) 'After all, Mr What's-Your-Name, I made a

8

hundred of them, didn't I?' I sit silent, not knowing what to say, even if I had the chance. She picks up her Scotch and throws it down her commodious hatch, visibly furious that I have turned in desperation to 7-Up. Like all people who enjoy a drink in the middle of the afternoon, she regards those who don't the way Jesuits regard pagans. But she's still not going to give up her performance, even if it kills both of us. She paces around the room, hands flapping like a seal's flippers, smoke rising in small mushroom clouds over her head, all temperament and talent and teeth. And fire and music. 'My *husbands*!' She pronounces the word the way most people pronounce Adolf Hitler. 'My first, as I'm sure you know, was called *Ham*! Ham Nelson! He suited the Ham but not the Nelson! No hero, he! I named the Oscar after him. He had a middle initial O, like David Selznick. He had a fat, epicene bottom. It made *mine* look like Charles Atlas's! Did I say *"had"*?' She explodes into a hard burst of laughter. 'I should have said, *"has"*! I saw him the other day. And first thing up, I looked at his fanny. It hadn't improved. So when I got hold of that statuette when I won it for *Dangerous,* I said to myself, as I turned it around, "Oh, *God,* its fanny's a dead ringer for Ham's!" Now I couldn't call the greatest acting award in the world a *Ham,* could I? So it *had* to be an Oscar!'

I think about Ham Nelson for a minute. A charming parasite, and blackmailer who conducted a dance band at the Hollywood Roosevelt, getting home at four A.M. every morning when Bette had to get up at six to go to Warner's. When she talks of him, all those sepia movie magazines of the thirties in which they were seen like two figures in a Valentine now seem more sadly inaccurate than ever. But she *did,* she said, love her second husband, Arthur Farnsworth, who oddly combined the jobs of flyer and night manager at an inn where she stayed. She said, 'When his mother buried him, the blasting kept me awake all night. The family crypt was

9

sealed up in a mountainside. How I longed to blast him out again! He should be waiting for me in Forest Lawn. But now I'll never have the courage to bring him west again.' I had a sudden vision of Bette, tossing and turning in a New England house like herself in *Beyond the Forest*, listening to the blasting of the power drills late at night that made way for her husband's grave.

Even Farnsworth, who she felt she would have stayed with forever if he had lived, doesn't provoke in Bette more than lukewarm memories. One sees her tragedy: she had to fight so hard in a world of men, she was afraid to seem feminine or sensitive and finally her natural vulnerability was locked in a mask of iron.

As for her third husband, William Grant Sherry, '*He* saw himself as a painter. *I* was supposed to be the great patron of the arts. Actually, I liked the way he looked on the beach in a pair of shorts. If you think you see a fool standing before you, well,' – this with a new stroke of a match under the table – 'I've got news for you. You do. But I'm grateful for one thing. Mr William Grant Sherry gave me a daughter.' She doesn't, or won't, say a word about Gary Merrill; he did help her adopt a son.

I turn to Miss Davis's movies as a *Titanic* passenger might grab at a raft. *Of Human Bondage*? 'The studio – Warner's – *fought* my doing that picture. But I loved Somerset Maugham's book, and I begged them to let me go to RKO. They finally agreed: I knew they were thinking, all right let her sink herself, we're tired of her anyway, nobody will believe in her as a Cockney waitress. Well, they *did* believe me. I put all my hatred of me into that part: I decided there could be no middle way, no glamour, Mildred had to be a bitch. And *God*, what a bitch! I was *disgustingly* good. I looked, as you "British" would say, a *fright*. My *hair!* I wouldn't let them take me within a hundred *miles* of a beauty parlour. Mildred was poor, she was maybe making two bucks a week, she was on her feet all day, she was dog tired at night, she was serving food, cheap English food, the worst on earth, and dragging filthy, dirty dishes, and she hated people as a result. Oh, if Mildred was going to have a man in her life he had better be exciting, strong, he had better make her feel wanted. And then she meets this weak sister, this *writer*, for God's sake!' She stops a minute, realising she is talking to one, and then continues. As she talks, one sees her tongue lashing Ham Nelson along with Leslie Howard, her co-star in *Of Human Bondage*: the husband at home, the actor on the set. No Loretta Young or Greer Garson here, saintly among rose and lily, gazing piously towards heaven. She is gloriously unfooled by self-regard: she has spent her life watching herself as others might watch Medusa in a mirror. She glories in her monstrosity.

'You've seen *Of Human Bondage*, of course?' Bette snaps. I reluctantly confess I have not. She lets out a cry. 'Ohhhh! I'll take care of that!' She rushes to a closet, drags out a print of the picture, and stands it up against my chair. 'Call me when you've seen it. And in the meantime, let's talk about something else!'

She rushes on to an entirely different picture, *Old Acquaintance*. She astonishes me by saying that the part of the novelist she played in that picture was closer to herself than anybody she had acted. The novelist was a picture of brisk, healthy, outgoing good cheer with a balanced shrewd mind and a cool absence of temperament. In this respect, at least, Bette is deceiving herself; the woman I am looking at is far more like the nervous temperamental popular writer played by Miriam Hopkins in the same picture. 'John Van Druten wrote *Old Acquaintance* with someone like me in mind,' Miss Davis says. I'm not courageous enough to tell her that she was the last choice for the part.

Instead, I cravenly change the subject and move over to *The Letter*, in which she played a Singapore memsahib who murdered her lover apparently under the influence of the moon. I ask her about the opening sequence, in which she shoots and shoots her victim outside the plantation house at night. 'The director, William Wyler, made me do that scene a hundred and six times. I kept running out of ammunition and that poor man who played my victim had to have a constant supply of white tuxedos. They were endlessly rushing up and brushing off his poor dirty face. And then the producer, Hal Wallis, printed the first take! To keep Willie happy, he told him it was take one hundred and three.'

I ask her how it felt to play a murderess. She looks at me straight in the eye, and I feel as though I've just stepped in the ring with Muhammed Ali. 'I *know* why you ask me that question. I'll say this – actresses hate playing murderesses more than anything. Even when Loretta Young hit someone over his head with a blunt instrument to save herself from rape in a picture, she cried and *cried*. But I've *never* worried about my image being dented. There are quite a few people I'd like to kill, right now. I'll kill *you,* for instance, if you give the name of a man who dropped his *Communist Party card* on my living room floor, directed several of my pictures, named everybody in the Unfriendly Ten and fled to Mexico to escape arrest!'

And what about *The Little Foxes*, in which Bette was exceptionally fine as Lillian Hellman's vicious southern woman, Regina Giddens? 'I *hated* every minute of that picture. Willie Wyler kept saying, "Play Regina charming. Let her kill with a smile. Remember Tallulah." Well, I didn't want to remember Tallulah. Bankhead was far greater than I in the part – I made the horrible mistake of seeing her on the stage – and I couldn't easily play a woman as charming who tells her own husband she wants him to die – and die soon. *Who lets him die . . . !*'

For a moment, the brisk little star in slacks fades away. The cigarette smoke dissolves, and I am looking at an overstuffed living room with potted palms and enormous, threatening furniture. A woman is sitting in the foreground, a spotted veil tied over her face like a caul, a medicine bottle standing uselessly nearby, while her husband crawls like a dying animal up the stairs . . .

'Are you listening to me?' Miss Davis's voice snaps. I reply, abruptly, that I don't have an alternative, and she slaps her thigh and bellows with laughter. She is pure Regina Giddens at this moment. 'I am talking, in case you're lying, about *All About Eve*. That picture saved my life. Professionally and personally. When I made it, I had been hit by a truck – the same truck that hit Margo Channing, that great goddamn ham I played. Oh, I don't mean a *real* truck. I mean, I had been hit by the knowledge, which is heavier than a truck for most women, that I was *forty*. And I knew Margo felt *every one of those years* hitting her and I felt down here in my gut every word she said when she told her lover, "I hate men." She hated them for staying attractive forever. From the day I was forty, I *screamed* every time I saw a mirror. It wasn't as though I was Hepburn. She could look great at a *hundred*. Sometimes I see my face in a shop window and I want to *die*.'

I feel like saying, if you looked at other people's faces instead, it might help, but again I turn coward. And I can't bring myself to lie that she looks terrific. She doesn't. But she is still more interesting to look at than just about anything outside of the Grand Canyon. She is a magnificent ruin, she is greatness in decline, but she is still undeniably great.

'. . . And then,' – a puff of her umpteenth cigarette and another Scotch down the hatch – 'I did *Another Man's Poison*. Right after *All About Eve*! I must have been out of my mind . . . a murderess in riding breeches?'

It is time to go. We have talked all afternoon. She signs her book of memoirs with a flourish, in a large, round, bold hand, surprisingly in bright green ink. She writes, 'I so enjoyed my interview with you.' How odd she should put it that way, as though she had conducted the interview herself.

Of course, I realise, she has. As I rise to leave, I can see she isn't only that bold, tough, fierce dame she likes to seem to be. I look into the pale blue eyes, alive with intelligence, and see another self, full of insecurity, vulnerability, bad nerves. She has given the same interview for over thirty years. The interview all stars cook up in different ways to pacify the press, to keep their secrets. I hold a thought of her as we drive back to the hotel. The nervous retiring girl who forced herself to be a demon to make it in show business; the thrifty New Englander who damaged herself financially to help a mentally sick sister and a greedy devouring mother. She wants to be a monster, I tell myself, so people will fear her; she knows what it takes to claw the way to the top. But scrape away the grease paint and there is a lonely unfulfilled woman. Suddenly I feel a dark wave of sadness.

Yet sadness isn't called for. It scarcely needs saying that only Katharine Hepburn and Garbo among the great screen actresses have matched Bette Davis's range and achievement. The essence of Davis's genius is not merely that she has given us an unforgettable personality, expressed in a striking array of theatrical mannerisms that identify her the moment her name is mentioned. Underneath the battery of technique, of sheer adroitness, there is the extraordinary truthfulness, the uncompromising realism. Whereas most stars have remained static, relying on a fixed, immutable personality that fades with the passing of fashion, she has survived because she has been able to adapt herself to successive decades, to 'become' modern again as each new decade is born. Today, in 1981, she is as imposing as ever. In the rugged conditions of television, with no time for rehearsal, for preparation, even for several takes, she is back in the kind of pressure-cooker atmosphere she knew in the early days of talkies. And the pressure suits her, supremely practised as she is; she is among the few names the television chiefs automatically think of, when they need a star in her age group to appear in a special.

She has, of course, never been in the conventional sense beautiful, but her face is more interesting than that: mysterious, intriguing, capable of an extraordinary expressiveness. She has the star's knack of imposing herself on every part, making it her own, and yet discovering unexpected depths in it, 'becoming' it so that she is able to convert herself into someone unlike her with striking intensity. She has often said in interviews that her hatred of the human being called 'Bette Davis', her unease with her own abrasive, strong and challenging personality, has made her want to lose herself in others by acting parts to the full; yet her own ego could not have managed these hiding places in imagined personalities unless it were itself possessed of great power. She has always had to impose herself in order to escape from herself. She has acquired power over producers and directors in order to bend the picture industry to her will. Only great popular acceptance could have made the exercise of that will possible. In the years when her public acceptance faded during the 1950s and 1960s, she was drastically frustrated in her aims.

Her early screen self was slender, vulnerable, eager and trembling with nervous excitement. Despite her lack of conventional looks, the face even at the beginning was mesmerising. Young people today who were born long after her zenith can identify with her when they see her movies. She has a character of great individuality, a kind of fresh anticipatory energy and sweetness. There is a feeling of courage about her. As though she would dare anything; her fear of so much of life was consumed in the audacity of her screen presence.

15

She was at her best under strong directors who controlled her and sought out the best in her. The great William Wyler, who was in love with her, managed to use her fierceness, her nervous mannerisms, with great creativity. The results were seen in her finest performances. As the frustrated Regina Giddens in *The Little Foxes* she suggested in every taut strained gesture the anger of a heartless, ambitious woman living in a world run by men. In *The Letter*, as a murderess, Leslie Crosbie, she was no less striking: in an early scene, she lies about the circumstances of her lover's death, with simulated tears, a damp handkerchief twisted in her palm, her words tumbling out in a stream of carefully rehearsed sentences; when she finally tells the truth, that she has killed the man deliberately, she speaks with a more mechanical, repressed emotional severity, making us see how she has willed both falsehood and truth in her life. And in *Jezebel* she rises above a rambling novelettish script to fashion a real character out of the selfish southern belle, Julie Marsden. Spoilt, defiant, petulant and destructive, Julie is a fully-rounded creation.

Only one other director brought Davis to this level: the pedantic Joseph L. Mankiewicz, in *All About Eve*. She has, of course, become more famous for this movie than any other, and it is a sadness that the Academy Award vote was split between her and Anne Baxter, depriving her of an Oscar for what was perhaps her best performance. As Margo Channing, the theatrical star in the Bankhead mould, a full range of her talent can be seen and hugely enjoyed: it is a dream of a part for a star. Margo, unhappy, vulnerable, absurdly generous, extravagant in all her feelings, insecure and afraid of the future yet capable of bold, transcendent bitchery, is a role 'made' for Davis, and she brings its gorgeously to life.

Often, Davis dominated pictures completely. Having

conquered Hollywood, she tended to select weak directors, sometimes effectively controlling them, sometimes
fatally. Her tendency towards exaggerated make-up
rivalled that of Kabuki actors, so that, aided by her
friend, the make-up artist Perc Westmore, who enabled
her to be any age she chose, she sometimes allowed
exaggeration: the bushy-eyebrowed face of the spinster
aunt in the early scenes of *Now, Voyager,* the harridan
whom Fanny Skeffington becomes in *Mr Skeffington,*
the carnival mask countenance of Baby Jane seem
altogether too extreme. She often plunged into self-
parody, outdoing parodists whom she despised. Yet she
could be capable of restraint, control, subtle make-up, as
in the neglected *Winter Meeting,* in which she convincingly, touchingly played a worn, virginal New York
poet, and in *Dark Victory,* in which she triumphed over
soap operatics in a sensitive, subdued performance as an
heiress going blind.

The gestures, the famous hip-swinging stride, cigarette
puffs, widening of the eyes at moments of stress or
humour, turning on a heel, the hand brushing back a
wing of hair, the nervous clenching and loosening of the
fingers, the Broadway British voice with its heavy emphasis on final consonants, all these are part of popular
culture, almost of racial memory. But too often her
quieter talents have been overlooked. Everyone remembers 'What a dumpppp!' and 'Fasten your seatbelts, it's
going to be a bumpppy night!' But one would do better
perhaps to recall the moment in *Dark Victory* when the
heiress finds the X-rays that tell her she has only a short
time to live; Miss Moffat's examination scene in *The
Corn Is Green* or her farewell to the miner-writer
Morgan Evans in the same picture when her face is
blurred with tears at the window. One can't overlook her
crippled wife in *Phone Call from a Stranger,* hoisting
herself up in a perfect simulation of a paraplegic, to
express her love of her humdrum husband who has

devoted himself to her, following a swimming accident. Or her unhappy Brooklyn housewife, plump, in shapeless summer dresses, winding up her hair in a long pigtail in *The Catered Affair*. The weight of the gesture, the heavy movement of the arms, the smudged reflection in a mirror are proofs of a great actress at the peak of her powers.

For years I've thought of writing this book. A biographer tends to become his subject while in the grip of the work. When I wrote *Charles Laughton,* I grew introspective, depressive, and even acquired a tinge of Yorkshire accent. When I wrote *Kate,* about Katharine Hepburn, I lost the weight I had put on while writing *Laughton,* became brisk and bossy, and started taking long walks along the Hollywood reservoir. When I wrote the life story of Ava Gardner, I . . . well, the less said the better. When I write about Bette Davis, will I start to chain-smoke without inhaling, will I become extreme and driven?

No wonder I took fifteen years to make up my mind.

One

HERS WERE stark and stony New England origins. In her film *Now, Voyager,* she takes out a picture of aunts and uncles, all of whom face the camera as though they are facing a firing squad. It is almost an autobiographical moment. Respect and honour were words used more often by the Davises than affection and love. The Davis family line ran like a fine-meshed chain right back to the sturdy anchor of Welsh Puritan settlers in Massachusetts. Wintry Davis faces and bony figures, complacent with self-denial, devoted to good works, the building of churches and wooden villages, gaze back at us from early paintings of the time. They founded Massachusetts on good, New World bedrock. They sailed clippers up and down the coast looking for whale as far as Bangor and Nova Scotia. They founded their dynasty with the same earnestness they might use to plant turnips.

On one side of the family were the Keyeses. English, they sailed from Britain to Watertown in 1634. Bette's uncle Reverend Paul G. Favor discussed her ancestry in an unpublished family memoir. Levi Keyes, he tells us, was Bette's great-great grandfather. Levi was the father of Harriet Keyes Thompson, who raised Bette's grandmother, Harriet Eugenia Thompson Favor, Harriet's own mother having died when Eugenia was only one summer old. In 1878, Harriet Eugenia Thompson married William A. Favor, of French Huguenot descent,

19

whose second child was Bette's mother, Ruth.

The Keyeses, Paul Favor tells us, were driven by a motor that propelled them, an engine of ruthless ambition. Favor describes Bette in describing her mother, grandmother and great-grandmother:

> This elemental driving force of the Keyes [women-folk] was a double power, the power of vision to see what they would accomplish, and the power to release an uncommon degree of energy which recognised no obstacle strong enough to deter them from achieving their ends.

Bette's grandmother, Eugenia, was the most formidable of all powers. She ran the entire family as though they were first-year pupils in a Sunday school. Her husband was admitted to her bed only to perform the act of procreation. Having endured this obscene penetration, excused only by the sanction of the Christian Church, she worked out her disgust in her control of her offspring. She was barely capable of admiration: pleasure in anything was quite beyond her grasp. Paul Favor wrote: 'She was not tyrannical or violent but she was as persistent as a flowing river and as irresistible. To escape from that river was as impossible as for logs to swim upstream.'

She launched her three children, Ruthie, Mildred and Paul, into life as a first lady might launch three battleships. 'She sought,' Paul writes, 'by precept and example to inculcate lessons of industry, studiousness, morality and religion.' The day was worked out with the aid of a large, ruled, black book in which everything performed was predicted and willed at the exact hours appointed.

At mealtimes, a gong rang and the children – and later the grandchildren – had to appear that instant or they were forbidden their food. They were not to speak in the presence of adults, even to indicate a stomach ache or headache. Music lessons were conducted with metronomic precision. The smaller children had a half-hour practice, fixed to the second; the larger boys and girls exactly one hour and a half. Piano and voice would be interrupted in the middle of a bar when the grandfather clock struck the appointed hour.

It is scarcely surprising that the children called grandmother, Madam. Madam Harriet Favor or Grandmother Favor were the terms used, not of endearment exactly, but of military recognition. Favor says, 'She had decided the kind of family she would have. And have it she did.'

It is significant that Grandfather Favor barely emerged on the scene. A mere stud, he materialised and hastily vanished, mostly to his club, while women dominated the family.

Bette's mother, Ruth, known to everybody as Ruthie, was as fierce and driving as Madam Harriet. She was, Paul Favor tells us, no intellectual at school. But she was Senior Commanding Officer of the Girls' Battalion. 'Short, broad-shouldered, like her father and her paternal grandparents, attractive in feature, magnetic and executive, Ruthie was the very soul of efficiency and leadership.' She clawed her way to the position of editor of Lowell High's *Monthly Magazine*. She wrote a score of tales for the magazine, starred in plays, upstaging everyone, painted and sketched with expertise and created every poster that hung on the school's green-painted walls. Ruthie was an 'artist': Paul Favor reminds us that she painted cups, saucers, bowls and pitchers with great industry and not a little skill. Ruthie's great gifts for decoration, ambitious but tasteful, flourished when Bette became famous. Her 'physical strength and perpetual motion' were felt in Bette's houses – she chose the antiques, selected and hung the wallpaper, ripped out rooms and remodelled them from top to bottom. She

21

was Madam Favor's daughter to the marrow of her bones.

Ruthie was the classic tomboy. She liked to be called 'Fred'. She wore her brother's trousers and work shirts. She dreamed of being an actor. She joined the Chautauqua classes run by Sadie Porter, daughter of the Baptist pastor of Lowell, Massachusetts. She learned acting, callisthenics, dancing and elocution. She emoted in plays in the family attic, with herself as the heroes, and wilting local girls as the heroines. When she turned villain – as the Wolf in *Red Riding Hood* – she terrified Miss Antoinette Birch into a fainting fit. As Tamerlane, in General Lew Wallace's *The Prince of India,* she excited the audience at the Chautauqua Auditorium in Ocean Park. Favor tells us that 'through her the great audience was transported to distant Persia . . . and brought face to face with one of history's thrilling moments. Her performance was followed by a storm of applause seldom equalled in Ocean Park's Chautauqua Assembly Hall.'

But these were childish exhibitions in the eyes of the stern Baptist Madam Favor and her stiff-necked brood. Madam Favor decided that the sooner this young lady was married, the better. The stage represented moral evil; the poison of grease paint, the lure of dangerous men.

Madam's approach to life had a melodramatic exaggeration – like the melodramas she despised.

After considerable research, examining pedigrees and photographs, and doing everything except applying a tape measure and a pair of callipers, Madam Favor finally settled on an appropriate husband for her far from willing daughter. His name was Harlow Morell Davis. He was, at the time he passed muster, approximately twenty-two years old. He was skinny, with a high, bulbous forehead, glasses, and a humourless cold efficient look. He was bedrock Boston down to the soles

22

of his black patent-leather shoes. He was a ruthless chauvinist who was brought up to believe that women were an inferior breed fit only to cook, sew and mother children. His brother, in an imitative spirit, dated Ruthie's sister Mildred – and also arranged a match.

Inevitably, Harlow and Ruthie were married after a regulation courtship. The wedding was solemn and cheerless. It took place at the family home in Lowell one month to the day after Harlow graduated in law from Bates College and secured a position with a shoe company where he remained a patent lawyer for the rest of his life. It may well have been said that nobody would have dared steal the idea of a shoe, male's, female's or infant's, from any shoe company that would engage Harlow Morell Davis as an employee.

The couple was not encouraged to live elsewhere. They were to make their home in the sombre, three-storeyed clapboard house – with its frowning eaves and blind windows that stared coldly out at the world on a maple-shaded street. After the small and formal wedding party, with only relatives admitted, a static array of Davises and Favors and nothing as inferior as a mere friend, the couple went on a honeymoon. No doubt Harlow Morell devoted himself to his husbandly duties with the same concentration he attacked the matter of a shoe patent. 'Ruthie was miserable, but she was sufficiently puritanical to be pleased by her state of mind. It must have been an unpleasant experience for both of them.

Its aftermath was sordid and depressing. A month later, Ruthie missed a period. Harlow Morell lashed out viciously at her, blaming her for this catastrophe to his career. This monster asked his young bride whether the child could be given away. She burst into tears, too appalled by his question to bring herself to answer it.

It is easy to understand Bette Davis's character when one sees that she was born of a father who hadn't wanted her conception. Knowing that she was born against obstacles, she regarded the rest of her life as an obstacle course. If she wasn't confronted by major problems, life seemed unnatural and she invented obstacles for herself. Peace and quiet, love and wanting – the consolations of most people's lives when confronted with the prospects of physical decline and death – held no appeasement to her spirit. She knew nature hadn't intended her to exist. Thus, she must make an overwhelming mark on the world: indeed, become one of the most famous people in it. Her whole life was a thrust towards glory – and heaven help anybody who stood in her way. It wasn't that she was cruel or crushing. She simply was fighting the battle against oblivion and infinity of darkness that she had been fighting from the moment her father reluctantly penetrated her mother's body.

It is typical of Bette's desire to seem to be tremendously dramatic and important even at the beginning that she has spent her lifetime believing she was born in a violent flash of lightning and clap of thunder. Actually, she was born Ruth Elizabeth Davis (on April 5, 1908) in a low whine of breeze and a sprinkling of rain.

Her first awarenesses were of the imposing house, with its fixed, unalterable, heavy collection of ornaments and furnishings, swept and dusted over decades until the very wood seemed to groan. She learned to dread the brisk, precise footstep of her father coming home, the cold slam of the door and the thin steely voice that needled her mother and humiliated her. She grew to feel an overwhelming love of her mother, who was a maverick in the rigid family: Ruthie was theatre-mad, gushing, fond of pretty dresses and fancy hair-dos, femininely soft and sweet, subject to fits of tears and outbursts of helpless rage. Just how much a baby comprehends the world beyond the urgent need for milk, urination, defaecation and love is not clear. But infant psychologists have taught us that conflicts of personality and

24

temper between parents can shatter a child's sense of security – make it self-sufficient and doubtful even from the first.

Lowell was not a beautiful town to grow up in. It was a mill town: Theodore Dreiser territory. Many years later, it gave birth to another kind of rebel: Jack Kerouac. Bette, who often expressed violence in her personality, was born in violence. Lowell was torn by strikes and riots, lootings and burnings in those dark years after the turn of the century. Smoke smeared the chill porcelain blue of the New England sky. There was scarcely a fancy window in the better parts of town that did not look out on dark, satanic textile mills built of forbidding grey stone far below. High-hat Yankees like the Favors were in the minority in Lowell. They lived in wide, lawn-fringed streets, shaded with maple and elm and oak: far above the common herd in those clean airy hills.

Eighteen months after Bette was born, Harlow Morell Davis more willingly fathered another child. He and Ruthie, in one of their rare judicious moments, had decided that just one child in a family was insufficient and unfair. Indeed, Harlow knew, there might be criticism within his company of his marriage and even doubts cast on his virility. Barbara, known as Bobby, the second sister, lived her life in the fantasy that her father had wanted her to be born for her own sake. But she soon learned that Bette was in every way more remarkable, and the knowledge crushed her and ultimately destroyed her.

There was a symbolic moment at the beginning. Bette, who at first welcomed her sister as a kind of doll, quickly asserted her power. She discovered on one occasion that Bobby had climbed into Bette's playpen and was sitting there with a complacent look on her face. Bette picked up the child and carried her the full length of the room, depositing her firmly on the parents' bed. 'And there you stay!' she is reported to have said, thus setting the

25

tone of her personality and her career from the outset.

Bette despised dolls, even though she went through a performance of cuddling one for a baby picture: she flatly refused to play with any such childish object. She had no interest whatsoever in collecting anything. She was devoid of infantile mischief and neighbour women shook their heads over her as she stared at them glumly from her pram, announcing that she was 'born old'. Although she became quite pretty, she was an ugly duckling at first, with her maternal grandmother's slightly bulging forehead, small nose and awkward uneven teeth that had to be fixed in a brace and still wouldn't set properly. She had a habit of bringing worms, beetles, snails and other disagreeable creatures into the house. On one occasion, Ruthie was giving an elaborate party with tea and cakes. Someone was heard at the door. Bette, aged six, marched in with great ceremony. She carried something to the table and placed it on the lace cloth. The women screamed. It was a dead field mouse.

By contrast, Bette hated stinging or predatory creatures. She dreaded insect bites, cats and birds, and she was as disconcerted by journeys in automobiles as any feline. Because her mother over-protected her, sheltered her from the world, she suffered for the rest of her life from physical cowardice. Under her seeming toughness and precocity, she was shy and frightened of everything. And then gave vent to sudden unexpected outbursts of savage temper.

She had a mania for orderliness. Her mother wrote:

Her passion for neatness began very young. One day when I was dressing her, she saw a tiny spot and quite a few wrinkles on her dress. She began to cry and would not be appeased. Finally I took out a fresh dress as an experiment and she became all smiles.

She was endlessly plumping up pillows and fixing drapes. A crooked curtain, a flickering light bulb or a speck of dust on a table drove her into bursts of rage. She was constantly straightening rugs, rearranging candlesticks on the table and fixing crooked paintings on the walls.

Bette's first school was the Wingate Private Kindergarten, which she attended at the age of five. 'She trudged off to school in the snow or rain or sunshine with equal eagerness,' Mrs Davis wrote. She was a good study and made friends easily, but she never let her fellow pupils get too close to her. She always remained at a distance; perhaps they sensed that her destiny would lead her far beyond them.

If there was one deep influence upon Bette's life apart from her mother, it was Madam Favor's. Madam Favor grew mellower and more kind with the passage of time. She taught Bette Bible stories. In a family-authorised life of Bette, long since forgotten, and buried in the pages of the defunct Boston *Herald-American,* George W. Clark wrote:

> Grandmother Favor knew all the sweet secret places in cool marshlands where could be found the first violets of spring. She knew the best grassy hilltops in New Hampshire, drenched in sun and whipped by the west wind, where one could live for long hours watching the march of white billowy clouds. She knew where the far off hills were bluest and where the salt sea spray whipped off the white caps at the seashore. And in drowsy summer days, she knew exactly how to help one pass the long hours in the orchard beside the old house in Lowell. But winter was the most fun when before the roar of a fire she'd read *Snowbound* out loud to Bette to the beat of a nor'easter against the clapboards.

Like a bird she was. Always in movement. She seemed to ripple rather than walk and to be with her was to be strangely content but no one could ever reason why. And if Bette Davis seems to flutter like a lovely bird sometimes now in her world of shadows, it is because of Grandmother Favor. And if on occasions she stamps her little feet, her eyes flashing, her throaty voice strident in range, it is because of Grandmother Favor, too, because she was one of many moods, of many fancies.

Madam Favor tried to break a certain dog-in-the-manger attitude of her granddaughter. Ruthie wrote of Bette:

What is hers is hers. She loves her possessions. She is generous to a fault in giving money, but not her things. She hates to lend anything, especially her books. She hates this in herself I think, but it is a deep-seated characteristic. When she is for some reason forced to lend something, she ends by saying, 'Keep it.'

War broke out in Europe in 1914 when Bette was six. She dressed up in a converted bed sheet her mother had turned into a nurse's uniform, and acted out scenes of being in the Red Cross on the Western front, with Bobby as her assistant or patient.

This was her first show of theatrical skill. Soon after, she made the gesture of visiting Grant's Tomb on roller skates. At an alarmingly early age, she could recite the first verse of *The Midnight Ride of Paul Revere*. All attempts to discourage her proved futile. One day, when the other children in the neighbourhood were playing, Ruthie found Bette sitting on the steps in the drifting flakes of an early snow, reading favourite passages of

28

verse by Longfellow to an audience of starving sparrows.

Bette saw her first motion picture at the age of eight: Mary Pickford in a heavy romantic. She adored it, weeping happily at its phoney sentimental situations. She was especially fascinated by the horrors of *Grimm's Fairy Tales*, which contained dire warnings to the improper and in which punishments were meted out to the wicked. She was intrigued by the correct sentimental novels of Louisa May Alcott, with their sober woodcut illustrations and poised puritan prose. She had an almost boyish interest in the plodding, historical romances of Sir Walter Scott and the purple velvet writings of Bulwer-Lytton.

In summer, the two girls were often in Maine at summer camp, enjoying canoeing, swimming, and plucking wild flowers on nature study walks in the forest. Theirs were innocent days of berry picking and pea shelling, clambakes and coasting. It was hard to go back to the family home at summer's end. As soon as Harlow Morell's unwelcome step was heard each sundown, the laughter faded and the merry runnings up and down stairs stopped. He even sat at a separate table during meals every night except Saturdays when he condescended to join his family. Meals were conducted in silence. If the children cried or asked for anything, his face grew black with fury.

Yet Bette's childhood was not as uniformly stark as Harlow Morell might have wished it for the good of his daughters' souls. As he rose in importance during the years of the First World War, the family moved from Lowell to nearby Winchester. It was a moderately pleasant town. Against the frowning wooden buildings painted grey to deprive the eye of pleasure, there were woods and rock climbs and an abundance of flowering shrubs. God-fearing folk even managed to loosen their stays a little in the warm compelling summers.

1918 finally brought a rift in the relationship of Harlow

Morell and Ruthie. They hadn't talked for months; they had lain next to each other in bed with as much intimacy as the carved stone figures on a Norman tomb. At last, they were forced to admit they could no longer keep up the pretence of marriage. The family's cast-iron world was shaken as though by a minor earthquake. Divorce was as unheard of in the Welsh Baptist Davis and High Church Favor families as in any Roman Catholic breed. Madam Favor held a grim family conference. Decisions were made in order to avoid the slightest hint of scandal. Harlow Morell would simply announce that his wife had left him. Even though in effect he had left her already by refusing her sexual communion, in those days the woman had to bear the brunt of the calumny.

As part of the arrangement, Ruthie left the house and took Bette and Bobby to Florida with an Irish nurse-maid. After the children were relaxed and softened by weeks of sun, sand and surf, Ruthie sat them down, took a deep breath and told them she had left their father. Their reaction was interesting. Bette burst into delighted laughter and announced, 'Now we can go on picnics and have a baby sister!' Bobby's reaction was less shrewd. She cried miserably; and in a sense never recovered from her father's disappearance from the family scene. Unlike Bette, she knew instinctively her father had wanted her to be born; despite evidence to the contrary, she clung to her fantasy that he was a kind and generous man; and knowing how close Bette was to Ruthie, she felt left out of that relationship. From that early moment, her tragic life – dogged by mental and physical illness, shattered marriages, breakdowns, a position as Bette's shadow – was laid out for that unhappy child.

Even at the age of nine, Bette seemed to know that, much as she would miss her father, his loosening of the bonds he had so religiously assumed, helped to insure her future. She probably never would have gone on the stage if he had remained in charge. He would have forbidden any such whorish frivolous indulgence. She would have been married off to a Boston banker or lawyer and grown fat raising a brood.

The next few years were marked by incredible restlessness of movement. In 1930, Ruthie wrote:

We lived in something like eighty houses: a record I believe. If there are those who take this with a grain of salt, I have a list of addresses and pictures of every place.

After the divorce, Ruthie became estranged from the upright family but gradually they softened in view of her plight and gave out small gestures of help. In 1919, mother and daughters were all stricken with Black Flu. When they recovered, Madam Favor copied out a list of schools advertised in the *Atlantic Monthly* and wrote to each of them in turn. She selected from the replies a letter written by a Miss Marjorie Whiting of the Crestalban School in the Berkshires, located between the Hoosac and Hoosatonic Rivers.

Crestalban was a proper place. It was a boarding school with an emphasis on vigorous outdoor living. It gave Bette the lifelong physical constitution that withstood the demands of her fierce and nervous nature. The first arrival of mother and daughters at Crestalban was unforgettable. It was a profound New England winter. The schoolhouse was a converted white clapboard farm with great red barns and a brown shingled house where lessons were attended. Snow was falling on the roof, making a picture fit for a Christmas card: Miss Whiting greeted them cheerfully in a small sleigh. The new arrivals rode over crisp, linen-smooth, whitened roads to their destination.

Twinkling and apple-cheeked, Marjorie Whiting, a niece of the artist Abbott Thayer, ran the school with her brother and three sisters, while the Whiting parents were the cooks. There were only thirteen children. Ruthie wrote:

Miss Whiting's brother Harry ran the farm . . . there the children learned the miracle of birth, watching the cows, the pigs and lambs, and here they learned the art of homemaking, sewing, as well as French and the three R's.

Mrs Davis recalled that eighteen out of twenty-four hours each day was spent out of doors; that the children, including Bette and Bobby, would take nude snow baths in the snow before breakfast and dry themselves off before a roaring fire; that they slept on a porch with snow for a top blanket; that they took classes on that porch, sitting in woollen bags and mittens with a steam-pipe under their desks to put their feet on. The children revelled in every moment – and soon learned sewing, mending, and cooking.

Bette made up her mind about everything. She played hockey and tennis with enthusiasm but little skill. She was better at swimming. She was a good student but not a brilliant pupil. She managed history and languages – but was hopeless at mathematics, chemistry and botany.

At the age of ten, she was at Crestalban on Christmas Eve while Ruthie was working as housemother at Miss Bennett's School for Girls, Melbrook, New Jersey. There was a Christmas party and Bette was Santa Claus. She wore the traditional red flannel cap and coat, cotton hair and beard, and cotton lining. Because Crestalban did not have the luxury of electricity the branches of the tree were decorated with large red candles. Bette reached out to fetch presents for the children. She noticed one of the candles had gone out and relit it with a match. The flame rose suddenly and caught the cotton of her sleeve. A moment later her costume was on fire. She snatched it off but the flames rushed up to her beard. Somebody threw a rug over her and stifled the flames.

She made her début as an actress. Her teacher shrieked theatrically, looking at her as she lay badly burned on the floor: 'She's blind! *Oh my God, she's blind!*' Bette stood up, her eyes tightly closed, groping around the room, touching the pupils' faces one by one to tremendous effect – before at last revealing to everyone's intense annoyance that she was perfectly able to see.

Her face *was* severely blistered, but after her play-acting nobody took her seriously enough to take her to the hospital. Instead, she was packed off on Christmas morning with the other children for a trip to New York. Cinders from the engine funnel flew into her face through the open windows and she screamed alarmingly during most of the journey. She was hugely enjoying her stardom. She thought she would die if her face ever healed up again. When her mother met the train, Ruthie flew into a fury. She screamed abuse at the teacher, only to be confronted by a staunch if damaged daughter who drew herself up to her full height and said, with the saintly hauteur of the Boy on the Burning Deck, 'It was my fault, Mother! Don't blame Teacher! They told me not to go near the Christmas tree! I disobeyed!' While her fellow pupils groaned, her teachers smiled at her sanctimonious announcement. Bette, basking in celebrity, was taken to the doctor. For fifteen days and nights her mother treated the ten-year-old's face with boric acid. An alarm clock was set to go off every fifteen minutes. The treatment left Ruthie exhausted and Bette almost a beauty. Bette screamed punctually around the clock. Mother dizzily told a reporter some years later, 'I think that's when Bette's eyes got big. It had something to do with the boric acid. The irises were enlarged. The eyes the world knows! Isn't that amazing?' Bette lost her top layer of skin following the accident and it never grew back. That gave her the strange 'bald' look that became famous, her extreme sensitivity to sun and windburn,

33

and to make-up with its toxic properties.

Her fiery accident not only made her identify with Joan of Arc but made her supremely conscious of her face. She was at once fascinated and repelled by it – as though it were someone else's. Drawn to it and yet terrified of mirrors. In later years, she would scream and hide her head if she accidentally saw herself on the screen. She never thought herself attractive, yet she was: her infectious laughter, her stylish, swinging walk, her trick of balancing herself on her heels and turning unexpectedly, her quick wit and wide blue eyes drew the attention of young bloods in their bearskins. She felt a flicker of encouragement at sixteen: boys with their slicked-down hair swarmed through the house, took lemonade with her on the porch from jugs clinking with ice chunks and gave her a spin on their bicycles. Her confidence grew: maybe she could fascinate. Looking in the mirror one morning, she was surprised to find she was a woman. Her teeth had been straightened by years in their steel braces, her eyes could probe like a hypnotist's when she chose. She was skinny, but she had heavy, voluptuous breasts. Life seemed horrific at twelve. At sixteen it seemed almost promising.

Ruthie dominated everything. She was 'psychic' and carted Bette off to a fortune-teller who predicted a great future for her. They were very close. One night, Ruthie was watching a movie when she had an overpowering feeling Bette was in danger. She spotted one of Bette's beaux in the theatre and insisted he drive over and pick up Bette from a dance. A bribe ensured his cooperation. Bette arrived home in a blaze of temper asking Ruthie what she meant by ruining her evening. The telephone rang. Bette heard the news: the boy she had intended driving home with had run off a cliff and been killed.

Bette returned to Crestalban and soon became just another kid. She grew up like Alice in Wonderland after swallowing from the Drink Me bottle. Her neck was elongated and her arms and legs grew skinny. She was so nervous with boys that in her own words; 'I couldn't get out even a bleat when I was with one. Oh, *awful*!'

At high school at sixteen, she quickly discovered that fierce intelligence and drive were no substitute for glamour or ease of manner. She was in peril of being branded a blue-stocking: not good for a high school girl. Skirts were going up and waistlines were going down. Girls started to smoke behind the gymnasium. Lips were bee stung. Colleen Moore was all the rage: her picture *Flaming Youth* would index a generation. Bette preferred *Little Lord Fauntleroy* and the prim throwback romances of Mary Pickford. She read proper books when other girls were rushing off to flirt with boys under Chinese lanterns after dances, or by campfires to the tune of Victrolas under harvest moons. She hung back from romantic invitations.

One evening, when Bette was sixteen, she had a date with a young, gangly boy named Henry Fonda. A friend of his dated Bobby. Hank's friend drove the Model-T and Bette and Hank sat in the back seat. She insists he kissed her; he insists with equal vehemence that he did not. She was very attractive to him, but he says that he was not attracted to her. The story has clearly got mixed up in both their minds. They never dated again.

This small but frighteningly intense girl fell in love with the theatre. Her most overpowering experience was seeing Blanche Yurka and Peg Entwistle in Ibsen's play *The Wild Duck*. Peg Entwistle's performance as the fragile and touching Hedwig moved Bette to tears. She told Ruthie: 'If I don't play Hedwig very soon, I'll die!'

Years later, when she learned that Miss Entwistle had in a melodramatic gesture thrown herself off the top of the Hollywood sign to her death because of failure in Hollywood, Bette was shattered.

The Wild Duck gave Bette her first intoxicating dream of stardom. She pestered Ruthie with her visions: soon, she would live in a country home; own a Packard car; diamonds; enough money so that Ruthie would never lack for anything; three strands of pearls; lots of clothes; world travel; the chance to be tall and dignified; an expert horsewoman; and learn to laugh like a lady. Her chief longing to be an actress was based on an intense mistrust of herself: her high, sharp laughter; her pinched face; her bulbous forehead; her quickness to anger; her fear of anything unknown; her mania for perfection; and the way that, though fanatically clean, as she always was, she usually covered herself with ink when she wrote letters.

Mother and daughters continued moving constantly in those years. The family gave little help financially and it seems that Madam Favor was less than generous. From Lowell to Winchester, from Ashburnham to Peterboro, from Southwest Harbor to Ogunquit and Ocean Park, the moves went on.

In 1924, Bette went to Cushing Academy in Ashburnham, Mass. There she experienced First Love. Harmon Oscar Nelson was not one of the Scott Fitzgerald boys with patent-leather hair and brisk suitings. He was awkward, weak, nervously charming, retiring and not very bright. He had no talent for sports. In a college where athletics were the certified cause of popularity, Ham was an outsider. But he was quite nice-looking, with a good figure, tall and slender. He had dreamy, romantically liquid dark eyes. His chief advantage was that he was a musician. He retained a fragile form of popularity because he was a leading light in the college band and ran various productions. He sang and composed and played several instruments. He seemed to have no interest in girls.

Bette was the first sophomore who attracted him. When they first met he said, 'Miss Davis, would you like to sing in the minstrel show?' She would and did. She had a frantic crush on him. But he was insecure with her, despite his interest, and Bette felt challenged. She told Ruthie, 'I'm going to get him if it's the last thing I ever do.'

It was uphill work. They sang in the glee club together but Ham was too wrapped up in his music. They went to dances. She was still waiting for her first kiss. She begged Ruthie for pretty dresses. Ruthie stretched the budget. Bette did and redid her hair. She wanted to be alone with Ham but in those days dances and parties were chaperoned like prison benefits. On Sundays, when during the coed hour the students were allowed to fraternise in a brief stroll through the grounds, she prayed for rain. Maybe she could achieve her objective under the sudden shade of an umbrella. There was a drought.

At eighteen, Bette gave her energy to play-acting. She wasn't expert, she performed like a sparrow, but she acted obsessively in everything she could: in theatres in Maine during summer vacation, in pageants, in every school play available. She and Ham Nelson drifted apart. She had to be an actress. Could she be an actress? She had to be an actress.

Ruthie wrote in her unpublished memoir:

As I look back on this part of my life I wonder what drove me on. Was it that through my daughter I would realise all of the many ambitions that were hidden within me? Whatever it was, my belief in Bette's ability certainly came true. Whether this driving desire to make her an actress . . . made her happy I don't know, but at this point nothing could have stopped either of us.

Even before she went to college, Bette studied dancing. She was a pupil of 'Roshanara', who taught at Mariarden, Peterboro, New Hampshire. Bette worshipped this English girl with the pretentious Indian name.

Ruthie worked hard as a photographic retoucher to pay for Bette's dancing lessons.

Through 'Roshanara', with her training in Indian dance, Bette learned the extraordinary physical discipline and control that marked her future work. The classes were held in the musty cellar of a church, from which, like moths from a chrysalis, the pupils emerged to perform in the summer on smooth green lawns.

Bette enjoyed the discipline of the work. She rehearsed a full eight hours each day. She learned 'Roshanara's' speciality, 'The Moth'. She wore white silk and danced on a special glass floor with lights illuminating her body. The audience applauded Bette wildly. Ruthie wrote, 'Bobby sat close to me as we watched Bette and we could not believe it was true. I've sat through many opening nights, but this was the most thrilling.'

While Ruthie took wedding and school pictures, Bette emerged as a star pupil. The summer vacations with their endless dancing lessons and weekly performances, were never forgotten. 'Roshanara's' early death came as a severe shock, terminating a period of great joy.

Bette returned to Cushing for the autumn term in 1925. The day she left Mariarden for the last time, the actor Frank Conroy made a remark without which no biography of a star is complete: 'Mrs Davis, if you don't put that child on the stage, it will be a crime. She has something that you can't buy, something that makes your eyes follow her even when she doesn't speak. And when she does, it is just added excitement.' Ruthie broke into tears, unable to reply.

Bette graduated with honours from Cushing. She made her way through her final year by working as a waitress at the college. There is a famous story that when she called her mother asking her if she could help out by waiting tables, she was horrified when her mother unhesitatingly agreed. By the time Bette dragged herself off to the cottage in Ogunquit where Ruthie and Bobby lived that summer, Bette was exhausted and had cried for two days.

That post-college vacation in Ogunquit was the last joyous time of Bette's life. It was a golden summer, without a day of rain. Bette became a lifeguard and started to look healthier. She and her sister ran about the rocks and small beach and teased the painter Stanley Woodward who was living there. Years later, Stanley Woodward said:

> I'll never forget Bette and Bobby Davis. Bobby was still at high school, and those two years difference meant a great deal to her. She was nervous and shy. Bette was the exact opposite. You never saw such energy! She did everything head-on. You could see what she would become. Her eyes were not really big. But she knew how to make them enormous when she wanted to win an argument. I think she fancied herself as a hypnotist. It took a painter to notice that!

The consuming ambition of every young girl with dramatic aspirations in those days was to be admitted to the severe discipline of the Eva LeGallienne school in New York. In order to enter the school, Ruthie and Bette moved to a modest apartment in New York City – Bobby still attending high school. Eva LeGallienne was a remarkable woman. A great actress, she was diffident and detached on the surface but fiercely committed to her art. There are several versions of what took place when the nervous, long-necked girl and her desperate show-biz mother arrived at Miss LeGallienne's offices. Ruthie wrote that 'this first experience was very humiliating and we never did see Miss LeGallienne.' But a more convincing version can be reconstructed.

While Ruthie sat in the outer office Miss LeGallienne's secretary questioned Bette in an atmosphere of sombre austerity. Bette was not invited to sit down. She was asked the names of books she had read on the theatre. She was given a play to read to Miss Le Gallienne. She was astonished to discover she was supposed to recite a speech by an ancient Dutch woman in a Dutch accent.

She entered the sanctum sanctorum. Miss LeGallienne, wispy but authoritative, had no interest in this awkward pale girl who seemed utterly lacking in the promise of style or presence. She did her best to discourage her by bombarding her with futile questions about her sources of income. Bette stumbled through the speech. Miss LeGallienne observed a nervous giggle and said, icily, 'Miss Davis. I can see that your attitude towards the theatre is not sincere enough to warrant taking you as a pupil. You are a frivolous little girl. Good day.'

Asked about this occasion recently, Miss LeGallienne said she could not recall it. 'There were so many young girls who came in looking for a break.'

Bette burst into tears and ran from the office. For days she was hysterical with rage and grief. Bette paced the New York streets, talking to herself, convinced she was going mad. She said later: 'I really was out of my mind. I had to be an actress. I wasn't an actress. I had to be an actress. Like a crazy pendulum, my mind swung from nauseating discouragement to furious rebellion. I would end it all. I would show the world, show Eva LeGallienne, Ruthie, the whole family. I would stun, startle, astound: give performances and become history!'

Eva LeGallienne's rejection following on her two brushes with death and her father's persistent suggestion she become a 'competent secretary' drove the dynamo of aggression, ambition and hectic desperation that compelled Bette into a career. One morning, Ruthie made her mind up. The only way to save Bette's sanity was to get her on the stage and keep her there. Shaking her daughter awake, she said sharply: 'Wake up, Bette! We're off to New York!'

'You're mad, Mother!' Bette said.

'Fix your hair!' Mother snapped.

Once Ruthie's mind was made up, there was no stopping her. If she couldn't get Bette into Eva LeGallienne's class, the next best thing was the John Murray Anderson-Robert Milton Dramatic School. Hugh Anderson was the executive director. He looked astonished at the determined little woman and her edgy, skinny, pop-eyed daughter as they swept past his secretary into his office. Ruthie put all her cards on the table. She said, 'My daughter wants to be an actress. You've got to make her one!' She took a deep breath. 'And I haven't a nickel. I'll have to pay on the instalment plan.'

Hugh Anderson was astounded. He was so crushed by Ruthie's determination he nodded weakly and agreed to Bette's admission. Ruthie continued to work as a retoucher. Bette rented a walk-up coldwater single on East 58th Street with a fellow Massachusettsian named Virginia Conroy. The two girls became fast friends. They ate at the automat, did their washing, dried their damp handkerchiefs by sticking them against the sunny windowpane and hung their underwear on a line strung across the room. They cooked over gas jets. One night, Ruthie came to stay. She refused to bundle with Bette and instead rigged up a bed out of two wooden chairs with her upright suitcase in the middle. In the early hours of the morning, Bette and Virginia were awakened by a crash. Mother had slid through the chairs and was lying with flailing arms and legs on the floor.

The Anderson School was a tremendous help. Arthur Hornblow, the legendary dean, was marvellous and so was the great George Arliss, who taught diction. He told Bette (advice she did not always remember): 'Remain simple in your diction. Never adopt that exaggerated English speech you often hear on the stage.'

41

Bette became a friend of a fellow pupil named Joan Blondell, who recalled later that Bette, all eyes and talent, was consumed with ambition day and night.

Bette appeared with Joan Blondell in a production of an obscure play written by Mrs Centlivre, the wife of the cook to Queen Anne of England, which Arthur Hornblow unearthed in an English attic. It was entitled *The Wonder, or A Woman Keeps a Secret*: an outrageous Restoration farce which involved plentiful scampering through bedrooms. Bette and Joan were cast as saucy Restoration girls, looking like Watteau milkmaids in their billowing dresses. The audience on the first night was dismayed by the racy dialogue and numerous goosing and wild escapes through windows. After an initial shock at the play being produced in such a soberly distinguished school, everyone relaxed and enjoyed the evening. The production cost just $47.00. It would have run more than three nights if, as John Murray Anderson recalled in his memoirs, 'Some busybody hadn't come in and attached one of the draw curtains that belonged to the theatre.'

Among the other pupils were Lucille Ball, Caesar Romero, known as 'Butch', Paul Muni and Anita Page, who later starred in *Broadway Melody*. It was a joyous atmosphere. The school only lasted for three years but they were three years which made history in the American theatre. Among the lecturers were Don Marquis, creator of archy and mehitabel, Robert Edmond Jones, Channing Pollock and Willy Pogany. It was a galaxy that shone its light blindingly on the brilliant students.

Bette had the finest teachers. In addition to Arthur Hornblow, she was taught dancing by Martha Graham. Miss Graham gave her the understanding of the use of her body, how to 'centre' her emotions that made her so magnetic in pictures later on. Miss Graham says: 'She had control; discipline; and at the same time electricity. I knew she would be something.'

Her mother fuelled Bette's drive. With a deserved scholarship, Bette decided to apply for work in the professional theatre. She had made a hit in *The Famous Mrs Fair*, her examination play, in which she had to change from a delicate ingénue to a tough society woman. Despite laryngitis, she had triumphed and Frank Conroy, an admirer of hers, gave her a letter to George Cukor, who was running a stock season in Rochester.

Two

BEFORE BETTE Davis leaves for her assignment in Rochester, let us pause and consider her at the age of nineteen: on the edge of her great career. Physically, she still has an odd, unfinished look. The mousy hair, the bald, burned-through face, the pale blue eyes that widen constantly at the emphasis of a point, the small mouth, long neck and famished figure do not add up to a picture of conventional prettiness. But she is immensely attractive: she exudes vitality, energy, wit and style. Instinctively, without forcing it, she has a kind of ice cold sexuality, intelligence combined with passion, sheer nerves with pointed reason. She is a picture of humorous aggression, with her vulnerability and terror of life, her definitive virginity, making her irresistible. Her movements, crucial to an actress's individuality, are already those of an original. She walks very quickly, very impatiently, with an odd combination of feminine looseness in the hips, a thrust of the large breasts, and a masculine firmness of step, an athletic resolution in the well-shaped legs. She is hampered by the long, heavy dresses of the time: an era that is reacting to the above-the-knee daring of the earlier 1920s. She will look better in the severely tailored clothes of the late 1930s and the 1940s.

Her character – her colossal, all-consuming ego – is formed. She has rushed into a theatrical career not merely because her mother wanted to and couldn't or because she herself could think of no other way except school teaching or stenography for a bachelor girl to make a living in that dark age. The theatre is a way of escaping from her great inner tensions and strains and from the harsh realisation that (disaster for a girl) she isn't a beauty. In the theatre, she can work out her inherited stormy power without making her mother's life unbearable and she can tuck away her cowardice – the weakness that lies under the violent temper. Aside from talent, she has all the necessary personal attributes to become an actress. She is consumingly self-obsessed, temperamental, a keen perfectionist and gifted with a prodigious memory. An audience, if halfway interested, inspires her. Whereas most people would dread facing a crowd, she is a typical actress in finding life intolerable without applause. It is as necessary to her as a blood transfusion to an anaemic child. She feeds on applause, laughter, tears. It is luck for her that she has emerged in an uncool period when unbridled romances and melo-dramas filled the stage. Today, in an age of elliptical, bloodless theatre, she may not have had an equal chance. She needs big emotions and big scenes as Bernhardt had done. That she will soon prove a comparison with that great artist is quite possible.

She is still without the experience of giving herself completely to a man. Ham Nelson, with his weak sexuality, his insecure masculinity, has proved to be an ideal companion for her. There has been no one else who mattered.

As Bette left for Rochester, soon after her birthday, on 27 April 1928, it was to be her first long separation from Ruthie. Ruthie, tied to one of a long succession of depressing jobs that were paying for Bette's career, could not accompany her on this occasion. The extent of Ruthie's emotional involvement with her daughter can be seen in an immensely long letter she gave her to take along on the journey. It contained not only minute instructions on how to conduct herself on the trip but a precise breakdown of everything that could happen. The note makes clear that Ruthie was, in spirit, on the train herself, sitting beside Bette, fussing lovingly over everything.

The letter begins:

Take twice, darling, to read all of this and check your things off as you pack – then read it over after you go to bed – the instruction part! [There follows a crude drawing of a smiling face like the moon: mother watching over her child.]
I'll be with you every step of the way. And I'll pray to God to watch over my little girl as I can't – *but you help there!*

The memorandum continues with a complete list of everything in the suitcases, including pink and orange pyjamas, towel ('do not use washcloth in train unless you purchase a little rubber case for it'), raincoat and boots ('may be pouring at Rochester'), pink kimono ('you should go to wash before donning dress'), and, rather oddly, 'black suede gloves in case of rain'.

There is a list of underwear, with instructions not to use the laundry in hotels but to wash the clothing herself at night, stockings, handkerchiefs, hair pins, safety pins, blue evening dress and green ('but I doubt if you could get into it alive'), black satin hat, black velvet hat, white felt hat for raincoat, grey hat, old sport hat, bathing suit, red practice dress, slippers, lavender silk and green chiffon hangers, 'and must look immaculate for breakfast on train!'

The letter contains further instructions on how to unpack in the train compartment, how to repack, and how to hang everything. There are warnings of men who make passes at girls without glasses, and on correct deportment with older people. One doubts if even a duchess in Jane Austen's world would have gone this far to cover the movements of a virginal daughter by carriage from the family mansion to a lady's finishing school in Bath.

Not content with all this, Ruthie gives Bette directions on life itself:

> When in Rochester (or anywhere) be *sure* to be your simple self – especially quiet and reserved at all times in public. This is *very* important as you are alone and so young, dear – people are ready to believe a girl – bright and young and alive – gay unless she is *very* conservative.

The effect of this massive instruction was overpowering. Bette was to arrive at the train exactly fifteen minutes to the second before it left; she was to get settled before the train whistled to announce its departure; she mustn't talk in the sleeping car to disturb other passengers; she mustn't undress and go to sleep unless she has correctly placed her clothes for the next morning; the porter must wake her exactly half an hour before breakfast to the second; she is to eat it from eight A.M. to nine, and no longer so as others would not be kept waiting; she was to tip ten cents on a dollar for meals, ten cents to each porter for carrying her bags upstairs, and if any of these were fresh, 'be sure to resent politely if possible but if not – not!'

Buried in this Tolstoyan missive is the most revealing instruction of all. 'Always keep fruit or crackers in your room – being hungry keeps me awake.' So there it is, spelled out in neon lights: she *is* Bette, and 'being hungry keeps *me* awake'.

Rochester was, as it is today, a bleak and depressing city, with square, brown, self-important office buildings, streets lined with starved trees, and winds that prowled angrily down the thoroughfares. But the Cukor-Kondolf

47

Company, as it was known, provided a good chance for a budding artist.

George Cukor was about thirty at the time; he had not yet emerged as a famous figure. In later life, he would become the remarkable director of such pictures as *The Philadelphia Story, A Star is Born* and *Gaslight*. Bette was cast immediately. Ruthie had predicted (she was 'psychic') that the girl who played the chorine Pearl in George Abbott's play *Broadway* would get into an accident and Bette would be needed to replace her. So bent was Ruthie on Bette's success that, if the original actress had not fallen down, Ruthie would have made her way to Rochester to push her. Bette even wondered if she had.

Broadway was a concoction about gangsters and their backstage molls in New York. Bette played Pearl, one of the dancers who shoots her lover in the back. Oddly, Marlene Dietrich, a lifelong fan of Bette's, began her career in the same part.

It was a small role, but a powerful one. George Cukor described Bette's appearance years later:

> The girl came down the stairs, delivered her speech, and fired her gun. Bette was incredible. She seemed to know this was her chance and she took hold from the first moment. I was worried she might be overdoing it. The other girl had played it toughly, coldly, but Bette had a mind of maniacal fierceness, and even seemed to be *willing* the actor to die. The audience was stunned. I realised that Bette had the same 'white heat' that Jeanne Eagels had – though I wasn't as impressed with Eagels as many people were. I was delighted with Miss Davis. I hired her to play right through the next season. But somehow she got it into her head that I sacked her on the spot as a reward for her efforts. She talked about it for years!

The engagement in Rochester only lasted a week. Bette got her next job with the Cape Playhouse, at Cape Cod. She had been promised a job by a smooth-talking youth in New York who claimed to be the Playhouse manager in order to get a date with her. When she arrived, there was no job. Fortunately, the director of the Playhouse hired her as a theatre usherette to save her from starving. It was not until Ruthie arrived and rented a small cottage (Bobby came along too) that life became tolerable.

Trying to contain Bette Davis as a theatre usherette was like trying to bottle thunder. She spent every moment during the performances of the Cape Players studying all the parts within her age range. Everyone noticed her. While the other girls who were acting as usherettes chatted about dresses, make-up, hair and girlfriends, she stood in the darkness at the back of the orchestra staring intently at the stage. If she had had to, probably she could have acted every part in every play perfectly. She badgered the director Raymond Moore to give her the chance to appear in something – anything. In her own words, 'I would willingly have been a deaf and dumb maid or a hunchbacked cousin locked in an attic room with meals left at the door if necessary.'

One of the producers of the repertory season was the dumpy, formidable Laura Hope Crewes, a snappish pudding of a woman who is best known for her role as Aunt Pittypat in *Gone with the Wind.* She had a high whining voice and a habit of smoking cigars on the sly. She suddenly found herself without a girl to play the part of Dinah in A.A. Milne's play *Mr Pim Passes By.* The part called for the actress to play a song entitled 'I Pass By Your Window' on the piano and to sing it at the same time. Miss Crewes snapped at her: 'You want to be in this play, don't you?'

Bette's smile was more eloquent than words. 'I have

one question,' Miss Crewes said. 'Can you play and sing "I Pass By Your Window" by tomorrow morning at eight o'clock?'

'Of course!' Bette snapped back. Her thoughts raced. She hadn't the remotest idea what 'I Pass By Your Window' was. What was she going to do?

She ran home. She told Ruthie, 'I've got to play and sing "I Pass By Your Window" by tomorrow morning.' Ruthie panicked. She took off in a beaten-up Ford – an ancient Model-T she had bought second-hand – and drove frantically to the only music shop in Dennis. They had never heard of the song. In desperation, she rushed off to Hyannis. There was a larger store there but they had neither heard of nor stocked the song. Ruthie lost control completely. She drove at a-mile-an-hour along every street in Hyannis peeking through the windows to see which of the occupants had a piano. With astonishing boldness she rapped on every door and insisted upon knowing whether any of the sheets of music lying on the pianos might happen to be the elusive song. One or two people had heard of it; nobody owned it.

By nightfall, she was at the end of her tether. She made up her mind to return to Dennis and inform her theatre usherette daughter that her chances of appearing in *Mr Pim Passes By* were negligible. But as she turned a corner, she uttered a prayer: at the sight of a church. Inspiration seized her: church organists usually stocked up tunes so they could play medleys at benefits. She invaded the church, discussed the matter with a parson, obtained the address of the organist, interrupted him while he was weeding his garden – and, to her apocalyptic delight, discovered that he had the precious score. He couldn't have been more astonished when a woman he had never met before flung her arms around him, kissed him, whooped with joy, and swept headlong into his house to pick up the music and make off to Dennis with it in a cloud of dust.

Bette sat up until three A.M. studying the music. She walked on stage at the first rehearsal and performed it perfectly. Unfortunately, once she started acting she waved her arms about like windmill sails. Laura Hope Crewes told her to imagine she had lead weights in her hands: that her mannerisms (later to become famous) would distract attention from the rest of the cast. That may have been what was intended. But Bette did her best to obey. 'I stood,' she said later, 'like a figure in Rembrandt.'

At the dress rehearsal, the lead weights disappeared and the windmill sails revolved. Laura Hope Crewes hauled back and struck her face. Bette said: 'My face burned and I counted to ninety-five.' The lead weights returned. She was triumphant in *Mr Pim*.

A great pleasure was meeting Ham again that summer. She had gone to see Norma Shearer in a movie melodrama and she was astounded when Ham sat nearby. She screamed like an ambulance siren and the whole audience shushed her. Ruthie kicked her in the shins.

She began dating Ham again. He was playing instruments in the Amherst band in the Old Mill Tavern on the other side of the Cape. During the days when there was no matinée of *Mr Pim* and Ham wasn't giving a daytime performance they whizzed about in his Ford and went swimming together. They lay chastely on the sand, scarcely touching, and talked their hearts out about everything. They knew they were right for each other. Only one thing bothered Bette. Ham was unwilling to see her in the play. His excuse was that he thought he would annoy her but she always suspected he was not interested in the theatre.

The earliest printed notice of a Bette Davis stage performance to have survived appeared in the Dennis *Times* on 21 July 1928. It was a review of a performance of a drama called *The Charm School,* given as a Methodist Church benefit at East Dennis' Sears Memorial Hall.

51

The review read:

> The junior players presented their first drama of
> the summer season and Miss Betty [*sic*] Davis was
> totally charming in the leading role . . . her com-
> edy was delightful and the applause that greeted
> her dramatic exit in the second act confirmed our
> opinion . . . In this play, Miss Davis' sister, Bar-
> bara, also took part as one of the pupils of the
> 'Charm School', who were all overflowing with
> vivacity.

At the end of the season at the Cape, after a glorious and
golden summer of theatre, romance and long warm
beach afternoons, she and Ham had to part. Despite the
fact that he was not the kind of strong and virile man she
most wanted, she loved his sensitivity, and she was
grateful to him for a lifetime for teaching her to love
music. His long, narrow, dark face, half-sad, half-
humorous eyes, and compact, smoothly muscled body
made a deep impression on her. She was almost in love
with him. But she had to think of her career: there could
be no question of 'seriousness'. Ham had engagements
elsewhere and she had to return to Rochester for the
next Cukor season.

She was cast in a show that was oddly named *Excess
Baggage*. The local *Times* printed the following item:

> Among the fifty actors and actresses who arrived in
> this city from New York in preparation for pre-
> sentation of *Excess Baggage*, a Broadway produc-
> tion, at the opening night of the season at the
> Temple Theater, were Frank McHugh, the leading
> man, Charlotte Wynter, the leading woman, Wal-
> lace Ford, and Bette Davis, the ingénue, a pretty
> blonde slip of a miss.

Bette's part in *Excess Baggage* was a much larger one than that in *Broadway*. She played Frank McHugh's wife. Wallace Ford told me years later:

> I got the impression Bette had been told to be shy, subdued in the part she played. But she didn't fool any of us for a minute. She was afraid to say 'boo' to a goose, butter wouldn't melt in her mouth – *for exactly five minutes*. After that, I took one look at her and said as she walked on to the stage, with her long goosey neck and her big eyes, 'Miss Ruth Elizabeth Davis, you're no goody-goody who's scared of her own shadow, you're thunder and stage lightning and goddamn greasepaint. You're going to be a *tiger* on the boards. Look out, world!'

The star of *Excess Baggage* was Charlotte Wynter. But she became excess baggage herself when she broke her ankle. The talk in the company was that her understudy, Miriam Hopkins, had sawed through the heel of Miss Wynter's left shoe.

She was certainly capable of it. It gnawed into Miss Hopkins's far from tender spirit in later years that she had to play second fiddle to Bette in pictures – after all, as she insisted on telling her friends to their barely concealed amusement, *she* had been the star of *Excess Baggage,* and Bette a mere bag! Miriam Hopkins was a pretty, blonde, ruthless bitch: hard-bitten, mean-tempered, a 'card' and a caution. She hated to allow anybody in the cast a half-ounce of attention from the audience when she was on stage. If an actress threatened to take over a scene, Miriam would rearrange flowers, wind a clock, straighten a picture, or even take out a book and read it to distract everybody's attention from the speech being spoken. Few could, in fact, upstage her. With her cat's eyes, mischievous sexy crinkly stare and tricky, swooping Southern voice, she had a captivating theatrical presence. She would fling herself into a chair, spread her legs wide as a stevedore's and throw down martinis as though they were lemonades. She could also be, if the pose suited her, the epitome of soignée elegance, using her beautifully curved back as expertly as a question mark. She was jealous, consumed with hatred, petulant, self-pitying, coarse, bloody-minded. And she was an actress of actresses, as Bette, who despised every bone in Miriam's body, had the common sense to admit.

Wallace Ford said:

Even *then* Miriam was afraid of Bette. She knew Bette was at least as talented as she, and that although she wasn't nearly as attractive, she suggested a feminine, sexy 'touch-me-not' quality that Miriam, with her bull-like aggression and tired, experienced bedroom look, couldn't match. She dreaded every moment Bette was on stage. The men were looking at Bette, not her. I'll bet my bottom dollar some of the young guys got erections looking at Bette. Miriam challenged them: they might have been looking at another man. When Miriam sat down she spread her legs wide. She wanted the men to look up her skirt: a lady she wasn't! But they did not like the gesture, it turned them off, it was too brutal. Bette crossed her legs daintily, hiding everything, and they had to have her. You should have *seen* the beaux at the dressing-room door!

Bette went on to appear in *Cradle Snatchers, The Man Who Came Back, Laff That Off* (in which she played a slavey) and *The Squall,* among other plays. The Rochester *Times* wrote of Bette's performance in the last production: 'The sweetheart was done with quite a bit of demure charm by Bette Davis, who gave us further evidence that she is likely to be a good actress in the making.'

Her co-star in the play *Yellow* was the tall and imperious Louis Calhern. Asked years later why, during the production of *Yellow,* Bette was suddenly dismissed from the season by George Cukor, Calhern said:

The trouble was that she wasn't too popular. She refused dates to the young men (I could have understood her attitude towards the older ones) and that wasn't considered kosher. She wasn't supposed to sleep around, but she wasn't supposed to be St Theresa of Avila either. After the performance at night, she seemed very uppity and Cinderella-like. She didn't drink (or, incredible as it may seem, even *smoke* in those days!) and she simply fled back to her lodging house. She was so grimly dedicated to work that it became boring. Of course, that dedication took her further than any of us. But it didn't make for comfort in an incestuous company like that. She was a terrific team *player* but she wasn't a team *person.* I think Cukor yielded to pressure in getting rid of her. She was *very* unpopular!

However, Bette landed immediately on her feet. She went to New York and joined the respected James Light at his Provincetown Playhouse, located near Washington Square. She was cast in a play called *The Earth Between*: a drama of incest set in Willa Cather territory, on a Nebraska farmstead . . . and she was so innocent she played the part of a girl in love with her father without beginning to understand the nature of the relationship.

It was her first real chance. The big critics were present at the opening night. It was an 'occasion' for the unknown playwright, a Nebraska boy named Virgil Geddes. And it was Bette Davis's début in New York –

even though this wasn't Broadway, only Greenwich Village.

Bette's Uncle Paul came to the opening night. He wrote:

> I well recall the mixed rain and snow in MacDougal Street 'where a man may call his soul his own and see who cares.' I sat with my sister, Mrs Davis, Bobby and several close friends of our family. We were really excited. Despite the weather the little theatre was well filled. A stuffy, rather forbidding little barn of a place, yet full of dramatic memories of bygone stars. It was a halcyon night for Bette. Telegrams, letters, flowers poured in.

By all accounts, Bette flung herself into the part of the daughter with extraordinary intensity, suggesting a delicate, vulnerable, fragile quality. The applause was tremendous. The only flaw in the evening, and it was a deep one, was the absence of Bette's father. She was in anguish as she noticed his absence, but partly consoled by the fact that he sent her a wicker basket of flowers.

She tossed and turned all night, bad notices whirling around her brain. But soon after dawn, Ruthie burst into her room in ecstasy and flung Brooks Atkinson's review at her.

Bette sat up, rubbed her eyes, and snatched up the paper, the all-important *New York Times*. Atkinson had written: 'Miss Davis, who is making her first professional appearance, is an entrancing creature who plays in a soft, unassertive style.'

Atkinson wasn't exactly calling her Sarah Bernhardt but Bette could make do with 'entrancing'. The *Daily News* said: 'The performances are good, particularly that of Miss Davis, a wraith of a child with true emotional insight.' St John Ervine wrote in the *Post:* 'Miss Bette Davis and William Challee ably suggest the disturbed minds of Floy and Jake.'

She was launched. No doubt about it, she was *launched*. And a dream came true: her dream of appearing in the company of Blanche Yurka. During one evening performance a pencilled note on the back of a blank form for ticket applications was pushed under Bette's dressing-room door. It read:

Bette Davis is asked to be at the Bijou Theatre at eleven A.M. tomorrow. Miss Blanche Yurka wants to see her.

It was a command which Bette Davis could only obey. Blanche Yurka, with her great, famished eyes, scraggly dynamic body and unkempt look was an empress among actresses. Entrée to her charmed circle was as treasured as entrée to Joseph Papp's would be today. Bette had never forgotten the impact of Yurka's production of *The Wild Duck,* with the ill-fated Peg Entwistle. If it killed her, Bette had to work for Yurka.

Miraculously, Bette was only committed to four weeks in *The Earth Between* – because it was set for a limited run. She dashed over to the Bijou Theatre in a state bordering on ecstasy. Blanche Yurka swept up to her like a great ragged eagle and embraced her in the wings of a dress. Bette almost broke into tears when the great star offered her the part of Hedwig in *The Wild Duck.*

It was almost too good to be true. The part of Hedwig had an intense meaning for her: the child whose father had not wanted her. Her joy was only slightly dented when she heard that she was a replacement for the talented Linda Watkins who, pretending illness, had announced she would not go on tour.

Bette rushed home to study the part all night, with Ruthie taking the other parts. She finally fell asleep in the morning, only to wake with a violent fever and headache. Every effort she made to get out of bed was thwarted. In those blessed days, doctors still made house calls. A physician pronounced her the victim of measles, which she had somehow skirted in childhood and adolescence.

The toughest phone call Ruthie ever made in her life was to tell Miss Yurka that Bette, who was sobbing helplessly in the background, would have to give up the part. Astonishingly, Yurka said in her typically abrupt manner, 'Mrs Davis, we'll wait.'

Years later, Blanche Yurka told me:

Bette Davis was by no means an accomplished actress at the time. Her mother, frankly, was a pain in the neck, and it's a miracle she didn't sink Bette's career from the outset. She was endlessly and sentimentally fussing over her. She was a weak, silly creature and, despite Miss Davis's loyal demurs then and later, she was the show-biz mother to end all! Even Bette, over eager and full of tears and tantrums, was a maddening handful. But one gets an instinct in this business. I knew Bette would be a great Hedwig. She would attack the part, not with technique, but with her nerves and with her heart.

It was true. Bette struggled out of her measles condition and sweated her way through rehearsals, despite two relapses in convalescence. There was no way she wasn't going to do the tour. The opening in New York was very successful, and in April, 1929, the company moved to Philadelphia. Bette's vibrant, heart-breakingly intense performance moved audiences to tears. *The Philadelphian* said: 'The strikingly effective portrayal in the production is that by Bette Davis in the role of the daughter suddenly brought to the knowledge that she is an unwanted child and that her supposed father had never been more to her than a provider. Miss Davis, wan, sickly, yet cheerful as the child should be, thrills us in the poignant grief that comes with the revelation of the child's great tragedy. Such grief could hardly be more helpless.'

The tour proceeded to Washington. The *Washington Post* said: 'Especially commendable was the selection of Bette Davis, a talented ingénue with a native sweetness and spiritual wholesomeness that blends ideally into a lovable character. Bette Davis is a young woman who is going to advance far in her stage endeavours. She was a profoundly sympathetic and appealing Hedwig and gained more by her simple natural charms than a more experienced actor could ever have hoped to do.'

In Boston, Bette played at her most intense in front of an audience which was filled with her personal friends and relatives. Her father came backstage but, inhibited and incapable of expressing praise to her face, that miserable man lauded all of the other players and made no reference whatsoever to her performance. The best he said to her backstage had been: 'You would make a very competent secretary.'

And this despite an overwhelming storm of applause; the chance (seldom allowed by Miss Yurka) to take her solo curtain; the chance to show those who had doubted her that she had the stuff of greatness.

He eventually relented when he got home. He wrote her a letter saying that he got a big kick out of seeing her in the show; that he was proud of her fine début; that he was most awfully tickled that she had the 'so nice Ibsen uptown engagements'. He fretted that she hadn't seen him for any length of time in the dressing-room; that she wasn't up to taking supper with him; that his bag had been swiped at the depot. And he added, 'By the way, you looked sorta peakéd to me. Take care of yourself so you won't crack up just when things are going so nicely. You need lots and lots of cream, milk, eggs, fruit, green vegetables – you ought to build yourself up – I was glad to see my so accomplished daughter do so well.'

The *Boston Traveler* led the local papers in a chorus of praise. It said: 'Miss Davis manages to wring this emotional part dry of its dramatic content without lessening Miss Yurka's role, and what a feat that is!' By now it was generally agreed that Bette had surpassed the fabled Nazimova in the role.

It was in every way a triumphant tour. It probably meant as much to her as anything else in her career. Although Miss Yurka was a disagreeable presence with a repulsive body odour when she sweated and had a habit of forgetting lines at rehearsal, which threw the rest of the cast into an uproar, she was a great and noble tutor. Bette learned much from Blanche Yurka: her use of stillness after great storming whirls around the stage, her sudden break in the voice in a moment of emotion, and above all the way she had of concentrating all of her power into her huge and brilliant, stormy petrel's eyes.

When the tour ran out, Bette was already established as an actress of promise. This was no mean feat in a period when, unlike today, Broadway was a galaxy of great stars and a showcase for the greatest dramatists of the age. It is painful to contemplate a list of productions in that period before the Wall Street crash. Whereas now there is the gruel of one-man shows, tuneless musicals, revivals and pastiches, pale echoes of burlesque or the Follies, in 1929 there was a giant's feast of pleasures. New plays by George Bernard Shaw, Noël Coward and Eugene O'Neill played with brilliant casts to audiences that savoured every word. Even Shakespeare flourished on Broadway – along with Ibsen, Strindberg and Pirandello. It was a time when intellectual content was not thought to be incompatible with entertainment.

It was a fine time for an actress to emerge. Bette could cut her teeth on the harsh perfectionism of rehearsals under commanding, demanding tutors. Given her New England love of discipline and taste for torture, she relished the hard work and slaved like a salt miner in front of an audience, collapsing, wrung out, into Ruthie's arms at the end of a performance. Miss Yurka's chief memory of her was:

> Gearing herself up to such a pitch that at times in the middle of a line I would almost freeze, thinking she was going mad right in front of me. She seemed so small and so frail. She and her mother ate the most dreadful food, probably because of the wretched money I paid her. She would leave the magical world of Ibsen and I'd see her and Mrs Davis at a hamburger stand in the rain. They seemed to be happy, laughing. I've never seen so much love between a mother and daughter. Much as I hated that dreadful Ruthie, I was on the verge of tears at the sight of them.

During the Yurka tour, Bette had played briefly as one of the young girls – spirited, laughing sisters – in Ibsen's *The Lady from the Sea*. Among the audience in Philadelphia was a successful young director saddled with the name of Marion Gering. He told me in Japan years later:

> I was very taken with her, and when I was casting a rather bad play called *Broken Dishes* by Martin Flavin, I thought she would be good as the daughter in the show. I asked to have her come in for a reading, and this frail, awkward girl kind of sidled into my office holding her mother's hand as though she were a child of eight. I realised that she had not been Hedwig for nothing: that she was *still* a baby, eager, tearful, spoilt, virginal and subject to wild shifts of mood. She stood there looking at me clumsily, poised on her high heels in an ugly little hat with an impossibly long neck that made me itch

61

to fetch an *axe*. She was very pale, and trembled, while Ruthie looked at her as though she had just given birth to her. The whole thing was totally insane but I told myself, 'My God, she's impossible, she's neurotic, she looks at once intellectual and emotionally backward, but she's got "actress" written all over her. She's *made of lightning*.' I had to have her, but I was frightened. Wouldn't she be too strong for the play?

When Gering gave her the part, Bette hugged Ruthie ecstatically. The show was essentially a vehicle for that perfect Milquetoast, Donald Meek, who was as nervous and virginally middle-aged as any tiny, bald, put-upon man he played in the theatre. It was the story of a revolt among the Bumpsteads, a fairly typical middle-western family. Like *The Earth Between*, the play was authentic Americana. It dealt in a mood of great sympathy and conviction with small town life and was very well played (the critics agreed) by Meek as the drudge who rebels against his family and by Bette as the daughter who aids and abets him and discovers true love in the process. It was generally conceded that Bette was triumphant in the final scene in which she denounced her tyrannical mother and the matriarch's hypocritical relatives in a powerful speech. Brooks Atkinson praised her warmly.

Even the Wall Street crash could not affect the success of *Broken Dishes* and despite the fact that Donald Meek lost his life's savings, he came on the stage the night the market plunged and gave a brilliant performance. Bette adored him for it.

A great thrill of those months was when Madam Favor descended from the utmost heights of Boston to see a performance. It was the first time that she had agreed to see Bette on a professional stage. At first, she sat primly upright in black silk in her orchestra seat while gales of laughter swept around her. But she soon gave in, and smiled a little. After Bette's big speech at the end, she joined the crowd in a standing ovation. It was one of the great moments in Bette's life to see her there, tiny, self-contained, and commanding.

Backstage afterwards, Madam Favor told Bette she was worried about Bette's appearance. She told her to be sure to take care of herself and eat well, before proceeding to the Davises' apartment on East 53rd Street. Bette went on to a theatre party and when she got home at 2:30 A.M. was astonished to find Madam Favor sitting up and waiting for her to congratulate her once again.

Broken Dishes ran for 178 performances. Bette was the toast of the town. She won the admiration of girls who identified with her part, wishing that they, too, could rebel against their families. It was a stroke of luck that she began her career with a role that excited sympathy in the young. Soon young women would be her largest audience.

Sam Goldwyn sent a talent scout to watch her performance and she was called for a screen test for *Raffles* in New York. But with her irregular features, awkward stance and (again) braces on her teeth, she looked atrocious and Goldwyn threw up his hands in horror. She was not upset. In common with all other theatre people, she thought Hollywood was an absurdly vulgar place where no one in his right mind would want to go.

Instead, she began to date eligible bachelors while still holding a torch for Ham. With Ruthie's reluctant approval she whirled off to the the Ritz-Carlton with a forty-year-old beau and laughed desperately over a cocktail which she was much too frightened to drink. She was spun off to a nightclub. She somehow got through the evening without losing her virginity. Her defence tactics were masterful. The forty-year-old beau disappeared.

Early in 1930, Bette went on the road tour of *Broken*

Dishes. She was in Washington when she was offered a chance to return to Broadway in *Solid South,* with Richard Bennett. The play opened on 15 October 1930 under the direction of Rouben Mamoulian. Bette was fascinated by Mamoulian, a brilliant and sophisticated Armenian just beginning to make a major name in the theatre.

He directed her meticulously. *Solid South* was an uproarious farce of the Deep South, dominated by the great Richard Bennett, father of the movie stars Constance and Joan, who was overpowering as a grandiose major careening headlong through his mansion and living out all the outrageous fantasies of the traditional Southerner in flowery speeches. Bette played a sweet young girl in love with Owen Davis, Jr., in a style of tender anticipation and joy. When comedy was called for, she played up expertly. It was Richard Bennett's play from start to finish but she made a small, certain impression.

When she was hired for the production, she showed her true spirit. Richard Bennett said to her with freezing disdain, 'I suppose you're another of these young ham actresses.' Bette replied: 'I've been up all night on a train. Unless you show me more consideration than this, I'll go home and we'll forget the matter.' As a result, she was hired.

There were curious incidents during the production. During one performance, finding a prop missing, Bennett broke off in the middle of a line and said, 'Stagehand, where's my cigar?' Bette also recalled an incident in which he spoke directly to the audience, glaring at it and saying, 'I suppose I'll have to tell you a dirty story to get you to laugh!'

Her reviews in *Solid South* earned Bette a chance for another screen test. She had the choice of continuing in *Solid South* or going to Hollywood. She was still hesitating when *Solid South* abruptly folded. Her mind was made up.

She was dubious about the test, but made it anyway. It was a freezing late November day. She had to take a subway to a remote suburb of New York. She was distraught with fear, knowing she wasn't photogenic. By the time she reached the stage to play a brief scene in Preston Sturges's *Strictly Dishonorable,* her nerves were unbearably taut. The director screamed, 'Action!' She fainted.

At last she came round – and delivered the classic remark, 'Don't worry! I do this quite often!'

Surprisingly, the test was a success: she won a Universal contract. But she didn't want to go to Hollywood. She tried hard to obtain a role in another play. She failed. And she and Ruthie decided to take the big chance and go west for six months to see what would happen. Hollywood still seemed to be the end of the world. And there was another problem. They had a year-long lease on their apartment and the owner refused to allow them to leave without paying the balance of the rent. This was out of the question since they only had $100 capital between them. They finally, after constant begging, obtained an agreement to sublease. But after two weeks they still had not succeeded in renting the flat and they were afraid they would have to be separated: a quite unthinkable possibility.

They were due to leave on 8 December 1930 for the Coast. The apartment still wasn't rented. On the 7th, while they were clinging together in a chair, crying softly with despair, the bell rang. The flat was on the main floor. Ruthie ran out and flung the door open so rapidly she forgot to dry the tears on her face. A tall, grey, sinister-looking man stood there. *'Show the apartment!'* he snapped.

Ruthie acted up a storm as she introduced the man to her famous daughter, extravagantly praised everything in her dismal home, and watched his face intently for a reaction. Finally he said, in a harsh, eerie near-whisper, 'Is there a closet that can be locked up and not easily reopened?' Ruthie looked at Bette. Was the man a murderer? Was he hiding stolen jewellery? What did it matter?! 'Yes!' Ruthie answered triumphantly. The man silently took out a series of $20 bills from his wallet and gave them to Ruthie with the words, delivered in an icy monotone, 'The maid must come and leave at twelve. Here's a hundred dollars for her. Leave your name on the bell and mailbox. Write the name and address of the person who will receive the rent, whether that's you or somebody else.' Mrs Davis commented in her unpublished memoirs, 'I wrote the name of a friend who had been kind, fearing if I gave the man a Hollywood address, he'd never send the money.'

As it turned out, the man paid his rent punctually and there was no word of an arrest. On the morning of 8 December, mother and daughter and their wire-haired terrier Boogum set out on their adventure to Hollywood.

Three

BETTE AND Ruthie had exactly $57 between them. Bette's earnings on the stage had been swallowed up in the cost of dressing properly for the role of an up-and-coming actress. $43 had gone in meals and preparing things for the new tenant. Ruthie allowed $10 a day for the trip which took five days. There was a brief stopover in Chicago, and everybody had to get off the train and change to the Santa Fe Chief.

The journey seemed endless. Mother and daughter had read their magazines within hours and their hearts began to sink. The parlor car was full of cigarette smoke and bar-room conversation unfit for a young lady's ears. Most of the time they gazed blankly out of the windows which were partly grimed with soot. When they opened the windows, cinders flew in from the steam funnel. It was very cold. The heating system was temperamental and frequently gave out. There were snowdrifts which had to be dug out before the train could proceed. Sitting up in the day coach at night meant that sleep was virtually impossible. The elegant first-class section with its art deco dining-room, mahogany fittings, travelling bookstore, barber shop and swarms of handsomely uniformed black attendants were several worlds away from the crowded, swaying day coaches, the snack bar, and the long lines at the bathroom in the morning.

Chicago, with its chilly, echoing station in those days before central heating, provided a bleak interlude. The papers were full of shootings and the people were rude and pushy.

By the time the train had chugged through the rolling wheat fields of Kansas, the parched deserts of New Mexico and the small farms, deserts and mountains of eastern California, Bette felt completely numb. She felt she had been on the train for five years. Much as she loved her mother, she wished her sister Bobby, who was at college, had been with her to exchange the funny, silly small talk that young girls enjoy. She felt desolate at the prospect of Hollywood but at the same time she was going to prove herself out there, along with all the other young Broadway actresses who were being enlisted for the new age of talkies. So she played with Boogum, and chatted with her mother about childhood days, and hoped things wouldn't be too bad at the end of the rainbow.

Bette and her mother were fascinated by the fact that they had arrived in the sub-tropics after having travelled 3,000 miles from the winds and sleet of the eastern states. They stepped down on a gravel platform next to a waiting-room office roofed with red tiles like dragon scales. A few wind-bent palm trees relieved the dusty anonymous shimmer of this strange place. Bette had been swept up in a fantasy of her own making: that a press corps would greet her with cameras and notebooks and eager questions about her love life. Instead, there was only one photographer, who disappeared quickly after snapping her with her mother poised on the carriage exit, looking decidedly awkward in their slanting hats, ankle-length dresses, and loose, ill-fitting coats.

They had been promised that a press agent would drive them to the Hollywood Plaza Hotel on Vine Street, where Universal Pictures had booked them. But no one turned up; they weren't considered to be worth such special treatment. They were forced to spend most of their remaining cash on the cab fare.

They arrived in Hollywood at a time of upheaval in the industry. Only three years earlier, the success of *The Jazz Singer* had rendered silent pictures virtually obsolete. By 1930, silent stars without stage training or with foreign accents had been driven in disgrace from the scene. Bette was an insignificant speck in a dust cloud of obscure performers that had blown in from the east. She realised she amounted to nothing; that she wasn't even remotely as attractive as the gorgeous girls she saw driving roadsters past her on the wide highway through the hills.

Her vision of Hollywood was fed by the picture fan magazines with their sepia-toned pages covered in purple prose and filled with photographs of handsome men and women swimming, playing tennis, and bouncing balls along a beach. She was soon to learn that Hollywood was the opposite of everything she had imagined. It was a town that knew little of leisure, entertainment, night life or culture. As Robert Benchley described it in the year of Bette's arrival: 'Hollywood [was] a flat, unlovely plain, inhabited by a group of highly ordinary people, all of them quite at sea and usually in a mild state of panic in their chosen work, turning out a product which, except for certain mechanical excellences, was as unimportant and undistinguished as the mass product of any plant grinding out rubber novelties or automobile accessories.'

There were no nightclubs and the only place where food was served after midnight was a lunch cart on Hollywood and Vine which offered egg sandwiches every other night. There were no speakeasies – nor even a cocktail bar. It was a long time since people gathered to, in Benchley's words, 'swap cocaine and pistol shots'.

For anyone used to New York, the distances were daunting. It took almost an hour to reach people, at a thirty-mile speed limit and often a steep climb in second gear up the sides of crumbling hills. New Yorkers who were disinterested in tennis, swimming, bed at ten o'clock and buckets of orange juice almost invariably turned into grumbling alcoholics.

Fear ruled everything: the fear of dismissal if the box-office results on a picture were not satisfactory. Fear of not having a voice that the microphone would flatteringly reflect. Fear of gaining an ounce of weight or a single grey hair. Fear of being named in a scandal that might offend the Legion of Decency or the women's clubs. Fear, above all, that talking pictures might be just a temporary phase and that those who had committed themselves to it would go all the way from millionaires to paupers in no time at all.

And beyond the fear there was the dream of fabulous incomes – for petrol station attendants and waitresses were suddenly living in palaces of marzipan and spit. A former secretary could find herself queening it over a copy of Marie Antoinette's Petit Trianon, with an 'eighteenth-century' garden thrown in for good measure. But the tumbril was always waiting.

Hollywood itself was a suburb of drab brown office buildings, pepper and banana trees, and apartments furnished in early Pullman. The Plaza Hotel was a far cry from the Plaza in New York. Its beige drab lobby offered speckled mirrors and turnip shaped lamps in shades that looked like out-sized pink pepper pots when Mrs Davis and her daughter walked into it on 15 December 1930. The room overlooked the wide, traffic-filled street, relieved only by the large red trolley car that clanked and swayed from downtown all the way to Santa Monica Beach. The heat was amazing; and already Bette's skin, with its burned-off outer layer, was drying and freckling badly. There was, as there is today, nothing quite as desolating for a stranger as a first day in Hollywood. Even in hard-bitten New York, people were more welcoming. Perhaps because of the distances between people's homes and the intense snobbery of property and money, the penniless visitor tended to feel, as he still feels, that he had been dropped on the surface of the moon. People were brusque and even downright rude to those who were neither rich, handsome, nor in the possession of a costly and ostentatious automobile. Even the presence of a dog, which would have provoked affection and pleasure in the East, was given an icy glance because it might soil a fake marble lobby or an asphalt pavement in the sun.

Ruthie testified that Bette cried from terror at the blankness and impersonal hardness of the environment. Her friends were left far behind – along with the theatre she loved. She didn't even *like* motion pictures. And she didn't dare tell her mother outright of her disappointment: that was the worst part. Mrs Davis wrote:

> Three years of praise and applause in the theatres of the East meant nothing here. Here you were guilty from the start until you could prove your worth. If we could have talked to each other about [our unhappiness in Hollywood], things would have been easier. But Bette retired into herself hating it all and I spent a period of trying to bolster up her flagging spirit.

The first day in Hollywood was tedious. Ray Jones, the photographer who had met the Davises at the station, turned up at the hotel to drive them to Universal Studios.

The journey took them over a canyon, past pink stucco bungalows and 'Moorish' mansions hanging to the edge of precipices. Universal Studios was not the empire it is today, with its black glass tower and its sprawl of enormous soundstages, its commissary where the inhabitants are gazed at inanely by giant blow-ups of the stars.

71

It was a disorganised scattering of wooden, verandahed buildings and rambling palm-lined streets. Purple mountains loomed over foothills that resembled giant sand dunes covered irregularly in scrub.

Universal had weathered the transition to talkies largely by re-releasing some of its silent classics with musical scores and sound effects. Its first part-talkie, *Lonesome,* was not the over-powering success hoped for, and instead of following that picture with more delicate love stories, the studio made a futile stab at *Show Boat* with mixed sound and silent sequences, and began to seek the big time with the ambitious and powerful *All Quiet on the Western Front* and the horror films *Dracula* and *Frankenstein.* Bette knew from the first that Universal wasn't in the same league as MGM, Paramount or the up-and-coming, feisty young Warner Brothers Pictures. Aside from *All Quiet,* there was little to indicate the greatness of Universal in the silent period.

As an obscure beginner, all she was asked to do was spend the morning posing for photographs in her street clothes, including (incongruously in the Hollywood sunshine) two silver foxes that had cost her her last nickel the winter before. She held Boogum high and embraced her mother and smiled obediently, all the time wishing she were thousands of miles away.

Ray Jones recalled an example of Bette's wit some years later. As they were leaving the photographic studio, he said to her, 'Who is your favourite actress?'

'Garbo,' Bette replied.

'Oh,' Ray Jones said, 'there's a letter in *Photoplay* this week in which a woman says she believes in Garbo in the same sense she believes in God.'

'That must keep Miss Garbo awake at night!' Bette snapped.

On the next day, a Saturday, Bette looked at Ruthie and Ruthie looked at Bette. If they were going to tolerate this place at all they had better get out of the hotel fast. Only a house would make the experience tolerable. They walked along Hollywood Boulevard until they found a real-estate office. A Mrs Mary Carr took them on a long drive through the hills looking at different homes. Although they had no idea how they would pay the first and last month's rent since they had only $1.50 between them, they were sufficiently good actresses to convince Mary Carr of their affluence.

At last they found a proper place: 4435 Alta Loma Terrace, a Grimm's fairy tale cottage with redwood door and eaves. They fell in love with it at once. But the rent was $80.00 a month. What could they do to afford it? Bette's salary was $450.00 a month but she wouldn't receive the money for several weeks: probably not until after the Christmas holidays.

Neither Ruthie nor Bette slept well that night. They had to have the house. They couldn't afford the house. They had to have the house. And how were they going to pay the hotel bill when they checked out?

There was an old friend of the Favors, Carl Milliken, who lived at the Hollywood Roosevelt, a fifteen-minute walk from the Plaza. Maybe, Ruthie figured, he could supply the money.

Ruthie woke while Bette was still asleep, exhausted by a flood of tears the night before, dressed silently and walked to the Roosevelt in the early daylight. She found Milliken on the tennis court in white flannels, playing with a Japanese coach. She walked straight up to him, looked him in the eye, reminded him who she was, took a deep breath and said very fast, 'It is absolutely essential that I have $400!'

Milliken instantly produced four $100 bills! Ruthie gabbled breathlessly that she was going to obtain a house and car and then she ran off, very embarrassed, while Carl issued a little homily: 'You must be frugal, you know. This town is a fickle mistress.'

Unwilling to disclose to Bette that she had turned herself into a beggar, Ruthie undertook a theatrical, complicated ruse. She walked over to the Western Union telegraph office on Cahuenga Boulevard and wrote out a message on a form that read: AM SENDING THE MONEY YOUR MOTHER ASKED TO BORROW. DAD. In order to make the message convincingly from a miser, she restricted it to ten words. She returned to the Plaza to find the room's door locked, Bette crying beyond it. She put the telegram under the door with the money. She heard Bette scream with delight.

Bette flung open the door, grabbed Ruthie and ran with her headlong to Western Avenue where they snapped up a brand new Ford on the spot. Bette never let on that she knew Ruthie had forged the telegram.

Once mother and daughter had moved into their pretty house in the hills, their spirits began to brighten. But they were dampened again just over a week later when they were confronted with a Christmas without friends or relatives, without snow or sleigh bells, without carol singers and children's laughter. Bobby came out on the train for a week and hated everything. Hollywood Boulevard was decorated with silver tinsel and papier-mâché figures of Santa Claus, reindeers and figures from fairy tales illuminated with bulbs in their stomachs. Wind-up phonographs in stores played carols through loudspeakers. The Davises braved it out with mother's favourite dish of roast stuffed goose and mince pie. They began to buy little things that reminded them of home: brass ornaments (which Bette always refused to polish), a print of a New England snow scene, flowered plates. Boogum frisked about happily, chasing chipmunks and raccoons, and skunks which frequently added their unique aroma to nights filled with the scent of jasmine. At least the New Year lay ahead. Until then, life was perhaps just tolerable.

74

Bette was to experience a rude shock when she reported for work after the New Year vacation. Although 'Uncle' Carl Laemmle was ostensibly head of the studio, this shrewd German-Jewish emigré had handed over the reins of power to his singularly uninspiring son known familiarly as 'Junior'. At the age of twenty-one, Junior was a depressing example of the results of nepotism. His sausage-machine-like approach to picture-making resulted in works of a surpassing mediocrity based ineptly on second-rate novels or plays. As an executive, he had about as much skill as the average caretaker. Almost everybody who used something for self-respect in Hollywood laughed at Junior behind his back.

Inevitably, for such were the *macho* demands of Hollywood executives, new starlets were subjected to a minute physical analysis followed by a completion guarantee. Perhaps fortunately, Bette failed to pass muster when Junior had her to his office. He opened his door, looked her up and down, and closed it again. The prospective merger was cancelled.

She went through the motions of a screen test. The director told her that her legs must be shown or she wouldn't succeed in Hollywood. He trained a camera on her and threw a powerful light in her face that made her squint abominably. She raised her skirt nervously, even though her legs were in fact very pretty. She claims that she saw the test, cried out and fled in horror from the screening room; but young actresses were never allowed to see tests in Hollywood.

She was put in the hands of the make-up man Jack Pierce, who specialised in monster movies and whose next achievement would be the horrific creature played by Boris Karloff in *Frankenstein*. Pierce did his best to turn Bette Davis into Jean Harlow. He dyed her hair a garish blonde. He plucked her eyebrows and painted artificial ones over her own. He took her rather thin lips and smeared them with lipstick to achieve a fuller look. He shadowed her cheeks to make them seem intriguingly hollow. She was handed over to wardrobe and given further tests in clinging satin dresses with large bows and bathing suits and afternoon outfits with eyeshadowing hats. She found the whole routine insufferable. 'Serious' and used to the commitment and intelligence of the Broadway stage, she found this dyeing, shaping and pummelling of her into a reliable sexy image utterly nonsensical.

In her dramatic tests, she played without the expected sexiness and coyness of the time. She acted with an edgy, uneasy, almost neurotic gaiety and sharpness. She was clearly too brainy: she exemplified Wilde's dictum that intellect destroys the beauty of any face. She played with her head and not with her emotions. People began to feel she wouldn't last in Hollywood. She was too high-hat. She was too 'Manhattan'. It was a relief to come home at night after these gruelling sessions and put up her feet and talk to mother about the good old days in New England before they had made this horrible mistake and come to California. Another consolation was that she and Ruthie began to make one or two friends. Reginald Denny was a well-set-up young Englishman who had been a great success as a comedian in silent pictures and was setting out on a career of being a tweedy, pipe-smoking, reliable friend of the heroine in countless pictures with 'British' settings in the talkie era. Denny met Bette in the University commissary. He told me years later:

Bette and I were good friends. There was no question of a romance: I was happily married with children and that rarest thing in Hollywood, a secure and comfortable home life. I knew Bette was hating it in Hollywood. She longed to go back to the theatre. But I encouraged her to stay. I knew that although she wasn't conventionally pretty she would outlive all the platinum blondes who were walking around trying to be noticed. Her face was made for the camera. It was amazingly 'open'. The emotions weren't hidden by deceit. You could read all her feelings in those hauntingly expressive eyes. I suggested to her that instead of fretting over lost theatre she should immerse herself in good movies. She should see the stars who counted: Garbo especially. Garbo had done very little in the theatre yet her face told millions about her most secret feelings. Bette, I felt, could do the same.

Bette heeded Denny's advice. She began to go with Ruthie to Garbo pictures, sitting in the balcony and gazing transfixed at the luminous face of that supreme Swedish actress, watching Garbo's instinctive, totally uncalculated style and grace. But it was clear to her from the start that she wasn't a phenomenon of nature as Garbo was. She would have to will, to force herself into success. Sheer brains and a hellish toughness would have to get her there.

It was around that time that Denny introduced Bette to a remarkable woman who for many years became her indispensable secretary, advisor, and friend. This was Bridget Price, a sweet-natured fan who would be skilful at dealing with any correspondence. Bridget seemed to know that Bette would soon be prominent. She waited around for the chance to be the right-hand woman of a star.

Bette missed Ham acutely in those first weeks in Hollywood. She longed to see him and wrote to him constantly in her bold, round hand in green ink on extraordinarily flimsy stationery. He managed to get a promise of a job as trumpeter playing in the official band of the 1932 Olympic Games which were to take place in Los Angeles. He promised he would come out the following year to set up the arrangements. Meantime, he wrote, he was very busy playing trumpet with a band in the East and he told her which new records to buy and wished he could have gone dancing with her.

She was in a constant state of virginal longing to be married and to become a mother; but Ruthie kept up the pressure to have her stay in Hollywood: already in her mind, Ruthie was counting the future dollars. Just after New Year's Day, 1931, Bette suddenly received a script and was asked to report to work. Her first delight at appearing in *Bad Sister*, from a novel by Booth Tarkington (a writer she admired) was dashed when she discovered that the script was a travesty of the author's whimsical Hoosier tragedy. She was to appear with a mediocre British actress Sidney Fox who had beaten her out for the leading role in *Strictly Dishonorable*. Bette's part as Laura Madison called for her to be an unhappy girl whose sister is the town flirt and gadabout. While Laura clings to the hearth with her knitting and her books, Marianne whirls about parties with gay young blades. The young Humphrey Bogart was cast as Valentine Corliss, a con man who degrades Marianne.

Bette found herself confronted with an uninspired director, Hobart Henley, poor dialogue and the motionless cameras of the time that were sealed in telephone booth-like boxes so airless the operators tended to faint in them. The soundstage was completely sealed off even down to the ventilators to prevent the slightest sound being heard from outside. Even so, a backfiring truck or automobile or a bi-plane flying overhead could penetrate the silence and ruin a whole sequence. The microphones were the size and shape of corncobs and were concealed in bellpulls, cigarette boxes, or uncomfortably between an actress's breasts. Bette had to wear a microphone in her bodice with a large black insulated wire attached to the wall which made it impossible to move in any direction. if she turned her face towards the leading actor, her voice would fade; she had to address most of her lines in the approximate direction of her stomach.

It is scarcely surprising in view of the conditions of shooting that Bette played the whole part in a whining, complaining manner that only too clearly revealed her dissatisfaction with the absurd mechanics of motion picture making. The *New York Times* correctly observed upon the picture's release at the beginning of April, 1931: 'Miss Davis's interpretation of Laura is too lugubrious and tends to destroy the sympathy the audience is expected to feel for the young woman.'

Long before the verdict was given, Bette knew the truth of it. She was also far from happy with the presence of Humphrey Bogart on the scene. In later years, she failed to agree with the perennial public adulation for this figure. She found him bad mannered, bad tempered, heavy drinking and downright boring. She also told Reginald Denny that someone should have told Sidney Fox she shouldn't play a Booth Tarkington story in a voice that reeked of Mayfair. Junior Laemmle told me:

Bette Davis has spent a lifetime saying that, referring to a supporting actor in *Bad Sister*, I told someone in my office while she was outside the door that she was 'about as sexy as Slim Summerville'. First, I don't know what she was doing eavesdropping at my office door! Eavesdroppers never do hear good of themselves! I never said anything of the kind. I said she could have changed parts with cornball Slim Summerville and nobody would have known the difference. That was closer to the mark. She was very bad in *Bad Sister*. When I was at the sneak preview in San Bernardino I saw her slipping out with her mother about halfway through. I'll take an even bet they were both in tears.

Laemmle, though much criticised by Bette, at least renewed her option despite the bad reviews of her performance and cast her in a more ambitious picture, *Seed,* which shrivelled quickly. It was directed by John Stahl, a manic sadist who sentimentalised everything he touched. *Seed* was a family story, the plot of which was so complex that it filled an entire column of the *New York Times* and still remains totally incomprehensible. Bette was reduced to a very subsidiary role as one of five children of John Boles, who was only about six years her senior. Much of the story consisted of the mother's problems with the father, who is trying to get off the ground as a writer. There is endless discussion about royalty cheques and manuscripts, none of which was of the slightest interest to an audience. Bette's chief contribution to the picture was cutting up, with forgivable relish, her father's novel into strips in one scene.

Shortly after *Seed* was completed, and released a mere six weeks after *Bad Sister,* Ham came out to visit and he and Bette began dating again. He deepened still further her love and knowledge of music. She was devastated when he had to return to New York, and hated working in her current movie *Waterloo Bridge,* a genteel romantic fantasy about lovers in the First World War, set in London, in which she played an insignificant support part only one name above 'Old Woman' in the printed cast list. Doris Lloyd, a British actress who appeared in the picture, said:

> I liked Bette. I could see her staying back after she'd finished her work for the day to watch the other players, widening her blue eyes and trying to overcompensate for her miserable part by vicariously living with the characters. Such ambition! Such hunger!

Bette was miserable with the director, James Whale,

whom she found indifferent, cold and rude and quite unimpressed by her talent. She was unaware of the fact that he was a fastidious artist whose British background in the theatre brought a striking authority to the evocation of London. Even a chamber pot under a bed or a patterning of wallpaper was scrupulously correct. *Waterloo Bridge* was a shadowy, haunting, poetic work reflecting Whale's almost feminine sensibility. Bette was lovely and fragile in the tiny part of the hero's brash sister. Whale, despite her disclaimers, directed her with considerable skill, bringing out her vulnerability as Marion Gering had done in the theatre.

The lease on Alta Loma Terrace ran out and Bette and Ruthie began a series of moves, with brief stays at Zuma Beach, Canyon Drive, Havenhurst Avenue in Hollywood, and San Vicente Boulevard in Brentwood L.A. It was part of Ruthie's nature that she was unable to settle anywhere for long. She became restive and irritable. A place that seemed a dream house one day would be fenced around with imaginary problems the next.

Bette had obtained a small foothold but she still didn't have a 'name'. She had to borrow constantly on her salary to make ends meet; to support her mother and sister. She gave an early interview to W.E. Oliver of the *Los Angeles Examiner* in 1931, saying: 'It is an ordeal in pictures after you've made a name on the stage. I can walk in any New York agent's office and they know me. Here I'm back where I was three years ago, getting a first foothold.'

Junior Laemmle confirmed that he felt he had made a mistake in increasing Bette's first option to twelve months at $450 a week. He immediately lent her out: to Columbia for *Menace,* an unbridled melodrama set in a gloomy old mansion in which she screamed and ran about, to an independent group for *Hell's House,* an undistinguished affair co-starring Pat O'Brien, and to

81

RKO for a pleasant rural comedy, *Way Back Home*. She was happiest at RKO, presided over by the benign Pandro S. Berman, who gave all of his productions a special quality. She also became a friend of the O'Briens and she and her mother often visited with them: she liked the bluff, outgoing Irishman with his big genial face and tremendous energy, his rapid line of talk.

Bette soon acquired another Hollywood friend: the young and sharply intelligent C.J. Wood, who, with his brother Vernon, would soon emerge as one of the most adept business managers in Hollywood. Wood got to know Bette and her mother very well and handled what little money Bette earned, investing where possible so that at least there was some interest on the meagre savings. For years, Wood was Bette's trusted advisor and intimate. He was introduced to her by Reginald Denny, who was one of Vernon Wood's clients.

With her career at Universal hopelessly abortive, Bette was finally convinced she should return to New York forever, and Ruthie was beginning to feel the same, when suddenly an astonishing opportunity arose.

George Arliss was at the time at the peak of his success as a Hollywood star. He specialised in portraits of a Rembrandtesque realism. Ugly, skeletal, round-shouldered with a beaked nose, darting, alarming eyes and an affected, high-pitched voice, he seemed to be the last person on earth who would ever make it in the movies. But he dug deep into a character, discovering resources in conventional lines and situations. He had seen Bette not only as a pupil in plays in the John Murray Anderson Dramatic School but in Blanche Yurka's *The Wild Duck* and in *Way Back Home*. He asked to see her as a possible fellow player in *The Man Who Played God,* the story of a pianist stricken with deafness as a result of an explosion whose joy comes from watching the people in Central Park from his window and reading their lips to determine the sad and touching details of their lives. Bette was to play a girl who adored him, fascinated by his elegant hands moving over the piano keys.

Unlike many actresses and actors, Bette had a remarkable capacity for being impressed by great performers. She was dazzled by him: he told her that she had been recommended by another actor, Murray Kinnell, who had been with her in *Menace;* he was too shy to admit he was fascinated and attracted by her as well. The interview went well. He wrote in his memoirs that from the first moment he met Bette Davis he clearly saw her quality; that she was the only actress he ever worked with who brought more vibrant responsiveness and interpretation to a part than was contained in the lines or was visible at first inspection. And, responding to Arliss's trust in her, his total conviction that she could play at a level equal to his own, she gave a performance alive with sincerity and intelligence. There was no bunk in her acting. She drove to the heart of an emotion. She knew *The Man Who Played God* was an important picture and perhaps, instinctively, she felt Warner Brothers would be her alma mater.

Warners was quite different from Universal. Instead of the feeble guidance of Junior Laemmle, Warners at Burbank, hard-bitten, tough, known in the business as San Quentin, was run by a no-nonsense, super-efficient team, headed by the tanned, blazered, wise-cracking Jack Warner, the quiet and persistent Hal Wallis, and the buck-toothed, nervously hypertensive Darryl F. Zanuck. Warner pictures were made without fuss, on scratch budgets and watertight schedules. Unlike haughty MGM, Warners made pictures about the poor. They dealt with the depression life as it was. They showed the misery of the chain gangs, the cruelties of the Ku Klux Klan, the rough life of an office girl who had to sleep her way to the executive suite, the gruelling pressures of newspaper offices or the horror of prisons and the slums that bred their occupants.

Warner Brothers needed Bette Davis because she was an actress without pretence. She was miles away from the high-falutin' girls who floated through society dramas with their noses in the air. Her gutsy, feisty, totally honest, hard-edged approach to acting melded with Warners' identical approach to picture making. Although she didn't know it then, she had found her home.

The Man Who Played God does not wear well today. It seems heavily sanctimonious and false and (except for the powerful moment when he realises he has been stricken with deafness) Arliss's performance is painfully dated, mannered, theatrical, false. Bette's playing is on two notes: of frantic gaiety and burning intensity. Her admiration of Arliss shines through her acting; it almost makes convincing the absurd theory that a girl of her age and character would fall in love with an ancient trembling gargoyle because of her fascination with his talent. The endless homilies and moral tags are scarcely improved by the feeble playing of the supporting cast, who seem to have just emerged from a Sunday School drama class. Only Davis seems to understand correct diction for the microphone: everyone else is fixed in slow motion, painfully aware they are being recorded. It is unjust that the *New York Times* critic wrote only one sentence about her performance: 'Bette Davis speaks too rapidly for the microphone.' Hal Wallis says:

Anyone who could hold her own with George Arliss in a scene and not look like a prop was outstanding in my book. Indeed, there were moments when you weren't looking at Arliss, you were looking at her instead. There was no question in my mind that she would go all the way to the top. She didn't just act with her eyes. She acted with her whole body: with every pore of that body. She was alive; she jumped out of the screen.

Bette and Ruthie were living at the time on Canyon Drive. Bette, overexcited by her new success, drove her recently acquired Auburn with such outright passion she was ticketed for speeding. On 16 February 1932, she was almost burnt to death for a second time. A battery short caused a sudden surge of flame to engulf her automobile as she was driving up to the house. She screamed and struggled with the door. Bobby, who had come to stay, dragged her from the front seat in the nick of time. The story was headlined in some of the papers' back pages: sure sign that Bette Davis was on her way.

At the same time as her narrow escape, she was also suffering from a jumpy appendix which caused acute spasms, sweating and vomiting. She was so terrified of losing work because of this problem that she postponed having an operation again and again.

During the period of her sickness, Bette found another friend in the beautiful and ill-fated actress Jean Harlow. Jean's lover, the producer Paul Bern, had committed suicide, leaving a note that indicated he was suffering from sexual impotence. Bette always refused to believe the story, and it soon became gossip in Hollywood that Bern may have had another motive: his common-law wife, who committed suicide the day after Bern, would have forced him into a situation where he would have to marry Jean Harlow bigamously. Bette gave Harlow a great deal of consolation in those harrowing days.

Because of the studio's excitement over *The Man Who Played God,* Bette was kept busy under contract; rushed into no less than five pictures in 1932. Of these, *The Rich Are Always With Us* had a special place with her because during the making of it she met and felt strongly attracted to a handsome young Irish actor named George Brent. Dark, brown-eyed, with a football player's build, he had come from the Abbey Theatre in Dublin to success on Broadway and in Hollywood as an uninspired but reliable leading man who could be an effective foil for high-powered actresses. Unfortunately, he was mean-spirited, tough, and handicapped by a wickedly vicious tongue. His sex appeal, hard to understand today, earned him a series of conquests that made him the envy of many Hollywood men. If one can seek an explanation of it, it may have lain in his masculine self-confidence, the aura of solid dependability and security. He was sturdily complacent and humorously self-satisfied. His static, stolid good looks combined with his bland, outgoing manner in captivating Bette.

But he wasn't responsive. He was already involved with the heroine of *The Rich Are Always With Us,* Ruth Chatterton, who made up for her small stature and plump, pouter-pigeon figure with a regal manner and an imposing expression on her undistinguished oval face that convinced audiences she was a great actress. It was a confidence trick that worked. Yet today, in the absurd Hollywood version of high society affairs that *The Rich Are Always With Us* perpetrated, Bette Davis, not Ruth Chatterton, is the one who is doing the acting. The only surviving scene of interest in their travesty of New York society is one in which Brent and Chatterton, visibly in love, are discovered in a bedroom. Brent lights two cigarettes at the same time and hands one to Chatterton. Writer Casey Robinson introduced the same device into the big cigarette scene in *Now, Voyager* that has become a kind of kitsch classic moment in film history.

In the later summer of 1932, Ham arrived from New York to play fanfares in turban and sash in the Olympic Games Band. Only two days after he arrived, Bette had to go East on a ridiculous promotional tour with the actor Warren William. Frustrated over the fact that George Brent was not attracted to her, that nothing that she could do could make him so, and that Ham's life seemed to be moving at odds with hers, Bette had a depressing stay in New York in bad weather, barely tolerating Warren William's ridiculously pretentious behaviour as a cut-rate John Barrymore.

Back in Los Angeles, Bette rushed through the shooting of her best picture to date: *Cabin in the Cotton*. At last, though she didn't like him, she had a real director: the ferocious Michael Curtiz, a brutal and savage Hungarian who addressed everybody including Bette as 'you bum'. He screamed his instructions on the set, was disgusted by any player who chose to take lunch, liked to work well into the night, and several times got into fistfights with his crew. He strode around in riding breeches, cracking a whip and pouring out a stream of foul language. He mangled his adopted tongue and peppered his phrases with a bizarre collection of malapropisms. Skeet shooting, polo and pictures were his passions. Bette spent the rest of her life repeating the well-worn story that Curtiz called her a 'no good sexless son of a bitch' and made her play a love scene to the lens of a camera. What she does not acknowledge is that he forced her into her best performance of the early 1930s. As Madge, the dizzy, selfish, peroxided Southern belle, she created a fully rounded character, at once ruthless, bold, and pathetic. She had little to work with in the script: an account of the conflict between labour and management on a southern plantation, symbolised in the internal struggles of emotion and conscience of a glum youth (Richard Barthelmess). Barthelmess, his face fixed and expressionless as a Japanese mask, plays with morbid passivity while Bette acts up a storm as his seducer. There is one marvellous scene, daring for its time, that succeeds in conveying a surprising degree of eroticism. Madge decides finally to corrupt her high-minded lover. Aware he is repressed, that he has sublimated his sexuality in his devotion to the workers, she lures him into a bedroom after giving a sleepy black maid

87

the afternoon off. Though played entirely at shoulder level, the scene conveys great power: Bette undressing in a closet, undoing the bow of her dress, and emerging, it is clearly implied, brazenly naked as her helpless admirer slowly and frightenedly whispers her name.

It is all the more extraordinary that Bette played this scene when she was still a virgin. But Ruthie had already decided the condition could no longer be tolerated, and Bette enthusiastically concurred. They discussed the matter as though they were talking about a merger. It was typical of Ruthie's nature that every step in Bette's professional and emotional career was planned on the same level of mathematical determination. Ham was earning on a regular basis: not much, but he was earning. He was a New Englander, so the Davises and the Favors would welcome him into the family. What was more, he had managed to sign a contract with the fashionable Colony Club to play trumpet in its jazz band. His salary had gone up to $100 a week. He could now be a husband.

Such were the narrow bourgeois considerations that Ruthie brought to bear on what should have been a spontaneous and warm coming together of a young man and a young woman. It was based on a shaky foundation of similar tastes and backgrounds, fondness, some physical attraction, and comparable salaries and prospects. Above all, it was based on a need for Bette to get rid of her troublesome virginity. At least on paper, it sounds rather like the acquisition of a first-class dentist.

Ham proposed to Bette and she surprised him by accepting instantly. Ruthie probably wrote his speech. Bette said in her memoirs:

I suppose I couldn't have expected Mother to suggest that we have an affair. Would that she had been wise. Would that Ham and I had been. I was hopelessly puritan, helplessly passionate . . .

The inevitable happened in August, a stifling hot month in Los Angeles. Perhaps because she feared she might change her mind, Bette opted for an Arizona wedding, since the California marriage laws called for a six-week waiting period. Ruthie, Bette and Ham set off together by car to Yuma, since Bette was terrified of flying. The journey was a dusty, miserable ordeal in those days before freeways. The Auburn choked and spluttered through 115 degrees of heat across the border. Bette drove, covered in sweat, Ham wilted in the front passenger seat, and Ruthie was in a terrible state in the back. All three were soaked to the skin when they finally reached their destination. They moved into rooms in a seedy hotel and soaked in baths of cold water. Then they met in Bette's room draped in counterpanes while their sweat-soaked clothes dried. Finally, in late afternoon, Ham struggled into his dirty rags and went out to buy a shirt and suit and wedding ring.

The wedding took place next morning, conducted by the Indian mission minister, Reverend Mark Schalbaugh. There was no press around, Ham temporarily lost the ring, two poodles raced around the room licking themselves vigorously, and steam trains tooted and shunted nearby. Bette, in a later description to the reporter Gladys Hall, said, 'I wore a limp beige dress, brown gloves and shoes, and carried two limp gardenias.'

That night, Bette moved out of her room into Ham's. She has described the total joy of her wedding night, of passion excused for the puritan by the institution of marriage. Next morning, she was fulfilled and more madly in love with Ham than ever. Now, she felt, there could never be any separating of them.

Four

ON THE face of it, Bette and Ham seemed to have a good enough recipe for a successful marriage relationship. Bette's earnings were not all that much higher than Ham's; they enjoyed the same things: music, movies, and taking weekend trips down to San Diego, where, after a difficult late Saturday night at the studio, Bette could relax on the magical ferry-boat trip to the grand old Hotel del Coronado, where Sundays could be spent mingling with the crowds in the lobby or swimming at the beach. Sometimes at night Bette would watch Ham conducting the Colony Club band when the conductor fell ill; and in the tradition of the time, a voice would announce her and a thin pencil of spotlight would swing around through the darkness and settle on the table where she sat with Ruthie and Bobby, enjoying the hot jazz under the light-studded ceiling.

These happinesses were extensively described in studio handouts and fan magazine articles. They were not invented but they only gave one side of the picture. Often, Bette would return home at night, irritable and worn out from hours of difficult shooting under hot lights. Her dream was of a husband who could simply put his feet up and read or doze by the fire while she relaxed completely. But in fact Ham was off to the Colony Club every night and would not return home until the early morning hours while she had to rise at 6:30 to drive over to Burbank from their house off Sunset Boulevard in

West Hollywood to go into make-up and costume fittings.

It was only on Sundays, and in the rare periods between pictures, that Bette and Ham had a chance to get to know each other. She longed for him to boss her, dominate her, take charge. She hated the fact that he complained because he had no dominance. And yet at the same time in many ways she regretted the fact that he had a career of his own which made it impossible for him to share much time with her.

When she suggested Ham should attend to tidying the house, he obeyed and she wished that he had not. It was as though she were constantly challenging both herself and Ham in order to achieve the kind of relationship which only a romantic could imagine would ever exist. She had already, unhappily, and for all her down-to-earth New England horse sense, begun to want the perfection promised by the fictitious scripts she played out in motion pictures.

Her attitude towards life was extremely cut and dried, far too hard and precise: she wanted life to be ordered but it was impossible to achieve that kind of order. She gave interviewers exactly the same story over and over again: it never varied because she wanted to act out a personality that was totally organised, cool, direct, and eminently sane. She still was an Easterner and always would be.

Her best friend, though she saw her seldom, was Robin Brown, a charming woman she had known since Cushing, and would know until the end of her life. New Englanders (especially her family) gave her a sense of security and firmness she never found in Hollywood people. She always tried to import into her life in Hollywood their stricter and more austere and sober virtues. The fact that Ham was New England made her forgive many of his faults, but she only wished he had a New England bedrock of firmness in his character. She in the very bones of her being had to win. Ham lacked her burning ambition; he could be happy just playing his trumpet in a sash and turban for the Olympic Games. Bette wouldn't stop until she was Sarah Bernhardt.

The chief problem was that while Bette's name became known, Ham's did not. He wasn't even a radio personality; he was fixed in the dreary existence of club or hotel performance. She wanted him to be in radio; she worked with him on Sundays on songs, hoping he would achieve a place in the Hit Parade; and one song they composed together, 'Riding on a Bus-top' was actually published. But it was a feeble effort and made no impression.

Ham's personality underwent a gradual but unnerving change. Deprived of a wife who could give him her days after a hard night's work, he had instead a wife who was constantly invited to parties which he couldn't attend with her, and whose name was being mentioned frequently in the press as an up-and-coming star. He became bitter and jealous. He started to whine with self-pity and sometimes even cried. There was an odd streak of femininity in Ham that made him fragile and clinging. His gangly charm disappeared and he lashed back at Bette even weakly hitting her when her contempt for him became too obvious. Within months, the marriage was in trouble.

There is no question that Bette slowly but surely lost her respect for Ham. As her income increased and his did not, she knew the score: that she would have to foot the bills. She didn't mind that, but she very much minded that Ham complained about it. In a desperate effort to appease him she agreed they would live on his salary, and that she would save her own with the aid of her business manager, C.J. Wood. Instead of moving into a house justified by her rising fame, they would live on the wrong side of the tracks in a modest house with a proper porch and clapboard front set back from the road off Franklin Avenue: a cottage rented from Cecil B. DeMille, who lived in vulgar splendour up the road in Laughlin Park. Bette's only luxury was a maid; a black lady named Adele Pfeiffer. Bette was able to give Ruthie a pleasant house of her own and a succession of automobiles. She dipped into her savings to satisfy Ruthie's greed for new possessions while denying herself virtually everything.

The pressures on her were constant. She was making five or six pictures a year; Ruthie's bills kept pouring in; Ham wanted new clothes; she herself had to dress well; C.J. Wood asked her constantly to try to invest more: she was forcing herself to improve daily as an actress. It is scarcely surprising that she became more fragile than ever, that she began to suffer from sudden and terrifying set-backs of health. At first, there was nothing more serious than an appendicitis operation two months after her marriage, but she began to develop sinus trouble, severe sore throats that caused her to lose her voice, headaches, fits of weeping. The extreme severity and neuroses of the Favor strain worked against her volatile and passionate nature and made her sick with exhaustion. She flung herself into her work with a kind of desperation that gave a special edge of anxiety to her acting. Often, there was a nervous, even a neurotic flavour in her performances when it wasn't called for by the script. Or, paradoxically, she would play an emotional scene in a clipped, precise, business-like voice that destroyed the necessary emotion.

Her technique was refined, her sensitivity to the demands of a part fascinating and remarkable, but there was a certain unevenness, a lack of composure in her performances that suggested the tensions and struggles of her personal life. Her acting was affected both favourably and unfavourably by her private torment.

And there were escapes from that torment in her social life. Since another man could not accompany her to premières or parties because that would cause excessive gossip, Ruthie went with her everywhere, often walking grandiosely ahead of her (in a far more expensive costume) in lobbies crowded with photographers and fans on movie first nights. Bette made a friend of Marion Davies, the adorable mistress of William Randolph Hearst, who invited her to a beach house at Santa Monica where Bette mingled with the famous. She discovered the arid delights of Palm Springs and La Quinta in the California desert, where there were palm-fringed swimming pools and weekend gatherings of directors and stars.

As for work, which in the last analysis meant more to Bette Davis than anything else, it was something of an ordeal relieved only by the occasional good script. In whatever little time they had together, Bette would ask Ham to read the screenplays and give his opinion; Ham, easily pleased, would be delighted with lines that Bette would savagely denounce as stupid and banal. When he became irritated by her wandering around the house in a trance-like condition 'becoming' her character, she would suggest that he read the male lead's lines to her while she responded with the memorised lines to be spoken by the heroine. Unfortunately, Ham was a poor reader, either stumbling over the words or trying to speak them with the florid emphases of a John Barrymore. When she criticised him with just points he would sink into a monotone. As a result, Bette would give up in despair and ask Ruthie or Bobby to work with her instead.

And there came another problem. Bobby was desperate to be an actress, to be a match for her sister. Consumed with sibling rivalry, she tried again and again, but she had no talent and the industry cruelly rejected her. Always unstable, subject to severe nervous attacks bordering on schizophrenia, she had a complete collapse sometime late in 1932. Ruthie took her East for treatments. She was in isolation for periods, hysterically screaming that Bette had taken away her chances for a career. The truth was that Bette, who put her family before everything except work, would have given many years of her life if Bobby could have been a success in pictures.

Life in the Davis household was scarcely eased by the fact that Bette found little or no pleasure in being rushed from one trashy picture to another. Warner Brothers, in common with other studios, owned its own theatre chains and pictures had to be made at express speed, and even back-to-back, to satisfy the demands of the theatre managers for a ceaseless flow of product. Of the pictures Bette made in 1933, the second year of her marriage to Ham, only one, *20,000 Years in Sing Sing*, was worth seeing. In this grim story of prison life, Bette appeared with Spencer Tracy, for whom she felt a profound attraction and admiration that has remained with her. (If anyone mentioned his drinking, she was ready to kill them.) Tracy had asked for her: he had seen *Hell's House* and had been fascinated by her odd, unpredictable gaiety. Bette, Tracy later told his friends, was nervous and restless during the shooting. At one stage, he said to her, 'You know, you could be the best actress in pictures today. I'll correct that. You *are* the most talented.'

'Damn right,' she snapped back characteristically. 'But who are we against so many?'

Tracy's biographer, Larry Swindell, wrote: 'They joked about their similarities – neither was handsome, and both had fierce tempers, and both missed the stage. They felt such rapport – it might have been that they were both Aries, and, in fact, had the same birthdate. Someday when they were rich, they planned to make more and better pictures together, but for one reason or another, they never did.'

Once more, the picture was directed by Michael

Curtiz, who made Bette's life miserable but who succeeded in wringing from her a performance comparable to that she had given in *Cabin in the Cotton*. As the convict's girlfriend, at once tough and vulnerable, she created a completely convincing and rounded character, alive with warm touches of detail.

A sadness of those months was that Bette's terrier Boogum died. The only cure was to obtain another pet immediately, and Bette acquired an adorable Scottie; later, a Sealyham, two poodles and a large Doberman pinscher were added to the pooch collection. Bette adored dogs and had wonderful fun with her family of quadrupeds. She found an escape from the problems of her life in taking care of them.

There were always headaches. One of them was a ridiculous journey across the country in February, 1933, aboard the Forty-Second Street Special: a train painted gold and made of fourteen cars that travelled from Los Angeles's Santa Fe station to New York and other cities on a sixteen-day junket to promote a current musical. The movie star, Laura LaPlante, the famous swimmer Eleanor Holm, twelve singing and dancing beauties and Tom Mix and his wonder horse set off on this gruelling expedition in winter blizzards. Frequently, the train was snowbound and the heating and water system broke down. If anyone opened a window, a mixture of snow and soot flew in. Bette, who always had a chest weakness, suffered from a series of miserable colds. She often had to address crowds from the observation platform at impossible hours of the day or night. It was a thrill for depression crowds to see the stars; but for Bette the only pleasure in the trip was discovering how famous she had become.

The separation scarcely helped the marriage to Ham. Yet they clung together, still romantically in love with each other in spite of everything. There was something touching and pathetic about this grim hanging on to the fragile raft of their relationship. Ham left the Colony Club and began to conduct dance bands in both Los Angeles and San Francisco; when he travelled north, Bette holed up in a depressing motel over weekends; but the divisions between them continued.

Much of her life was spent in longing for better scripts. Very gradually, her character was changing. Instead of the serious, subdued, but intense creature she had been, she began to become more edgy, dramatic, prone to exaggerations and to chain-smoking without inhaling: closer, in fact, to the Bette Davis we know from her screen performances. Her emotions, forced back while she still had her virginity, now took charge of her and she became almost violent: fierce and driving in her frustrations. She began to prod and irritate. Her need for improvement maddened people even while they admired her or adored her.

She was utterly different from the phoney, artificial women who ruled Hollywood. She was 'human', abrasively honest and exhaustingly outspoken; she appreciated talent, and was as quick in detecting or denouncing stupidity and mediocrity. If a young supporting actress was struggling, she would help her with her lines. But if she discovered incompetence in a fellow player, she would scream blue murder at her unfortunate victim.

She was a great fan of her friend Jean Harlow and watched her in everything, calling her to tell her how fascinated she was with her performances. It intrigued her that Harlow could subdue a pleasant, modest nature in the appearance of a harsh, slangy golddigger: the type Harlow made famous in pictures. She admired Gable, and continued to worship Garbo. She was a movie buff, and regretted she did not have the luxury of the MGM stars, for whom vehicles were constructed with fanatical care.

She saw all of Hepburn's pictures and again felt admiration: Hepburn seemed to treat RKO like a country club, serving picnic lunches on the set and airily selecting all of her own scripts. She loved and envied Hepburn's face. She read constantly, consuming book after book and expressing extravagant enthusiasm for writers she admired. She loved the works of Somerset Maugham and doted on the poems of Carl Sandburg.

She became obsessed – her life was a series of obsessions – with the thought that she must go to RKO – Hepburn's studio – to star in the role of Mildred, the bitter cruel waitress who taunts the crippled London intellectual in Somerset Maugham's *Of Human Bondage*. She pestered Pandro S. Berman, genial head of RKO, to take her on for the picture version; most other actresses were terrified of the part, convinced that playing a bitch would ruin their careers. She felt she had nothing to lose, and, given her current misery and frustration, she was in the correct mood to act the part. She has admitted that she often taunted poor, weak Ham Nelson the way Mildred taunted her victim.

Somerset Maugham knew her work and was supportive of her ambition to play Mildred. But Jack Warner, a cold and ruthless man behind his good-natured front, refused to let her go. Finally, he became so irritated by her constant phone calls that he gave in with a groan. And again she almost lost the part because the British actor Leslie Howard, a cool and disdainful man, didn't want her and considered her a nobody.

In the weeks it took Bette to induce everyone to let her play Mildred, she discovered she was pregnant. She would willingly have given up the supreme opportunity to make *Of Human Bondage* if she could have been the mother of a child. But to her horror Ham, who at that moment destroyed much of her feeling for him, told her she must get rid of the baby. She suddenly realised he was terrified by the expense and ashamed to think that she might have to pay the costs of raising a baby. Also, she feared, he was anxious that his meal ticket would be lost. A further shock came when Ruthie also opposed the idea of a baby. In a bitter passage in her memoirs, Bette wrote, 'I saw Ruthie's point . . . I saw everyone's point . . . I understood everything intellectually. I was wretched emotionally. I did as I was told.'

Doing as she was told involved, obviously, an abortion. There is no question that this operation, discussed by her on television recently, affected her health and upset the emotional basis of her marriage. She struggled through a laughable example of trash called *Fashions of 1934*, through *The Big Shakedown, Jimmy the Gent* amd the slightly superior *Fog over Frisco* before at last she was able to escape to RKO for *Of Human Bondage* in the spring of 1934.

The director of the picture, John Cromwell, said later:

The first day I met Bette Davis I knew she *had to be Mildred*. What struck me most about her? Her courage. No other actress in Hollywood would have dared face a camera with her hair untidy and badly rinsed, her clothes cheap and tawdry, her manner vicious and ugly. She worked like a dog on her Cockney accent, she made you feel she had been on her feet all day and much of the night as well, serving food: the most exhausting of jobs for a woman, and the most humiliating. She said to me, 'A girl like Mildred must look ill: she has tuberculosis and she's poor.' I told her to do her own make-up any way she wanted so long as she didn't overdo it. After all, Mildred couldn't seem to be literally dying, she had to have the energy of pure evil. I sensed a desperation in Davis. It wasn't just the desperation of an unhappy woman whose marriage was going wrong. She was frightened, really frightened that the worst thing of all would happen to her as an actress: that she would become bored with her work, that she would develop a block and would lose her career. Mildred was her chance, once and for all, to make the big time. And yet I never felt she was overdoing it. My faith in her was supported by the knowledge that her greatness would be tempered by discipline.

It is hard to believe that Bette was still, at the age of twenty-six, when she played Mildred, in many ways a sheltered and unworldly girl whose mother's love and whose constant employment at a major studio had cut her off from the realities of the depression. In portraying Mildred, she clearly drew from her memories of being a waitress at college, so that when she came home from work in a scene one could feel the ache in her feet, in every bone of her body. She drew on her own streak of shrewishness to show Mildred's vicious anger. Although Leslie Howard's impossibly defeated, passive Philip was hard to believe, he wasn't far removed from Ham in his character. All of Bette's buried frustration emerged in her acting. The result was a performance without compromise. And there was a problem in this. Leslie Howard, who was critical of Bette's Cockney accent, was jealous of her and cared little for her. She had to put up with his maddening indifference – and that indifference, along with the determination to convince him she was his equal, gave an almost manic edge to the hatred she conveyed in acting with him.

Somerset Maugham was the first to praise her performance. But audiences were disconcerted by it. The preview was a disaster: people filed out angrily muttering that it was a dirty picture: they couldn't believe any man could accept such verbal lashings: it was perverse, ugly, against nature. The producer Pan Berman made radical cuts and changes but *Of Human Bondage* still failed at the box-office and the picture, apart from Bette's performance, hasn't stood the test of time.

Back at Warners, pleased by the reviews of *Of Human*

Bondage, Bette plunged into a new series of movies of which only two, *Bordertown* and *Dangerous*, made a real impression.

In essence, *Bordertown* was just another heavy dark melodrama of the kind in which Warners specialised: later remade as *They Drive by Night*. The murder scene was brilliantly played. And in the courtroom sequence, when this larger-than-life villainess had gone insane, Bette ranked with the greatest stars. She could have acted the scene with hysterics but instead more frighteningly conveyed psychological breakdown through subtle gestures and intonations. Perhaps because her own nature was so hypersensitive, so delicately balanced, and because she knew Bobby's torment, she could provide a convincing glimpse of a psyche that had gone over the edge. Her definitive playing of the scene proved that she was not merely a broad player of melodrama. She grew in stature through this part. In doing so, she defied the director, Archie Mayo, who had a weakness for purple passages. It was a distinct case of an actress triumphing over a director.

Dangerous, made several months later, was a sentimental fantasy about an actress of the Jeanne Eagels variety who feels haunted by a 'jinx' – some mysterious force which drove her to destroy others and herself and over which she had no control. She is first seen hovering on a street corner in the darkness near a theatre, where she is spotted by a handsome architect (Franchot Tone). The architect picks her up, rehabilitates her, gives her a break by financing a play himself. But, helpless because of her self-destructive streak, she smashes her car into a tree on the first night. It emerges that her fellow victim in the crash is her discarded husband, who remains in love with her despite her total lack of interest in him. A laughable ending has her returning to her injured husband, who smiles at her wanly through a hospital window.

This tissue of nonsense would have sunk most actresses at the start, but Bette gave the role of the actress an extraordinary realism. In scenes that were flat and mechanical, she conveyed a range of naked feeling, sometimes daringly mixing emotions: all the way from cynical humour to despair in the course of a single dramatic moment. For all his professional skill, and it was considerable, Franchot Tone was static and waxen alongside her amazing virtuosity. In *Dangerous*, more than in any other picture up to that time including *Of Human Bondage*, the special quality that Bette offered could be seen most clearly. It was a courageous disclosure of feeling, a truthfulness of word and gesture, a nakedness in which the audience seemed to be seeing her thoughts without any intervention of technique. The technique fell away and exposed the nerve of suffering. It wasn't a calculated method. It was acting achieved through empathy with character and audience. Only a person with this degree of nervousness and hypersensitivity, risking her own well-being in the commitment of her playing, could have achieved this level. And always the emotion was tempered with intelligence, giving the more critical members of the audience the feeling that they were encountering somebody they would enjoy meeting. Other actresses had an equal appeal to the masses; few had an equally strong appeal to the critics.

For all its faults, *Dangerous* brought Bette great satisfaction. And the picture earned her extraordinary reviews: although critics were severe about the manufactured nature of the production and its soap opera lines and situations, they justly praised the firmness and honesty, the emotional depth and range of the central performance. It was manifestly clear that Bette would be in the front running for an Academy Award when the awards were given out in February, 1936.

* * *

By the late summer of 1935, Bette Davis was established as one of the big international stars. And this resulted in countless fan magazine articles, photographs of her posing with her dog, Tippy, swimming in somebody else's pool (which the studio pretended was her own), being seen at 'nightclubs' which in fact were corners of old nightclub sets, living the kind of life a star was supposed to live in the depression: a life of pure fantasy, spun out of celluloid. Her acting off-screen had to be as effective as her acting on. Gradually, she learned the secret of giving press interviewers the image which she and Warner Brothers needed to sell to the public: an outgoing, cheerful, witty, no-nonsense kind of woman, with an answer for everything. No indication here of the pain, the nerve-wracking strain of her life with Ham, her mother and sister; no hint of dire quarrelling, of sudden threats of departure, of makings-up under stress. Nor was there an inkling of the humiliation Ham felt at being ignored by people at premieres or parties who treated him like some manager, agent or obscure hanger-on, who shook Bette's hand or embraced her while almost literally pushing him into the background. Nor could anyone discover in those glowing absurd articles an inkling of Bette's shame at the treatment of her husband and her longing for him to be as successful as she. Even though she tried to ignore it, it was painful to have a husband earning $100 a week when she was earning $1,000.

Nobody seeing her smiling in photographs and at social functions would have suspected her intense dislike of most Hollywood people and Hollywood talk with its emphasis on fashion, make-up, scandal and intrigue. It wasn't often disclosed that she much preferred staying at home listening to Bing Crosby records, reading Somerset Maugham's short stories, poring over her latest ill-written script or adding touches of New England to her living-room in the form of brassware, Toby mugs and decorated plates. She liked to argue, wrangle, ride horseback and work in training guide dogs for the blind. None of this particularly interested the magazines. There wasn't much you could make of her loving fog, rain, argumentation and onions.

She had reached that minimal point of power at which she could actually ask for parts. Whether she was given them was another matter: she had wanted to be loaned to RKO, where Pan Berman would have had her play Elizabeth to Katharine Hepburn's Mary Stuart in *Mary of Scotland*: a chance to beat her envied rival hollow in the championship stakes. She had wanted to play Alice in Paramount's crazy-house version of *Alice in Wonderland*, with Gary Cooper as the White Knight, but Warners had refused to let her go. Now she became fascinated by the part of Gaby Maple in *The Petrified Forest*, which had become a big Broadway hit that summer. On this occasion, she got her wish.

The Petrified Forest was a typical mid-thirties melodrama about a cross-section of society trapped in an unlikely milieu: in this case, a filling station in the Arizona desert. Robert Sherwood, the author, brought together a frail intellectual Englishman, a yearning waitress-poet, a bored society woman whose lifelong hunger had been to play the nun in *The Miracle*, her dreary husband, a snarling gangster and his henchmen and an ancient, wiseguy grandpappy. The conception was purely theatrical and scarcely inspiring, the writing was heavy and pretentious. Nevertheless, the story had a basis for a good, high-powered movie.

Bette was the perfect choice for the fragile waitress, Gaby, whose yearnings for a literary career and a trip to Paris had a touching quality of hopelessness. Because of her experiences at Cushing, she knew what it was to be a waitress; her love of poetry also needed no stimulation.

She had acquired a forceful new agent, Mike Levee, along with her improved status. Levee called her one

Sunday and told her, 'Hal Wallis wants you for Gaby!' She was thrilled and called Jack Warner at home in an excited state: 'This is wonderful! How can I thank you enough?' Impulsive as ever, she rushed on, 'It's a great honour. The finest honour I've received. My only concern is Leslie (Howard). Will he work with me again? He hated me in *Bondage*!'

Warner reassured her. Howard would give no trouble: her career had improved tremendously; Howard would be forced to respect her. He had been cast while still appearing in the play as the highbrow Englishman Alan Squier, and had told Warner at the time that Bette would be quite acceptable to him.

A problem was that Howard could only spare a few weeks to make the picture in Hollywood because he had to return to New York to appear in a new play. When Bette met him on the first day of work in October, 1935, she found him, for all his protestations, as cold and aloof as ever. She lied to the columnists that she adored him; but they seldom talked during the length of shooting. And she disliked Humphrey Bogart who was cast as the gangster Duke Mantee as intensely as she had when they worked before. He drank, he was unruly and rude. He was gruff and impatient with Bette and talked only of making enough money in California to buy a yacht and sail off into the blue for good. With her dedication to work, she was disgusted by his lack of interest in picture making and his cynical attitude towards the studio.

The unit was transferred by train in savage autumn heat to Red Rock Canyon, a gruelling location that was made to stand-in for Arizona. The white sun, the wind-blown sand, the swarms of flies that burst from the earth and the trees in small black storm clouds drove the cast almost mad with irritation. Bette, with her sensitive eyes and skin, suffered from severe eyestrain and freckling and burning. When she inhaled the fine gritty dust, her sinuses acted up badly.

Leslie Howard, a stickler for contract terms, refused to work on Sundays, which infuriated the director, the fat, edgy, manic Archie Mayo. Worse still, Bette herself went on strike. Her throat and sinuses were so severely inflamed that she could not perform at all. When the production manager screamed at her that she should go to work, the other cast members rebelled along with her, and Genevieve Tobin, Leslie Howard and Bogie all retired to the local hotel for the day.

Another problem of the shooting was that Leslie Howard disliked the director so sharply he would not appear on the set at the time called for each morning. He would be an hour or two late on several occasions simply in order to annoy Mayo. This childish behaviour irritated Bette. Moreover, she became increasingly sick. She developed a cold when the hot California autumn suddenly changed into a chilly damp winter. Her cold worsened so that she had to be shifted around in the schedule and some of her scenes were shot using a double. As if this were not enough, she slipped and sprained her ankle entering the petrol station set one morning. She limped badly and had to drop out of more scenes. She clashed with Mayo over the interpretation of her lines and in particular over the use of her voice. She pitched her voice very high; he objected to what he called its 'Mickey Mouse squeakiness'.

There was worse to come. To match the dust of Arizona, Mayo had a wind machine blow a toxic substance called fuller's earth all over the set of the petrol station exterior. Bette protested that in her condition she couldn't face this. Mayo insisted on proceeding; as a result, she often suffered from headaches and nerve rashes and became so ill she was afraid she wouldn't be able to finish the picture.

Back in Hollywood in the midst of her increasing sickness, the studio offered her a script. The production manager, Tenny Wright, brought it to her on the set in a break between scenes. It was so atrocious she wanted to throw up. It was a version of Dashiell Hammett's *The Maltese Falcon* entitled *The Man with the Black Hat*. When Frank Shaw, unit manager on *The Petrified Forest*, handed it to her, she glanced through it and impatiently tossed it into her dressing-room.

When Jack Warner's secretary called her the next day asking her for a quick response on the screenplay, she said that her lawyer, Martin Gang, would see Warner to discuss it as she 'most emphatically would not'. Gang failed to turn up at the meeting. Bette took sick and cabled Warner from her home on Franklin Avenue that she needed a rest, that all the weeks on *The Petrified Forest* breathing in fuller's earth had made her ill and exhausted. and she was sure that 'anybody else' could play in *The Man with the Black Hat*.

As soon as she was back at work on *The Petrified Forest*, Roy Obringer, the studio's legal authority, went to see her on set between takes to remind her of the legal obligation she had to appear in anything the studio cared to send her. She became nervous and fretful, smoking constantly, and said, edgily, 'Valerie Purvis in *Hat* is wrong for me. There are hundreds of artists you can select for the part. I'm exhausted from this picture – *can't you see I'm exhausted*? I need a rest – my nerves are bad.'

Jack Warner refused to accept this excuse and ordered her to report to the producer, Henry Blanke, to discuss her wardrobe fittings on the picture on 2 December. She did not report to Blanke, sending another telegram announcing that she was 'physically incapable' of doing so. Obringer replied by telegram – all this across a distance of less than ten miles – saying that the studio doctor, Carl Conn, would be coming to examine her that night to see if her 'incapability' was genuine. He reminded her that her contract specified she submit to medical examinations at any time the studio chose to send a doctor to see her.

At six o'clock on 2 December, Dr Conn drove over to her house and found that there was nobody at home. Obringer protested by telegram. She cabled Obringer from her sister's house saying that she was unable to be home when Conn called; that even if she had been home she would not have allowed him to examine her; that she was not ill and did not claim to be; and that she wanted a rest.

What annoyed her more than anything else was that she would be expected to make a taxing, challenging and important picture like *The Petrified Forest* and then, because of the pressure to supply the exhibitors with product, have to mug her way through junk like *The Man with the Black Hat* right after it. What was more, she was genuinely exhausted, her nervous irritability more extreme than ever. Bobby was still mentally disturbed and in and out of sanitariums. Her mother was equally upset that this kind of pressure should be applied by Warners. Ham Nelson, conducting his combo every night in Hollywood, tried his best, after rising late in the morning, to calm Bette down in his ineffectual, gangly way.

It was not a very happy house, that modest Cape Cod cottage named by Bette, The Nelson House on Franklin Avenue. A husband who came home exhausted at all hours of the morning was not the ideal companion for an actress whose nerves were frayed. Her temper can only be imagined when she discovered that the studio suspended her on 3 December for failing to report to wardrobe. But she couldn't afford to be suspended: her mother's bills and Bobby's were heavy, and she had to make sure they had everything they needed in their separate homes. Moreover, she had already borrowed against her earnings, so heavy had her burden of debt become.

On 6 December, fretful, furious with Warner, she had

108

to begin work on *The Man with the Black Hat*. And Jack Warner tossed her a bone: he yielded to her six desperate written requests to let her appear on Al Jolson's Shell Chateau Radio Program, acting out a high-powered scene from *Dangerous*. 'But she mustn't,' he coldly told Roy Obringer, 'do anything from any material other than that film.'

As it turned out, she played her scene from *Dangerous* with such earnestness, such feverish attack and style, that Al Jolson, an unpleasant man, actually clapped her at the end of her delivery.

Bette had hoped for some rest after babbling her way through the imbecilities of *The Man with the Black Hat* (later retitled *Hard Luck Dame* and then *Satan Met a Lady*) and the *macho* hauteur of her co-star Warren William. But no sooner had she retired to Franklin Avenue in a state of nervous exhaustion than she was told that a crisis had developed: Kay Francis had refused to appear in a nonsensical farce named *Cream Princess* which was due to start at any minute. In this emergency situation, Tenny Wright rushed the script to Bette's house where her maid Adele received it. When she returned home, Bette had to laugh. The note from Wright was: 'Please ready yourself immediately for *Cream Princess*.' She couldn't believe the title, and called her friends to laugh over it some more. She had to play a former cafeteria cashier who pretends to be the madcap heiress to a cosmetic fortune and has an affair with a reporter played by George Brent.

Although she acted with her customary flair, Bette was even more disgusted by this trash than she had been with *The Man with the Black Hat*. Many scenes were shot at the Toluca Lake Country Club golf course, in harsh sunlight that made her peel; she had to shoot several other scenes at Santa Monica Beach, where her sensitive Easterner's white skin suffered more and the hard glittering light beating off the Pacific Ocean gave her a severe case of eyestrain: so bad a headache she could scarcely proceed. On 7 February 1936 she walked off the set, cabling Tenny Wright from home that she was 'dead after five days and nights of work . . . I cannot work tomorrow . . . I cannot do myself justice.'

She hated the cameraman, Arthur Edeson, and for years refused to have him on her pictures. His harsh, realistic style of lighting made her look quite unattractive: always a danger since she did not have perfectly photogenic features.

She had been in bed for several days in February when she received word to attend the Academy Awards. She struggled out of bed, feeling sick, and discovered she hadn't a single dress worthy of the occasion. Her dear Ruthie selected a particularly ugly gown. Ruthie, of course, dressed magnificently for the occasion.

Bette said later that she felt completely numb when she heard her name announced as the winner. She made her way awkwardly to the stage. She knew only too well, as she stood alongside the Irish star Victor McLaglen, who had won for *The Informer*, that she had won in a sympathy vote because she had lost for *Of Human Bondage*. She despised *Dangerous* and wasn't overwhelmed at being awarded for her performance in it but she also knew she had reached the summit: that she must now fight desperately hard to retain her position. From that moment on, she would more consciously assert her power; she *dared* not make any inferior pictures in the future.

No sooner had she received the award than Bette took the train to New York to attend the 1936 Democratic Convention at Madison Square Garden. She rushed through the final scenes of *Cream Princess* in order to make the trip. Roosevelt was the idol of her existence and when Big Jim Farley asked her to appear in his support it was more exciting for her than being given the Academy Award. She arrived at Grand Central in intense cold, to be greeted by a swarm of reporters. The Warner press agent Charles Einfeld was appalled when she launched into a violent attack on the Hayes office, which censored motion pictures, and the problems she was having with scripts as ridiculous as that for *Cream Princess*. 'Cream Princess!' she laughed. 'What a title! Surely *that* calls for censorship!'

The press was delighted with her outspoken remarks. Most stars merely rattled off carefully memorised stock answers and gushed about their co-stars and future vehicles. The press had never met anyone like her before: she had a mind of her own, she was prepared to attack her bosses, she knew a good script from a bad one. She was even prepared to attack a movie in mid-production and probably imperil its commercial release! The reporters adored her and applauded spontaneously when she was through. Publicist Charles Einfeld shrivelled with embarrassment.

Typically, Bette had refused the usual suite at the Plaza or the Ritz Towers and preferred the simple, quasi-British Algonquin, with its echoes of the famous Round Table, its powerful intellectual associations. No other stars stayed there. The suites were cramped and the room service slow. The lobby was small and cluttered and fans could easily gather round. But Bette knew instinctively that the Algonquin crowd would pay her little attention. They were far too sophisticated to be impressed by anything as ridiculous as a Hollywood picture star.

No sooner had Bette gone up to her suite than a telegram was slipped under her door. It contained a message that drove her into rage and laughter. Jack Warner wanted her to return at once on the five-day train journey to shoot a new sequence for *Cream Princess* (re-titled *The Golden Arrow*). This would show her and George Brent and a cabbie sporting outsized shiners on their eyes.

This was the last straw. Bette cabled back that even if this meant the end of her career as an actress, she would not give up her trip to New York and the Democratic Convention to return to Hollywood to shoot this imbecilic scene. Warners could damn well wait until she was good and ready to shoot the sequence when she returned.

It was the first serious indication that Bette had assumed the power, will and resolution of a star. Winning the Oscar had changed her overnight from a determined mouse into a lioness. She knew that if Warners dropped her, she could sign with any other studio in town. At last, she had found security; she had achieved at the very least a high degree of courage.

She called Martin Gang, her attorney, in Hollywood and gave him lengthy instructions that he was to convey to Jack Warner immediately. Now that she had an Oscar, she expected to be given an income and working arrangement commensurate with her importance as a star. She must have three months' vacation a year; she must have a considerable salary increase – health and money had become obsessive concerns by 1936 – the right to do an outside picture once a year (she was still fretting over being refused the chance of Queen Elizabeth to Hepburn's Mary Stuart); to do four broadcasts a year – like most stars, she loved the prestige and excitement of radio – and more consideration over scripts the studio would offer her.

Martin Gang outlined all of these requests in a letter to Jack Warner, who promptly told Ralph Lewis, the studio lawyer at the Warner's attorney's, Preston and Files, that he would tolerate no further nonsense from Miss Davis. He would not allow a new contract since the old one was perfectly valid; and Miss Davis would come back for retakes on 18 April or she would be suspended indefinitely. Lewis felt the letter Warner drafted was too brusque and that it should only be sent if Bette still further refused to appear for the retakes.

Receiving no reply to his letter, Gang called Lewis and was told, subtly, that little response was expected from Jack Warner. Fearful of his relationship with the studio being affected, Mike Levee prevailed upon Bette to return to work on the date appointed. She fumed at her vacation being cut short, but agreed when Levee pointed out she might have more chance to negotiate if she did the 'black eye scene' obediently.

Meanwhile, Hal Wallis was preparing for her a picture called *Mountain Justice*, based on the story of a girl in the backwoods who killed her parents. He rushed forty pages of script to her at Franklin Avenue and called her for wardrobe. A.A. Chang of Preston and Files, acting on behalf of Ralph Lewis, broke the news to Martin Gang that Bette's requests were rejected outright.

When she discovered she had returned to Hollywood for nothing, that she could gain nothing from her futile cutting short of a vacation she so direly needed, Bette's fury had no bounds. Here she was, an Oscar-winning, world-famous star, and the studio would do nothing to reward her at all! And she raged at Levee for having deceived her into thinking that if she came back she would be given more reasonable terms of work. She accused him of kowtowing to the studio because he was afraid of antagonising its executives.

No sooner had Bette settled down to reading *Mountain Justice* than the studio decided temporarily to withdraw the script because of legal problems and replace it with *God's Country and the Woman*, another rural subject, about a tough girl running a lumber kingdom in the northwestern states. Bette wasn't very interested in the property, and in fact all she wanted to do was join Ruthie in Hawaii, where her mother was expensively vacationing on Bette's money.

Mike Levee constantly pressed her to go ahead and make *God's Country and the Woman* and she gave a

113

radio interview on KHJ on 24 May to the critic Edwin Schallert saying she was 'looking forward' to doing it. At a meeting in Levee's office on the night of 2 May, he told her that he was sure if she met Warners in an amicable frame of mind and did what they wanted she would get a new contract. Martin Gang told her to fight the studio instead, and on 21 May, Levee prevailed in a quarrel against Gang and wrote dismissing him from any and every service on Bette's behalf. That same day, Bette cabled Levee to 'have nothing further to do with the negotiations; she would attend to them herself.' Levee resigned, saying, 'she's more grief than the commission's worth.'

On 18 June, A.A. Chang of Preston and Files sent Bette a continuity of *God's Country and the Woman* with a reminder that her present contract made it essential for her to go ahead and do it. She was told to report for wardrobe at ten A.M. on 19 June. She hired a new lawyer, Dudley Furse, and summoned Vernon Wood to accompany her to a meeting at the studio on 20 June with Jack Warner, Hal Wallis, Roy Obringer and Ralph Lewis. Warner had called the meeting in a last-ditch effort to persuade her to undertake the picture.

Everyone was seated when Warner said, sharply, to Bette: 'Why will you not work in *God's Country and the Woman*? I'll make you a reasonable offer. I'll give you your favourite Sol Polito as cameraman. I'll increase you from $1,600 to $2,000 a week. I'll try to find better stories for you and I'll add Sally Sage* to the stock company. What more do you want? Be a trouper, Bette. Agree to do this picture!'

Bette rose and paced about the room, puffing characteristically at a cigarette. 'My attitude,' she said, 'may be *right* or it may be *wrong*! But I'm willing to take my chances on the public rejecting me, on my *losing face* with the public, by not being in pictures in the event I don't get the terms I want! I don't want to hold up
*Her double

114

production of *God's Country and the Woman*! I am *willing* – yes, *willing*, to return and start the picture provided that on completion I am *assured* I will be given a new contract along the lines *previously requested*!'

Warm and conciliatory, Vernon Wood said he hoped there would be an early settlement. 'Mr Warner,' he added, 'won't you consider Miss Davis's value to the company? Considering Miss Davis's potential, are we asking too much in $3,000 a week?'

Warner snapped, 'I don't want to get into money matters! I've made a fair and reasonable offer.' Bette said to Hal Wallis, 'You wouldn't lend me to RKO to do *Mary of Scotland*. Why?'

Wallis replied, 'We didn't think the part was important enough for you. It was only one scene. It would have done you more harm than good.' Jack Warner added, to no one in particular, 'We build stars here, Give them every chance. Then they turn around and demand everything. I repeat my offer. $2,000 a week. And I'll do better. Six additional yearly options for another six years going up to $4,000 eventually. I can't top that.'

Bette wheeled round. 'That's *a seven-year contract*!' she shouted at Warner. '*A five-year contract* is long enough! *And after five years I'll be too damned old to be in pictures*!'

Jack smiled. 'How foolish of you, Bette, to believe you'll be too old then. You'll only be thirty-two!' '*Thirty*!' she snarled back, and for a moment, they laughed.

'You'll be at your best,' Warner said, 'with five years added to your career!' He then offered her twelve weeks' vacation without pay divided into one six-week and two three-week consecutive periods. Up to then, all of her payless vacations had been split up in small segments over twelve months.

Bette wasn't satisfied. Now her strongest motive became clear. '*I'm entitled to more money*!' she snapped. 'I don't think I'm asking for too much.'

Jack said, 'You're being obstinate and arbitrary.'

Bette fumed, 'I want more money, the chance to do outside pictures, or I'll take my chances and get out of pictures for good.'

Wallis wrote on a slip of paper, 'Let the first term be two years only: give her $2,000 and then $2,500.' Warner shook his head as he read the note.

Davis told Vernon Wood, 'We're leaving.' As they walked out, Jack Warner told Wood, threateningly, 'I want you to fix this.' Wood assured Warner that Bette would make *God's Country and the Woman*.

But she would not. Denied everything she wanted, especially the money and the chance to do outside pictures, she told Wood on Sunday to call Wallis at home and tell him she was refusing all of Jack Warner's offers. She wrote a lengthy letter to Warner on 21 June saying that she was mainly objecting to the money she was being paid; that she had no desire to be off the list of players; that she knew he could stop her from working, a great unhappiness to her because she enjoyed working; after her vacation in New York she was so rested it hurt; and 'If I'm worth anything to you at all you can't mind letting me know in writing. If I'm not this letter is in vain.' She went on to say that she didn't want the loan-out clause in order to be her own boss. She insisted she did not want to be autonomous. She said she'd like to have a boss give her orders, someone she could look up to, whose authority she could respect 'as much as I do yours, Jack.' But she knew change would do her good, that she could work better with new directors, new casts, and, she added significantly, 'I also am ambitious to be known as a great actress. I *might* be one. Who can tell?'

Vacations, she continued, were important to her because they broadened her intellect and she had never been out of the country. What was more, she was essentially a high-strung person who must have rest. In

116

mid-letter, she suddenly changed course on money, saying unpredictably that she would take even less than she was getting if she could have her rights to vacations and loan-outs. She wrote, 'You asked me to be level-headed and I believe I am. I am more than anxious to work for you again but not as things stand. As a happy person I can work like hell – and as an unhappy one, I make everyone around me unhappy.' She recognised, she continued, that in a business with a fickle public to depend on, the money should be made when it's possible, since later the public may 'tell you to go to hell'.

Jack Warner had heard it all before. He didn't bother to reply either by telephone or letter. Instead, Roy Obringer wrote to her: 'Unless you report for *God's Country and the Woman*, you will be suspended and damages charged against you.'

She left Obringer's letter unanswered. Days went by. Jack Warner ordered another rude note from Obringer, then suddenly relented and called Bette to give her one last chance. He said, 'Once more, please don't break your contract, Bette. Public opinion will react against you! You are being foolish! Change your mind before it's too late!' She hung up on him quickly and the rift seemed to be final. Jack Warner suspended her immediately. He refused to allow her to appear on any radio shows, knowing how deeply this would wound her. She sent a telegram to Warner apparently trying to appease the situation by fibbing and said she was 'awfully sorry' about all that had happened and, 'I would have enjoyed very much playing Jo Barton in *God's Country and the Woman*.'

Bette began to panic. She was most afraid that her dressing-room, that holy of holies for a star, would be taken away from her and given to someone else, thus causing the impression at the studio that she was through as an actress. She called Jack on an impulse and begged him not to let the room go. He atypically gave in and told

Tenny Wright on no condition to touch it in any way.

In this awkward period, a Polish producer, Ludovic Toeplitz, who operated out of London, offered Bette a chance to make two pictures in England. He had read the headlines and decided to take advantage of her rift with Warner. She accepted at once. But unfortunately no such arrangement with another producer could possibly be regarded as legal. It was a vain gesture of rebellion, and in her heart Bette knew it. She packed her bags at once.

Five

LEAVING HOLLYWOOD was certainly a major problem. Bobby was still suffering from mental disturbances, and Bette hated to leave her. She told her business managers, Vernon and C.J. Wood, to take care of her mother and sister, and, of course, the rent on 5346 Franklin Avenue would continue to be paid to Cecil B. DeMille. Ham, between jobs, would go along on the trip. It was the first sustained time they would have together in a long while. It was a last ditch effort to heal the rifts in their marriage.

Bette had never flown before and flying in those days was exceptionally uncomfortable and hazardous. For some reason, perhaps to avoid reporters, she and Ham set out on their journey to England via Canada instead of by the more comfortable route on the Santa Fe Chief and Twentieth Century Limited to New York. They got aboard a miserable milk plane that made an all-night trip to Vancouver, touching down at all kinds of improbable places along the way, and tossed about by the slightest turbulence. The trip was so unpleasant that years later, when Bette made an extraordinary emergency flight to her second husband, she announced she had never been in a plane before. Clearly, the earlier experience had been completely blotted out.

Bette arrived in Vancouver with her nerves in shreds. She was confronted by the very thing she had hoped to evade: a gang of trench-coated and fedora-hatted reporters demanding to know the details of her clash with Jack Warner. She lost her cool completely, and instead of taking a comfortable middle course, she once more denounced the studio and everyone connected with it for forcing her to do trashy pictures. Overlooking her radio interview with Schallert and her cable to Jack Warner, she now turned savagely on *God's Country and the Woman*, dismissing it as 'some nonsense about a lady lumberjack'. Far gone though she may have been, exhausted, desperate and strained to the breaking point, she could scarcely have told the reporters her principal battle was also for money. But the press headlined that fact anyway.

The Warner representatives in Vancouver were faced with an impossible situation. Warners had cabled them that only one overall interview would be allowed at the airport: the general press conference. But as soon as Bette checked into the hotel with Ham the prominent local feature writers and radio interviewers besieged the hotel demanding to be given her time. A local Warner chief talked to Roy Obringer by long distance and was sternly forbidden to allow anyone near Bette. Told this, she instantly went to the nearest radio station, announced herself, and appeared without warning on a show in which she said she would no longer tolerate the Warner behaviour and was going to England at once to start an entirely new career.

Bette and Ham took the Canadian Pacific Railroad to Montreal: a spectacular journey through mountains, across plains and past lakes that had her excitedly glued to the window of the compartment throughout. Without the strain of work, without the tension of the soundstage and the worry about her future career, Bette was more or less able to relax. Ham was joyful again. Together, the couple became exhilarated at the idea of Bette having a new career in England where she was so loved. One may guess that the buried romantic side of their relationship was restored on this spectacular trans-continental journey.

They attracted enormous attention when they boarded the British ship *Duchess of Bedford* bound for Great Britain. Fellow passengers talked for years about seeing Bette, tense and pop-eyed in slacks, and Ham, looking tall and awkward in a cardigan and heavy brown trousers, striding the deck in the teeth of high winds. The couple didn't care who stared at them. They arrived in Britain on the fourth anniversary of their wedding – and that was entirely appropriate. They were truly married once more.

Meanwhile, Warners' lawyers in Los Angeles, Preston and Files, hired the distinguished firm of Denton, Hall and Burgin in London to act on their behalf against Bette. Denton, Hall and Burgin sent an emissary to the north of England to serve Bette with an injunction preventing her from making the film for Toeplitz. She ignored it completely. Blissfully disregarding the fact that she had no business to be proceeding with this new venture at all, she embarked on a tour of various parts of England and Wales, where she tried to find some of her distant relatives, the Davises, without success.

In London, she had a pleasant meeting with Toeplitz and the former silent comedian and director, Monty Banks, who was married to Gracie Fields and was to direct *I'll Take the Low Road* with Douglass Montgomery as Bette's co-star. She proceeded with Ham for a lengthier journey that took in Blackpool, the Lake District, and the west of England. People would stare at her as she made her leggy compulsive entrance to various inn dining-rooms, hair in a scarf, wearing a sweater and swinging skirts, briskly digging into steak and kidney pudding or sausage and mash. Wherever she went, she attracted people not only because of her fame

121

but because of her irresistibly natural, down to earth, talkative behaviour. Unlike many stars, she did not pretend that fame was a burden to her, nor did she hide ostentatiously in hotel rooms. She went everywhere and saw everything, and what the hell if people gaped transfixed at her presence.

She loved England, and England loved her. Indeed, it is possible that the warmth of feeling for her was even greater in England than in America. It was partly to do with the fact that she had a very nearly English accent and didn't seem unbearably a Yank. She had perfect manners, rare in visitors from Hollywood, she read books, she was well informed about politics and if she wasn't exactly an intellectual that was all to the good. She was a tweedy, tough, opinionated, humorous and vital person with whom countless English women in the middle class could identify. What was more, at a time when emotions ran closer to the surface than they do today, women who were highly and publicly sensitive, who wrote impassioned letters and made scenes as a matter of course also felt they were one with her. They could escape their own problems by seeing her luxurious suffering in the huge, shimmering silver and white images of the screen. Their own pain seemed less significant when Bette was fighting feminist battles Up There for all depression girls.

Bette knew in her heart that her trip to England was not much more than an expensive and controversial furlough. She made the best of it. The case was postponed and postponed again. She and Ham went to Paris where she revelled in being dressed by well-known couturiers for Toeplitz's first film *I'll Take the Low Road*. She thanked God she had lost ten pounds.

It became clear by September that Warners was going to take her to court if she continued to proceed with the picture. She was running out of money. She had had to pay for Ham's as well as her own trip from America since he had no cash of his own. Because she was a star they had had to travel first-class all the way. Normally, anyone earning over $1,000 a week, as she was, in the depression would have been able to save sufficiently to make the trip possible. But the costs of her mother's extravagance and Bobby's hospitalisation had proved to be still more crippling in the past few months. Moreover, Ruthie was talking of coming to England. Though Bette didn't mind, indeed would love to see her mother, she knew who would be paying for that.

Meantime, Bette had to find an important barrister to defend her. Unfortunately, she made a poor choice. Sir William Jowitt, later Earl Jowitt, was a distinguished member of the bar. But for reasons that remain mysterious, he did not handle the case with his usual distinction. It can be said in his defence that the case was perhaps indefensible. However, having taken it on he failed to make anything of it.

Bette was represented by the solicitors Morris, Munton and King. Warners' lawyers, Denton, Hall and Burgin cleverly engaged Sir Patrick Hastings as their barrister. Hastings was unquestionably one of the most skilled advocates in Great Britain. His particular speciality was ridiculing the opposition. Judges were fond of him because he combined a remarkable grasp of the letter of the law and a superb memory with an icy sense of humour that demolished pretence and exposed the tiniest weaknesses in an argument. He had a formidably striking appearance, heavy browed and saturnine, and a vibrant voice that could strike terror in almost anyone. His weakness, used as a strength, was failing to take anything seriously which suggested the unusual or the foreign. This again appealed to judges, especially when they had a traditional British doubt about the virtues of 'continentals' or Americans.

Bette knew that she faced a formidable enemy in Sir Patrick. Sir William Jowitt, she discovered to her horror, required a retainer of several thousand pounds which she did not have. In Hollywood, all her savings, and they were meagre, were tied up in insurance policies to secure annuities for her in later life. Cashed in, they would have been virtually worthless. The Wood brothers advised her she could not afford to pay her attorney the equivalent of $10,000.

In this hour of extremity, not knowing how she would defend herself, Bette needed the moral support of Ham more than she ever needed it before. Somehow, she felt, she would raise the money to defend herself. But it would be useless fighting the case just for herself. She was buoyed up by the thought that Ham, whose love she had so happily regained, would be at her side every minute during the agonising experience of a trial.

But Ham was already growing restless. He was nervous about being dependent solely on Bette for money. His masculine ego was abraded by constantly being referred to as 'Mr Davis'. Much as he loved Bette, he hated having to be with her at all times and cast under her shadow. He would have to take a back seat when she was being interviewed. But *he* was an artist too – even if it was only as an obscure musician and band leader.

It is heartbreaking to realise that this fresh attempt to patch up the marriage cracked apart that September. The worst shock Bette had received in a shock-filled life came when Ham suddenly announced he was going back to America on the very verge of the trial. He wanted to be his own man again, to start earning again, and he had been offered a job of band leader in Hollywood. She begged him to stay. He would not. And then, to add insult to a crashing injury, she had to pay his expensive fare home.

It is probable she reached her lowest ebb when she saw Ham off on the ship to America. She was emotionally drained, sobbing helplessly, when she went down to the pier and saw the vessel draw out into the icy autumn sea. Fortunately, Toeplitz put up a basic amount (repayable) to enable her to proceed with her defence. But she had to pay for a small room at the Park Lane Hotel when he discontinued payments on her suite.

It was a drizzly, bleak October day when Bette, watched with a mingling of envy and fascination by a crowd of housewives, stepped out of a cab and ran with hips characteristically swinging up the depressing stone steps and along the depressing stone halls of the Law Courts in the Strand. She walked quickly to the plain wooden bench where she was to sit for the next two days, dressed very simply in tweeds and a beret. From the moment she took her place, she settled on a theatrical actress' ploy: all day long she looked directly into the judge's eyes with a challenging wilful stare as though she wanted to force him to do exactly what she wanted. It was a device that misfired.

Neither the prosecution nor the defence acted admirably in the case. Despite the fact that Bette had won an Oscar and was by now world famous she was an American – and Americans were not taken seriously by high-class British legalists in that day and age. Nor indeed were movie stars of any description: pictures were simply empty-headed diversions for the masses and Hollywood was a synonym for mindless vulgarity. Moreover, Sir William Jowitt and her lawyers had absurdly allowed Bette to use as a point of defence that the studio had forced her to attend a dinner for Roosevelt. This nonsense could be dismissed at once since in fact attending a dinner for her idol represented the summit of her ambitions.

Opening for Warners as plaintiffs, Hastings neatly disposed of this foolishness. He also played on the fact that Bette's salary of over $1,000 a week was fantastically large for any person in those years and seemed like a king's ransom in England. Commenting on the statement that Bette was a kind of slave, he remarked, to general amusement, that if anyone wished to enslave him at that price he would be perfectly willing to give the offer his consideration. He called her 'a very naughty young lady'.

He thus unfairly skirted the issue which was that Bette was being compelled to make pictures in which she had no interest. Had Sir William Jowitt a better grasp of the case, he would have put it to the court that Bette's career was being ruined by the very studio which built her up. He would have cited plot details of some of her more dreadful movies and particulars of the idiotic characters she had to play. He made no such plea.

Sir Patrick pointed out that the case was of great importance to the film industry because the contract referred to was essentially the common form across the Atlantic. He struck home when he said that what Bette was trying to do was tear up her contract wilfully and without approval for no reason at all. He made fun of Bette's complaint that she worked long hours; he emphasised that she was earning two to three thousand dollars a week when he knew perfectly well she was not; and Jowitt, though correcting the figure in his address, failed to raise an objection. Sir Patrick reminded the judge that there were clauses in the contract making it impossible for Bette to perform for anyone other than the plaintiffs until 1942. He said he was surprised to discover that the presidential dinner to which she objected (laughter in court) included five state governors, four United States senators, and three cabinet officers and celebrated the anniversary of the birth of Thomas Jefferson. Nobody, he continued, thought that it was a breach of contract to suggest to Miss Davis that she should accept the invitation. 'I cannot help thinking,' he added, 'that Miss Davis is letting her imagination run away with her.'

Turning to the position in law, Sir Patrick pointed out that awarding damages against Miss Davis would be

126

futile. There was no way of assessing damages over a period of seven years. All Warners wanted to do was make sure that 'a competitor of theirs does not take their personal servant' – Bette sat up at the word 'servant' as though she had been stung – 'whom they had brought up and used in competition with them.'

Jack Warner smilingly took the stand, looking as though he was about to burst into song on the vaudeville stage. Sun-tanned and dapper in an elegant three-piece suit, he was a great contrast with his wan and washed-out, staring-at-the-judge star. He announced complacently that he had built Miss Davis 'up almost from oblivion to what the company thinks is a very great height.' Sir Patrick asked him, 'How much, Mr Warner, do you estimate the damage in money from Miss Davis walking out?' Jack Warner replied, 'That is impossible. But I can tell you this: any film of ours in which she appears is worth six hundred thousand dollars or seven hundred thousand dollars gross in the world.'

Warner went on to say, lying, that the first complaint he had had from Bette was in 1935 when she said that a part which she was playing was not so big as previous parts which she had been given. Apart from the incorrigible pun on *So Big*, the statement, as anyone who remotely knew Bette Davis would recognise, was nonsense. She would have complained from the very first day she set foot in the studio.

He went on to add a piece of information that was entirely superfluous and already known: that she had won the Oscar for *Dangerous*.

Instead of trying to show that Warner had grossly exploited Bette, forcing her into far too many pictures a year of poor quality – a statement that would have rocked the industry's foreign image to its foundations – Sir William Jowitt feebly asked 'The prize for *Dangerous* is the highest honour the industry has to give?' 'Within the industry, yes,' Jack Warner with equal fatuity replied.

Warner did not improve. Nor did Sir William. The conversation went as follows. Jowitt: 'Is Miss Davis ambitious to become a great actress and is she very much interested in her profession?' Warner: 'She is ambitious to become a great actress and she is very much interested in her profession.'

Jowitt: 'Do you agree that film making calls for great qualities?' Warner: 'It calls for unique qualities.'

After this inane exchange, Jowitt at last got down to brass tacks – more or less. He asked, 'Isn't it heartbreaking for an actress to play a part that she feels to be unsuitable for her?' It would have been better had he confronted Warner with details of inept parts, but at least this was something. Warner's reply was bizarre. He said, 'Knowing how difficult it is to get film scripts, I myself, *speaking as an actor* [sic] would be willing to give and take with any producer in the matter of parts.' As if this were not enough, perhaps unrivalled for sheer gall as a statement, he went on to lie that he had bought *The Petrified Forest* specifically for Bette to appear in.

Sir William Jowitt now started a red-herring. Exactly where he obtained his information is not certain, but he asked the ridiculous question: 'Is it true that your brother Harry Warner asked Miss Davis to sign an undertaking that she would not divorce her husband for three years?' Jack Warner replied with the only sensible statement he had made so far: 'I have not heard of that and I am sure my brother never did such a thing.' But he could not resist making a hypocritical addendum: 'That would not be publicity, it would be bad taste.'

With Jack Warner's evidence, the proceedings, perhaps fortunately, came to a temporary close. Exactly what thoughts were swirling in Bette's brain as she returned to her room at the Park Lane Hotel can only be conjectured.

The case proceeded the following day. Gerald

Gardiner, representing Toeplitz (who disgracefully had not even bothered to appear in court) rose and announced, irrelevantly, that allegations of criminal conduct amounting to bribery had been made against Toeplitz and there was no evidence of such charges. In summing up, Jowitt said, to titters in court, 'Miss Davis could not, if she wanted to, become a waitress in a Lyons tea shop or a hairdresser's assistant in the wilds of Africa, if there are any hairdressers there.' This total *non sequitur,* eccentric and unfunny, must have caused Bette a shiver or two.

He listed a number of complicated cases including, bizarrely, Wolverhampton and Walsall Railway Company versus London and Northwest Railway, 1891, and, just as oddly, 'Rely-a-Bell Burglar and Fire Alarm Company Limited v. Eisler (1926)'. What a case of two railways suing each other and a burglar alarm company accusing someone of appropriating it had to do with Bette Davis only Sir William Jowitt and God could possibly answer.

It is scarcely surprising that Sir Patrick Hastings omitted any mention of this Gilbert and Sullivan affair in his memoirs. The fact is, the case should never have been fought in the first place. Bette's London solicitors should have advised her to go at once back to Hollywood and forget the matter since her contract was watertight and could not be varied. The only advantage in the case would have been to draw attention to exploitative and sexist attitudes in Hollywood. No such purpose was achieved. Since Bette herself did not appear as a defendant in the witness box, she was deprived of the chance to give the performance of a lifetime. In every way, it was a disastrous occasion and it goes without saying that she lost.

She was faced with $25,000 in legal debts and no hope for the future. Her picture was called off. But fortunately, Jack Warner's wife, Ann, a charming woman, was fond of Bette and reminded her husband of Bette's great financial potential for the studio. Warner was nothing if not money-minded. Making a grand show of mercy, he 'forgave' Bette and invited his erring star back to Hollywood. He basked in public approval while Bette went to Rottingdean in Sussex to consider an appeal. She took up cycling and, chronically accident prone, forgot to turn a corner and skinned her knees bare. Next day, she caught a severe cold and spoke through her nose to the press: 'I won't attend the rehearing because my hypnotism didn't work on the judge the first time. Silly of me, wasn't it? I am not a good hypnotist.'

Recovering from her cold, Bette wandered the beach in a drizzle and finally made a phone call to her mother to come over and keep her company. But as abruptly she cancelled the invitation. She realised she couldn't afford to appeal and a chance meeting with her old friend George Arliss made up her mind for her. Hearing she was depressed and sick, he had come to see her and offer her tea and sympathy. He told her to go home and make her peace with Warners. She sailed for New York in November.

In Manhattan, she gave interviews to the press, saying that she was back for five more years of work and that's all there was to it. She once again stated she hadn't been fighting for money and fewer pictures. She met her mother in New York and had an uneasy reunion with Ham, who was working between jobs in his usual uncertain manner as an artists' manager. When she arrived in Hollywood, she felt a wave of relief. It was 18 November 1936, late autumn, and the sun was still shining warmly. Bobby and her friends, the Bill Greens, met her off the train. Maybe the future wouldn't be so bleak after all.

Six

INSTEAD OF preparing an elaborate vehicle for Bette's return, Warner's gave her a low budget picture – but a far better written one than most. At the time Bette had left for Canada, the writer Robert Rossen had made an outline for the producer Lou Edelman of a new script, *The Men Behind,* based on the trial of Lucky Luciano. Rossen worked slowly and methodically, and Hal Wallis added Abem Finkel and Seton I. Miller to make up a trio of writers for the property. By November, they had a first draft and Hal Wallis decided to assign the story to Bette. Renamed *Marked Woman* – he had the title changed so that it would be more overtly a starring vehicle for Bette alone – she would play Mary Dwight, a dance hostess in a sleazy New York nightclub, who is branded by the mob. Her character was based on an actual figure in the Lucky Luciano case, and the writing was accurate, hard-hitting, audacious in the best Warner Brothers manner.

As soon as Bette was settled into The Nelson House, at the end of November, and Ham, their differences patched up, got a job conducting his combo at the Blossom Room of the Hollywood Roosevelt, Hal Wallis and Jack Warner called her in for a very amicable discussion. She told them she was excited by the script, feeling that at last she would be making some progress in her career, and impatient to get back to work at her old studio she had fought with for so long. But then one of those irritating, silly, inexplicable accidents that marred her life took place.

A messenger who was supposed to take the script to her failed to do so. Tenny Wright was to follow up with a call to see whether she liked it, but, distracted by the problems of five pictures being shot at once, he failed to act.

As a result, Bette did not receive a script until two and a half days before production began. She called Wallis when she found Warner had gone out and he in turn raged at Wright and had a script rushed to her.

She sat up until three A.M. reading it. She couldn't sleep the rest of the night. Ham, exhausted after his stint at the Roosevelt, complained because he could not rest. Bette was wildly excited. She had seldom encountered such vivid, sure writing and character drawing. She called Wallis and rushed in for her tests. But the dark rings under her eyes, caused by nights of sleeplessness, forced Wallis to order the shots to be completely redone.

She plunged enthusiastically into work. The first day back was exciting: the crew applauded as she came on the soundstage. She was warm and protective with a young and nervous actress named Jane Bryan who played her sister, a well-brought-up girl destroyed by contact with gangsterdom.

Jane Bryan says:

Bette was absolutely spectacular. She was so patient, so considerate of me that she was almost *living* the part of being my older sister. She knew I had *terrible* nerves – still do! – and that making pictures for me was *torture*. I was lost in admiration for her. I had to tell anyone who asked that Bette was the most unselfish star I could imagine. Anyone else would have ridden roughshod over me. She did everything in her power to help me and she stood between me and the director.

132

I got to know her and her mother and sister very well. I used to go to their house on Franklin Avenue with its proper front porch and I *adored* Ham. He was so gangly and sweet! But it was impossible, their marriage. And Ruthie was restless and bored. She turned to Christian Science at that time, and so did Bette. Not many people know that.

There were problems on *Marked Woman*. Bette's voice, always strained because of the constant flow of speech she addressed to everyone all day off the set on every subject under the sun, threatened to give out on her.

She used an old trick of pitching it in a higher register. As a result, she tended to sound 'singsong' and affected and the director Lloyd Bacon begged her to talk in huskier tones. She had no rapport with Bacon at all, nor he with her. He was a man's director, and here he was directing a story about women! Luckily, the script saw her through. And there was the delightful diversion of seeing Mayo Methot, a fiery hard-drinking small-time actress who played 'one of the dancehall girls, falling headlong and ill-fatedly in love with Bogey.

Hal Wallis, as so often before, strengthened the picture by having some scenes retaken. There was a sequence in which Bette and Jane Bryan had a quarrel over Bette's profession. Bacon played it very flat. Hal Wallis asked Bette and Jane if they would redo it: Bette was to sit in a chair and Jane was to sink to her knees and fling her arms about her and sob, 'I didn't mean it! I didn't mean it!' and hold Bette close and drop her head on Bette's lap as Bette gazed sadly into the camera and then protectively down at her kid sister for the fade out. Bette responded at once to the suggestion and played the scene with extraordinary tenderness. Jane had already become her 'kid sister' in real life.

Before the picture was done there was a major row. No Bette Davis movie would have been complete without one. There was a scene in which she was badly beaten. She insisted on going into the make-up test with bandages on and her eyes blackened. She had been to a doctor to check the correct way she should look. But Wallis objected to the test, writing in a memorandum, 'The last make-up test of Bette with bandages on and her eyes made up is absolutely horrible . . . we are not making a comedy . . . she should have her eyes discoloured and slight swelling on one cheek . . . let's stop trying to make her look too horrible looking.'

There was some comic relief on the picture. An actor who played one of the henchmen of Eduardo Ciannelli provoked Hal Wallis's annoyance because he gave such a bad performance. 'Who is that monkey?' Wallis asked Lloyd Bacon. 'Why the hell didn't you get a menacing looking character? He looks like some five dollar extra man. Couldn't you see he wasn't right for the part of a gangster?' The reply convulsed Bette and the other players. 'I'm sorry to tell you,' Bacon said, 'that he is one of Lucky Luciano's favourite gang members. We put him in the picture for realism!'

Jack Warner loved *Marked Woman*. For years, it was one of his favourite pictures. An incorrigible punster, he ran into Bette one day in a corridor and said, 'It's terrific. There's a sock in every foot!'

This response, soon to be echoed by audiences and critics alike, encouraged Bette to write to Warner on 6 January 1937, that she was in bad financial trouble. She had hoped to pay her legal expenses in England without taking an advance on her salary, but the bills arriving from London were crushing and she realised it would take her a year to pay them. She begged Warner to advance her $14,000 on her salary so that she could meet her immediate bills. He could make the cheque out to her London solicitors, Morris, Munton and King, direct and deduct $700 a week for twenty weeks. She added that the whole experience had been a severe worry to her. And she added an interesting last sentence, 'I am thrilled to death about *Jezebel*. I think it can be as great, or greater, than *Gone with the Wind* . . .' Jack Warner agreed to the advance, lying to the press that he had paid for everything.

Bette was referring to a development that had just taken place. In February, 1935, a play entitled *Jezebel* by Owen Davis, about Julie Marsden, a ruthless Southern belle who steals men from their women in the antebellum period, had been submitted through the New York office's Jake Wilk. It had been done on the stage with Miriam Hopkins. Walter McEwen of the story department in Hollywood sent it to Hal Wallis with the words, 'It [the story] is not very good . . . But it could provide a good role for Bette Davis who can knock the spots off the part of a little bitch of an aristocratic Southern girl . . .' Wallis agreed, but the snag was that Miriam Hopkins was determined to play the part on the screen and jointly owned the rights with Guthrie McClintic. At the time Bette referred to being 'thrilled to death' at getting a chance at Julie Marsden, Hopkins and McClintic were locked in a violent quarrel: McClintic wanted to sell the play on any terms, Hopkins only if she could do it. Miss Hopkins held up negotiations for several weeks, and when she heard Bette Davis, whom she still envied savagely, long after their working together at Rochester, would want to play it, she made further violent objections. It was not until the spring of 1937 that she finally yielded for $12,000 and only when Walter McEwen lied to McClintic that she would be first choice for the part when a satisfactory script was finally completed.

Meanwhile, the deadly studio pressure rushed Bette into another gangster picture: *Kid Galahad*. She quailed when she heard Curtiz would direct it but there was nothing she could do. She was consoled by a tight, fast-moving script and by the cast: not by Bogey again, but by Edward G. Robinson and her beloved Jane Bryan. It was a typical Warners programmer: a story of the boxing rackets directed with hard, slambang efficiency and pace.

Already, in this second picture after her return, Bette had begun to assert a formidable degree of power. Irving Rapper, who later became director of two of her most famous pictures, *Now, Voyager* and *Deception,* recalls that *Kid Galahad,* on which he was assistant director, offered his first chance to meet her. He says, 'I asked the script girl, "What's Bette Davis like?" and the girl rolled her eyes towards heaven. "Oh God, don't ask me!" she replied.' Now Rapper asked Michael Curtiz for his comment. 'Son-of-a-bitch don't ask me,' he also said. 'You'll see her when she comes in.'

Rapper's first sight of Davis was unforgettable: blue eyes wide, long neck stretched out, body thin and angular, she ran on to to the set as though on to a tennis court, formidably geared for action. Edward G. Robinson had to throw her bodily against a table. She struggled with Robinson, then fell back. Curtiz screamed at her, 'That's not the way to fight him, you goddamn bum!' And Bette screamed back, 'You show me what you want me to do and I'll do it!'

Curtiz, who had been a strong man in a circus, stood there while the tiny Robinson looked at him in terror. 'It's OK, Eddie, throw me,' Curtiz said.

'But if you struggle,' Robinson replied, 'that's the end of me!'

Bette had to laugh at the sight of the runtish actor trying to throw Curtiz's 195-pound body across the room. Everyone else broke up when Curtiz did a hilarious imitation of Bette, complete with swinging hips, snapped-out delivery, and frantically puffed cigarette. Robinson pushed him. Curtiz ricocheted off the table and almost knocked Robinson over. Then he said to Bette, 'Goddammit, bum, this is what I want.' She nodded and stood in position. Robinson pushed her with all the strength he had used on Curtiz – she weighed barely 100 pounds. As a result, she ricocheted so violently she flew clean across the set and into Irving Rapper's lap as he sat watching the scene. She screamed, 'My *God!* Who are you?' And he said, 'I'm the dialogue director.' And she replied, 'Thank God you caught the ball!' And they burst out laughing and became good friends.

Jezebel was still being scripted when *Kid Galahad* was being finished, and it was impossible for Bette to proceed with it. And at that moment she suffered a grievous blow. She lost what would undoubtedly have been the greatest of all her triumphs: the part of Scarlett O'Hara in *Gone with the Wind*.

It is interesting to speculate on the contradictory reasons given why she lost the role. The most convincing one seems to be that David O. Selznick, who had bought the property, was considering Errol Flynn as Rhett Butler and Warner had agreed only on condition that Bette played Scarlett; her conviction that Flynn was wrong for Butler was so intense she would rather surrender the chance than have Flynn act in it. Jack Warner characteristically rewarded her by casting Flynn opposite her in two pictures in the next two years.

In her memoirs, *The Lonely Life*, Bette says that during one of her many quarrels with Warner she saw a copy of *Gone with the Wind* on his desk and said, 'I bet it's a pip!', thus encouraging him to turn it down. Another version has Selznick deciding Bette lacked the sheer physical beauty which could explain Rhett Butler's total infatuation with her over a period of years. Whatever the reason, she wasn't in the running after the first few weeks.

Would Bette have made a good Scarlett? She herself is

convinced she would have been a triumph in the part. Certainly, excellent though Vivien Leigh was, she became somewhat monotonous and strident in the less satisfactory second half. Bette could have brought greater resources of thought and feeling to the picture's development. But it is possible that her lack of sheer beauty might have told against her in the long run. The essence of the book and film, the reason for their immense success, is that they are hinged on one theme: Rhett Butler's consuming sexual desire for Scarlett and her maddening refusal to commit herself totally to him. The reader and the film-goer are kept in a torment of irritated suspense during long stretches of what amounts to literary *coitus interruptus*. The formula worked to perfection because Margaret Mitchell convinced us that Scarlett was not only a perennial tease but a physical prize for which most men would be prepared to kill if necessary. For all her great talent and attractiveness, Bette Davis could never have answered that description.

Bette enjoyed making *Kid Galahad* – even though it was in essence a programmer. But she was annoyed that she had to follow it with a tiresome soap opera, *That Certain Woman,* in which her only consolation was working with the director-writer Edmund Goulding, an amusing and mannered English homosexual who shared Curtiz's entertaining capacity for acting out the scenes for both the actors and the actresses. In a sequence in which she had to kiss Henry Fonda, he played her part with a conviction that had everyone doubled up with laughter – and Fonda red with embarrassment.

After *That Certain Woman,* Bette was in a state of exhaustion, barely weighing 100 pounds, and on 15 March she fled to the La Quinta Hotel near Palm Springs, refusing to come back, but Hal Wallis insisted she must – by 28 March. Dudley Furse, who had long since replaced Martin Gang as her attorney, wrote to Wallis that she had low blood pressure, a result of the flu

138

Ruthie with her young baby, Ruth Elizabeth Davis, born 5 April 1908.

Three generations of 'Keyes women folk': Grandmother Favor,
Ruthie and young Bette.

'This small but frighteningly intense girl fell in love with the theatre,' Bette in a school play.

As a life guard that golden summer in Ogunquit.

Miss Davis in Hollywood.

In a scene from *Bad Sister,* her first film.

In *The Man Who Played God* with George Arliss.

Of Human Bondage. Somerset ▶ Maugham was the first to praise her performance.

'the firmness and authority, the emotional depth and range':
Bette in *Dangerous*.

Winning her first Academy Award in 1936. She named the
statuette 'Oscar' after her husband's middle name.

A Warners promotion shot. Although now a hot property, Warner Bros still wouldn't agree her terms.

6

As a spoilt Southern belle in *Jezebel* co-starring Henry Fonda.

With Humphrey Bogart
in *Dark Victory*.

The Private Lives of Elizabeth and Essex with Errol Flynn.

In *All This and Heaven, Too* with Charles Boyer.

she had suffered from after *Marked Woman*. She wrote to Wallis, 'Give me a week more . . . I must have a brief chance of being something more than a jittery old woman.'

He did not give her the week and she had to return for *It's Love I'm After*, directed by Archie Mayo and written by Casey Robinson. It had a most amusing idea: Basil Underwood and Joyce Arden are a successful, seemingly Luntish acting team, whose romantic performances, particularly in *Romeo and Juliet*, cause a sensation on the stage. But offstage they are constantly locked in a battle of wills, hating each other and fighting violently for the survival of one ego against another. Olivia de Havilland played the part of a young girl with a crush on Basil. Bette was a feisty Joyce Arden, matched with a fierce-tempered Leslie Howard as Basil Underwood.

Oddly, the film's situation was altered in real life: Leslie Howard, who looked so wan and delicate, was a passionate woman chaser in private who could give some points to Errol Flynn. He made Olivia de Havilland's life miserable by almost literally begging her to go to bed; but she was staid and virginal, and if she hadn't yielded to Errol Flynn, she certainly wasn't about to yield to Leslie Howard.

Bette's rows with Leslie Howard were as fierce off-screen as their on-screen conflicts. But they both broke up laughing in the middle of a Romeo and Juliet scene, and from that moment on their friendship was soldered up again. They had the greatest professional respect for each other, and Howard told Bette it was 'a shocker' that she wasn't going to be Scarlett. She couldn't have agreed more – and soon after that he was cast as Ashley.

At home, she still had crosses to bear. She would come home pale and worn out after a day of flinging herself into scenes to find no husband to greet her: Ham was busy conducting at the Blossom Room of the Hollywood Roosevelt, and didn't get home until two or three in the morning. A light, restless sleeper, she would wake on his return and sometimes could not sleep properly the rest of the night. In the morning, she had to be up very early, sometimes around seven, to drive to Warners for make-up over the old Cahuenga Pass. She would wake Ham, who needed to sleep until noon to recover his strength for the gruelling task of standing conducting his band for six hours every evening. They scarcely saw each other; she couldn't even attend his performances because she would have attracted too much attention, and might have thrown him off balance; and besides, she was too tired. Even Sundays were difficult because she had to shoot late into the night on Saturdays by an old studio rule and she needed to sleep all day afterwards. She could only envy stars like Katharine Hepburn at RKO and Garbo at MGM who were treated like queens; Garbo would never work at night, and Hepburn would stop production for hours while she served elaborate picnic luncheons. Even Errol Flynn on her own lot was able to escape to the West Indies or to Mexico the moment a picture was finished, and Humphrey Bogart also had his yacht. But her life was still severe, pinched, unglamorous: her house was still small and in an unfashionable district, her mother (not that Bette would ever resent it) was still spending money as fast as Bette could earn it, on jewels, clothes, cars, expensive vacations; Bobby was still suffering from mental illness, and the sanitarium and psychiatric bills were crushing; there was the $14,000 paid off to Warners for the London legal bills and the fact that the trip itself had not been entirely paid for by Ludovic Toeplitz; and Ham's job meant it was impossible for them to enjoy more than very brief trips to Palm Springs and La Quinta. Life was agonising; and never more so than when she saw the way the studio was handing her low budget pictures, and when she realised that her marriage was heading rapidly for the rocks.

Their early romantic life had been so warm, so innocent and fulfilling: by taking her virginity, Ham had
earned her undying affection. But she, even at this stage
of her career, was earning $2,000 a week – she still had
not attained her original goal of $2,500 – and he was
earning $300 a week at the Roosevelt. In those unen-
lightened days of the mid-1930s, a woman who was
earning more than a husband could not pay the bills
without feeling a deep inner resentment; in her memoirs,
Bette lashes out at men who have their wives pay the
household bills while spending their money on clothes.
Today, a liberated woman would not resent supporting a
husband; but the stigma forty years ago was almost
Victorian. She claims that Ham overcompensated by
attacking her physically, and that he had to assert his
manhood by making her unhappy. But if these physical
fights did take place, it's certain it was because her
temperament – challenging, infuriating, domineering –
irritated him unbearably. Because he was watching what
increasing fame and success were doing to Bette: changing her from a pallid shy wren of a woman into a
powerhouse full of hatred and anger and drive. The
woman he had married was rapidly ceasing to exist, and
it was a torment to him to see it.

He made a valiant attempt to save the marriage, gave
up his band, and joined an advertising agency. But it
didn't help. Obsessed with her work, Bette was, as his
later divorce evidence painfully made clear, no longer
attracted to him.

She enjoyed playing the light comedy of manners but
immediately afterwards the brief honeymoon with Warners suddenly came to an end. She moved to Santa
Barbara for a rest when Hal Wallis offered her a slangy,
Joan Blondell-like part in *Hollywood Hotel;* and she
flatly refused to play it. She felt, she told Wallis on 17
July 1937, that the offer was a great mistake; that she
had had only four weeks of vacation after *It's Love I'm*

After and that she wasn't fit enough to tackle another picture; that she had hoped for a complete rest at the beach for the twelve weeks she was allowed, after making three movies in five months; and that she was still feeling the effects of these pictures and the harrowing ordeal of the court battle in England. She was only a mere 104 pounds, and must regain her weight; surely Joan Blondell could play this nonsense instead? In a confirming note, she said, 'I'm sure you must believe me when I tell you I've been through a little bit of hell.' The letter, dashed off in her bold, rounded hand in garish green ink on pink paper, still breathes anxiety and mental and physical exhaustion forty years later.

Wallis ordered her to appear for wardrobe on 28 July – or she would be suspended. It seemed as though her whole fight had been for nothing; she had obtained three superior programmers, that was all; and *Jezebel* seemed as far away as ever. She failed to turn up for wardrobe, and when the studio demanded to know why, her secretary, Bridget Price, called to say that Miss Davis had been so severely burned while sunbathing at Carpinteria that she had a case of sunstroke. Her mother and Dr C. Horace Goshow confirmed the statement; according to a friend, Bette was simply putting on a performance worthy of those she gave on the screen, in order to avoid acting in the dreaded *Hollywood Hotel*. She was also drastically upset because in revenge for her behaviour the studio was forbidding her to do one radio show after another: a familiar way of punishing rebellious stars.

The row grew louder: when Roy Obringer insisted she do a Warner Brothers radio show on KFWB she declined on the grounds that she had not been allowed to do the Chase and Sanborn Show or the Lux Shows. Finally, in October, she traded.

Nevertheless, there is another side to the story. Bridget Price wrote to Jack Warner and Hal Wallis on 29

July that Bette had second-degree burns, and that she was feverish and fretful – particularly that she was getting second billing to Leslie Howard in *It's Love I'm After*. She wrote, 'Bette asked me to express her deep regret to you regarding her present illness: I do feel that this enforced rest although painful at the moment will make her really strong and well for the first time in a year!' She went on, 'If you can wait for Bette's recovery she will give her very best to her work, even to *Hollywood Hotel,* as she always does even though she thinks she isn't right for a picture.'

The sunstroke won the battle, and she didn't work again until *Jezebel* was scripted in the autumn. The rest at Carpinteria did her some good; she gained weight; and she began to feel that in *Jezebel* she would have a chance to become a very great star.

Miriam Hopkins had at last relented, and Robert Buckner, a dignified and elegant gentleman-writer, produced a smooth first-draft screenplay of *Jezebel*. But it did not solve the problem of a rambling, diffuse structure, or the fact that it was impossible to sympathise with Julie Marsden, the spoiled little Southern vixen; Buckner solved the problem by hitting on the idea that at the end of the picture she is regenerated by suffering. Edmund Goulding was supposed to direct the picture, but he disliked the script and dropped out; Hal Wallis had a writer named Clements Ripley work on it, with another writer, Paul Muni's brother-in-law Abem Finkel, supplying additional pages. Finally, there came the problem of obtaining a leading man; Hal Wallis wanted Jeffery Lind, later known as Jeffery Lynn, who was appearing in a play in Chicago, but negotiations broke down and instead – fortunately – cast Henry Fonda. Bette, who had liked Fonda during the shooting of *That Certain Woman,* was very pleased indeed.

Wallis hit on the bold idea of hiring William Wyler, then under contract to Sam Goldwyn, to direct the picture. Wyler was at that time one of the two or three most important directors in Hollywood. In his early thirties, he was a virile, driving man, compelled by great energy, ruthless in his attack, a perfectionist who would take scenes over and over in order to achieve perfection. Small, impish, with a darting, wickedly smart sense of humour, he was extremely attractive to women. From the moment she met him, Bette fell in love with him, and there is no question that he upset the balance of her life at the same moment as he drastically enhanced it.

Hal Wallis recalls that Bette impulsively entered into a love affair with Wyler. There is no doubt that his blunt Jewish looks, fierce drive under a seemingly quiet exterior and, most importantly, incredible grasp of her potential as an actress overcame her fear of him and enslaved her as only she could be enslaved. She became convinced (she always had the power to convince herself of anything) that this would be the most complete and permanent relationship she would ever know. Wyler had recently been divorced from Margaret Sullavan, whose wilful, mercurial, unreliable and perverse nature was the exact opposite of Davis's. Wyler had more in common with Bette: both were disciplined, severe spirits, dedicated to achieving extraordinary levels in their working careers. Yet in some ways Wyler was as incompatible with Bette as he had been with Sullavan. He was born in Alsace Lorraine, which made him almost as German as if he had been born in Germany. There was a strictness and coldness in Wyler behind the genial driving personality that resisted most earnestly the endless fire and fever of Davis's nature. Neurosis in a woman irritated him, as it irritated most German men; he was infuriated by Bette's tortured spirit, even when he most admired her. He was at once drawn to and exasperated by her. Bette was partly excited by the idea of being dominated by a man at last: the woman in her was excited. But her mind and her ego found it impossible to accept that domination. She was afraid. Afraid of being consumed by Wyler. She herself wanted to be in charge of everything: even a visit to the hairdresser or dentist irritated her because someone else was in charge. She was torn as always by conflicts of desire and what was best for her. The tension exhausted her. She was running too fast on her shaky engine.

Fear of exposure and fear of being consumed ate away at Bette's fragile health. She lost weight and played many scenes in *Jezebel* with a darting, stabbing intensity that no doubt resulted from her state of terror.

Bette was under very severe pressure during the making of *Jezebel*. Her marriage to Ham was steadily distintegrating, and she must have thought wistfully of the days when they were just an ambitious young couple starting out – before her career as a star had placed her so far ahead of him. Wyler was everything Ham was not: rich, famous, domineering, unafraid, secure, and prepared to confront her head-on in any argument. His judgement, she recognised, was better than hers. For the first time in her career, since John Cromwell directed her, she had found an artistic guide, who could bring out the best in her.

And Wyler hit, right at the outset of their working together, on a brilliant notion. He brought in Walter Huston's tall, loosely-constructed son John as co-author, rewriting the last half of the picture in its entirety to deepen the character of Julie Marsden and make her regeneration believable. Wyler talked to Bette intensely both at the studio and on the evenings they were able to spend together, teaching her how to control her energy and enthusiasm, how to tame her too desperate anxiety to do every sequence as perfectly as possible. His memoranda to Hal Wallis and the line producer Henry Blanke at the time indicate this. One reads (15 October 1937): 'She comes in during the morning eager to do it right, maybe to overdo it . . . and I tell her to take it easy. I tell her a scene is important, but not every scene . . . so she learns not to act everything at the same pressure, as though her life depends on it . . .'

He taught her to modulate her style, to allow herself soft as well as overweening passages, and to adapt herself to Henry Fonda's more static, subtle approach. Wyler's love of endless takes, always so infuriating to the studio front office, proved effective in her case, because he simply drained her energy by having her rush in and out of rooms dozens of times until she acted like a normal person. Her anguished state of mind might have ruined her performance, but he taught her, with great patience and skill, to use the stresses she was suffering from to enhance her interpretation.

This patience and this cunning meant that the production moved very slowly indeed. And when Henry Fonda arrived, ten days after production began, that star soon made clear that he would have to be released as quickly as possible, because his wife was expecting their first child who turned out to be Jane Fonda. Bette's nervous strain resulted in a small red swelling, a kind of pimple on her face; and no closeups could be shot of her for several days. Worse, her make-up, which was highly toxic, inflamed the spot still further and she became ill, returning home for several days until the production, with Fonda becoming increasingly fretful, slipped twelve days behind schedule.

As a result, and in order to release Fonda, much of the movie had to be shot out of schedule. Bette developed a 'charley horse' that made it impossible for her to film the important ballroom scene, in which Julie shocks New Orleans society by wearing a red dress, on the days appointed. The sequence had to be postponed again and again. On the night of 20 December, after eleven consecutive hours of very slowly shooting disconnected pieces of sequences, Bette became hysterical, collapsing in floods of tears in her dressing-room. Her conflicts over Ham vs. Wyler, her misery at the constant re-arrangements for the birth of Fonda's child, Wyler's tough driving of her and her devotion to making Julie her greatest role had again upset her precariously balanced nature.

A month behind schedule, the production dragged on through the cold damp winter of 1937, into the later hours of Christmas Eve and into the New Year. Bette was frayed, exhausted, ill, and then she was stunned by a jolt of bad news. While she was still shooting on New Year's Day, 1938, her father died suddenly in Boston and she could not be spared for the week or more it would have taken to attend the funeral.

Tormented by the fact that she could not go to Boston since the cumbersome picture was by now twenty-four and a half days behind, she had to shoot exteriors on rainy days on the backlot, and she came down with bronchitis and a miserable cold. She had to shoot a strange scene in which she sang along with the plantation blacks,* and her voice, always troublesome, gave out, so that she had to rehearse for days on end and then struggle to match up shots with days of sickness in between. By 17 January the picture still wasn't finished and Hal Wallis decided to let William Dieterle finish the picture. Bette shouted with rage, saying that after all she had been through she would not tolerate anybody else taking the picture on. Much as she hated the work, she was by now not only in love with Wyler, she was enslaved by admiration of his talent.

By the end of January, 1938, Bette was so sick that her Doctor Noys told the studio in a memorandum dated 30 January she would be in no shape to begin any picture in the near future. Indeed, he added, he was amazed she had managed to struggle through to the last day's shooting of *Jezebel*. Her condition did not allow for the kind of nervous strain she had undergone. She should have two months off, whether her contract allowed for it

*Cut from most versions.

or not, 'because she is going on grit alone'. He added, 'She is not actually medically ill, but her general physical and emotional make-up is such that if we rush her into another picture she will be in danger of collapse.'

She had her two months off, in February and March, when her affair with Wyler ran into trouble. She evidently was terrified by the idea of being consumed by an ego even larger than her own. She had no desire to work. When the studio's Benjamin Glazer brought a trashy story called *Comet Over Broadway* to her front door in March, she had her maid tell Glazer she was in bed and could not get up. Glazer returned later in the morning and she had gone out; her maid Adele said she had gone to Bobby's house. But when Glazer arrived there, Bette was also missing. Not surprisingly, he reported to Jack Warner, 'I believe we are getting the old run around.'

She gave an elaborate dinner party at the Beverly Hills Hotel to raise money for the Tailwaggers Club – a dog lovers' organisation. The guest of honour was Howard Hughes. She says in her memoirs, discreetly, 'I became involved in a catastrophic relationship . . . he was extremely attractive and one of the wealthiest men in the West – or East, for that matter.' She says that she met him for the first time at the club.

At the time, Hughes was in his thirties, handsome, overwhelmingly wealthy, a great flier whose pictures *Hell's Angels* had been the ultimate in aviation movies. But Hughes was nervous, awkward, shy, and self-conscious. Bisexual, he hid in corners at parties and was clumsy and ill-at-ease with women. He was like a great gangly country bumpkin. Women wanted to mother him.

His physical self-consciousness was so extreme that he suffered from sexual impotence. It came as a considerable shock to Bette when she discovered this. He had been through an enormously publicised romance with Katharine Hepburn. No doubt competing with Hepburn in an affair with Hughes fascinated Bette. But there is no certainty that his relationship with Hepburn was ever consummated.

Hughes romanced Hepburn in a very old-fashioned manner. He dipped his wings when he flew over her house; he even taught her to fly. As fanatically private as she, he was always dodging in and out of cars, trains, planes with her in an attempt to avoid publicity which, like Garbo's, inevitably resulted in an excess of it.

When Hepburn went off on a tour of *Jane Eyre* in severe winter weather, Hughes followed her by plane at considerable danger to himself, and put a fresh emerald on her dressing-room table every first night she performed.

There is no evidence that he treated Bette with equal attentiveness and indeed he soon returned to Hepburn with whom, it seems, he had more personal empathy. But in one respect Bette Davis was closer to him than Hepburn.

Yet curing an impotent male, after the bitter disappointment of the relationship with Ham, was very far from being what Bette wanted. Wyler drew her back quickly from the complicated, struggling personality of Hughes.

And then came severe shock. Ham Nelson, threatened, maddened by Bette's attraction to Wyler, and still more exasperated by her fascination with Hughes, suddenly went off the rails. He decided to bug the house he now shared with her on Coldwater Canyon and with the aid of a well-known private detective fixed up recording devices – discs in those days – in the walls of the bedroom and living-room to be able to prove the physical detail of the affair.

He obtained a sound truck to which the wires were

attached, leading from the recording devices, and late at night he parked the truck in a secluded side street just behind the house. In an agony of mind that could scarcely be guessed at, he listened to the couple together. As he listened, on that dark street at night, he could suddenly endure no more. He raced down to the back door, let himself in with a key, and burst into the bedroom. Hughes tried to punch Ham in the face. He flubbed it. Ham said that the instant his recordings were released Bette's reputation as a star would be ruined because in those days adultery was a sin so serious that the Legion of Decency could wreck a career if they discovered it. The scene, at once grotesque, comic and nightmarish was followed by one even more extreme. Ham blackmailed Hughes for $70,000 in return for agreeing to destroy the recording.

Hughes hired a professional gangster to kill Ham, but then discovered that Ham had advised the police that, if he were murdered, Hughes would be held responsible for the killing.

The ghastly episode destroyed Bette's relationship with Hughes as Ham had hoped it would. Hughes, hypersensitive and sexually insecure anyway, turned in desperation to a series of affairs with men whose challenge to his potency would not be so severe or threatening. Bette was scarcely able to sleep and retreated to her sister's house. Hughes rushed a cheque to Ham for the demanded figure and Bette had her business manager C.J. Wood write a cheque for $10,000. Then she took a loan on future earnings and, as a matter of honour, paid Hughes back the full $70,000. Hughes never forgot the decency of the gesture, but, fabulously wealthy though he was, he wasn't decent enough to pay her back. Instead, he indulged in the absurd theatrical gesture of sending her a single flower periodically for the rest of his life on the anniversary of the repayment.

Seven

Jezebel ESTABLISHED Bette as a very great star, Wyler's fanatical direction paid off: Bette's interpretation was startlingly vivid, making Julie Marsden's petulance and drive understandable and sympathetic. She was justly praised for it and won her second Oscar for it the following year.

In June, 1938, Bette began work for the fair-haired, elegant director Anatole Litvak in *The Sisters,* a contrived romantic melodrama about the fortunes of three young women in the early years of the twentieth century; third choice after Irene Dunne and Ginger Rogers, she was cast as a girl who falls in love with an impoverished newspaperman and moves to San Francisco at the time of the earthquake. She played opposite Errol Flynn; he replaced Fredric March, Franchot Tone and George Brent – all of whom refused the picture. Flynn was earning $4,500 a week to her $2,250; no question which was the larger star, or who was more admired by Jack Warner. Although she wasn't his type, Errol made a conventional pass at Bette which she pre-emptively rebuffed. Her absenteeism was more remarkable than ever; even though she was playing in high summer, she became ill with influenza, and lost her voice again on 27 June; Jack Sullivan, the assistant director, acidly wrote a memorandum to his superior Tenny Wright saying, 'I don't know whether she's sick or getting too much social life.' This was a sly reference to the persistent studio

151

rumours that she had been dating Howard Hughes.

And once again, the extraordinary rivalry between herself and Miriam Hopkins flared up. Miriam was fuming that Bette had played in *her* drama, *Jezebel,* and now she began accusing her recently acquired husband, Litvak, of having an affair with Bette at the same time he was directing her envied and hated enemy. Actually, her charges were groundless: Bette was by no means 'over' Wyler, and it was not until some months later that her fascination with Litvak developed into a brief and ill-fated, much gossiped-about affair.

Miriam Hopkins was a remarkable personage. With her crinkly hair, snapping eyes, contemptuous mouth and Southern drawl, she was as pretty and cruel as a sleek Persian cat. She was jealous – consumingly so of Bette – ruthless and much too intelligent for her own good. Her drive and ambition had earned her success in such movies as *Dr Jekyll and Mr Hyde, Becky Sharp, The Story of Temple Drake, Trouble in Paradise,* and *These Three.* She acted even her most trivial scenes with a fierce intensity belied by her cool dismissal of her film performances in private: of all stage – and literature – snobs, she was among the snootiest. She never quite reached actual stardom; the failure of *Becky Sharp,* an adroit bowdlerisation of *Vanity Fair,* suggested to everyone in Hollywood that she wouldn't warrant a picture on her own. Maybe audiences picked up that she was too 'intellectual' and high-hat, that she was a Southern belle slumming vigorously in pictures. And she also lacked that ice-cold sex that Bette had to perfection.

Litvak was a Russian who had made his name quickly with his polished direction of *Mayerling,* a romanticising of the famous historical episode with Danielle Darrieux and Charles Boyer. He was everything Miriam was not: gregarious, charming, tactful, with a passion for the glamour and luxury that still existed in Hollywood in 1937. He loved nightclubs and parties; she hated them.

Inevitably, too, he would fail to have a rapport with Bette because her life was so cramped, so dark, so meagre, with Bette's penny pinching and her troubled sister, and the small, unpretentious house on the wrong side of the tracks rented from Cecil B. DeMille. Litvak wanted to enjoy Ciro's, the Trocadero, the Clover Club, cocktails and laughter; and Bette was interested in rushing home from work to kick off her shoes and devour a script more hungrily than she ever devoured any meal or kissed any lover. Her affair with Litvak lay in the future.

In the late summer, Bette was busy pushing for the role of Judith Traherne in *Dark Victory,* a play in which Tallulah Bankhead had flopped, and which was currently owned by David O. Selznick, who planned to co-star Katharine Hepburn and Fredric March in it, or possibly Garbo and March, with a screenplay by Philip Barry. In January, 1938, Walter McEwen, head of the Warners' story department, bought the play from Selznick for Kay Francis at a price of $20,000; but Miss Francis turned it down because she was mortally afraid of playing a dying woman. The story dealt with an heiress to a fortune, a typical 1930s Park Avenue brat, who is stricken with a fatal disease: a cross between *My Man Godfrey* and *One-Way Passage.* Casey Robinson, perhaps the most gifted writer of women's scripts in the business, had been hoping to do the picture for three years, and had mentioned the possibilities of it to Bette. He longed for Spencer Tracy to play the doctor who diagnoses the heiress's ailment and falls in love with her; and she, who had loved Tracy and who still admired him almost more than any other actor, was hugely excited by the idea.

Instead, Jack Warner decided to avoid the difficult negotiations with MGM that hiring Tracy, who was under contract to Metro, would involve; and he was also afraid of Tracy's alcoholism. He chose George Brent, his favourite stopgap for virtually every picture then being made that lacked a leading man. The choice was more intelligent than it may have seemed. Brent exuded integrity, warmth, and a quiet, composed good humour. Although by no means a great actor, he had a gift for playing foil to major actresses, and he could certainly be a convincing doctor: nobody in pictures had a more polished bedside manner. Despite her disappointment over Tracy, Bette was pleased by the choice. Warners raised her salary to $3,000 a week, due to rise in annual increments until late 1949; and Jack Warner personally wrote to her that he would, at long last, sweep away the remainder of her $14,000 loan. She further saved money by continuing to have no agent in the wake of the unfortunate Mike Levee.

There was no question that Bette was in anguish after Ham had walked out on her. It is easy to imagine her state of mind: her rage and contempt for him, particularly over the blackmailing of Hughes, had been followed by remorse; both David Lewis and Hal Wallis recalled that she was fearfully distressed by the collapse of her marriage as she began preparing for *Dark Victory* three weeks later.

No sooner had she begun the picture in October, than she experienced another trauma. She had been quarrelling with Wyler, who wanted her to marry him most desperately, but who was also seeing a beautiful young girl named Margaret Tallichet. One evening, when Bette returned home after a day of shooting, she found a letter from Wyler, which had been hand delivered, on her entrance hall table. She was too angry with him after their latest collision to open it.

A week later, she finally decided to read the letter. She put it down and burst into tears. It said that unless she agreed to marry him immediately, he would wed Margaret the following Wednesday. The day she read the letter was a Wednesday. And the moment after she finished it, a radio announcer stated that William Wyler and Margaret Tallichet had been married that same morning.

Bette did not return to the set for several days. She refused to see anyone. She realised that not opening the letter was the most serious mistake of her life. It is extraordinary to reflect that her next picture with Wyler was entitled . . . *The Letter*.

For those who made *Dark Victory*, Bette's absence was most infuriating. Edmund Goulding wrote to Hal Wallis on 26 October 1938: 'We were advised (from her home) that she would not appear when we were on set in the morning, ready to shoot lineups that had been rehearsed and arranged the night before. On each occasion it has been necessary to rush actors from their homes and dig into the script out of continuity . . . wait while the actors come from their homes, wait while the actors learn their parts, and on the last occasion complete a new set and install new plumbing . . .'

After receiving this note, Hal Wallis sent for Bette, but she failed to appear at the meeting. He was annoyed; but there was nothing he could do; and her absence remained unexplained until she called him and told him she was leaving the picture for good. He was horrified, especially since she had been interested in playing it as soon as he told her Kay Francis had declined it – and she even told people she had begged for the part for years. She explained that she was heading for a nervous breakdown, and empathised with the stricken Judith Traherne so completely that she couldn't bear any more talk of disease and death. Wallis talked her back into the picture, explaining to her how to use her anguish creatively in her work. She went back on the set very courageously indeed, and played with a nervous vulnerability and sensitivity, a sense of open, daringly expressed pain and despair that she never equalled before or since.

She and Brent and Goulding worked together very

well, hampered only slightly by the cameraman, Ernest Haller, who took inordinate amounts of time arranging lights. Only occasionally, as in a quarrel scene in which she wheeled around in a doorway and threw down a muff, shouting at Brent in anger, was there evidence of over-acting, and this was quickly corrected; but for the rest of the movie she performed with restraint and subdued realism.

In the wake of Wyler's marriage, she needed someone desperately. George Brent was the stopgap in life as he had been in the picture. He was indispensable male company. Bette was still heading for a nervous break-down. He remembered that she, still recovering from Hughes and smarting over the loss of William Wyler, needed strength and calmness instead of fire and brimstone; and that they had an affair which lasted the length of shooting of *Dark Victory* and a year beyond. By now, he said, she was still firmly separated from Ham Nelson, and about to face Ham's divorcing of her; and he recalled they spent many evenings together at her house in Coldwater Canyon or at his home after the day's work. It was commonplace for stars to have brief romances with their fellow leading performers; and these were often privately smiled on by the studios, to help give conviction to the love scenes. Only the columnists had to be cautioned to silence, because Bette and Ham were still married, and any hint of adultery might upset Bette's career, in an age when bluenoses still ruled America.

The affair with Brent was a problem. Temperamentally, once again, they were ill-matched: she was more than ever all fire and fury and sudden unnerving switches of mood, and since this was 'real' life or what passed for it in Hollywood, he did not have the saintly static waxen calm called for by a Casey Robinson script. He was human, too; acid and sharp and unable to cope with the behaviour of a temperamental and nervous woman. Her

156

tightness with money annoyed him as well. He couldn't understand how she could live in a modest house, even though at $1,500 a month the Coldwater Canyon residence was costing ten times more than the cottage on Franklin where Ham still lived. He did not know that her mother and sister were such heavy burdens that even at $3,000 a week, $1,500 a month rent was difficult to pay out. And then she had to dress according to her new status, drive an expensive car, be seen, now and again, in expensive restaurants and nightclubs . . .

If *Jezebel* propelled Bette into major stardom, then *Dark Victory* undoubtedly confirmed it. The number of articles devoted to Bette in fan magazines and women's glossies notably increased. Her fan mail grew so massive that her ever-loyal and devoted secretary, Bridget Price, had her time cut out answering it; and she was frequently interviewed in the press and on the radio, expertly fielding questions about her impending divorce. In England, her fame grew enormously and she was voted most popular actress by many magazines across the world. She had cause to be gratified by her role of Duse of the Depression, Queen of the Warner lot, and Rival to Garbo, but she was still displeased by her salary, dwarfed by Loretta Young's and Charles Boyer's and Marlene Dietrich's, and even by Ginger Rogers's. It is dismaying to realise that, when she played opposite Charles Boyer two years later in *All This and Heaven, Too,* he was earning $12,500 a week: thousands more than she was.

Even while she was meeting the taxing histrionic problems of *Dark Victory,* problems that required every ounce of skill and concentration she possessed, she was under pressure to climb into hooped skirts and tight bodices for *Juarez,* her next picture, in which she played the ill-fated Carlotta of Mexico. Al Alleborn, assistant director to Dieterle, constantly annoyed her on the set of *Dark Victory,* asking her to come to wardrobe; and even

157

when costume designer Orry-Kelly approached her personally, she declined. Clearly, she realised that her performance as Judith Traherne would be affected by any sudden assumption of an entirely different woman's wardrobe and wigs, and she wisely postponed the tests until the principal photography of *Dark Victory* was completely over.

. And that end of shooting was greatly delayed because, despite George Brent's supportiveness, she was ill again. She told Hal Wallis she still wasn't 'over' Wyler. She had walked out on the love of her life and it gnawed at her. *Juarez* had to be postponed again and again – all the way into December, 1938.

A year earlier, Hal Wallis and Jack Warner had concluded arrangements for buying *The Phantom Crown,* a biography of Maximilian and Carlotta of Austria, and a play on the same theme by Franz Werfel. As early as 1935, Wallis had talked about the idea of making a movie about Maximilian, Carlotta and Juarez with Max Reinhardt in Salzburg. After some discussion with Luther Adler for the part of Juarez, Wallis decided to give the part to Paul Muni, who had been greatly successful in two other biographies, *The Story of Louis Pasteur* and *The Life of Emile Zola.* . On 12 October 1938, when Bette was working on *Dark Victory,* Wallis offered her the part of Carlotta, the ill-fated Empress of Mexico; the part was small, but she had always begged for a chance to play character roles; and there was a bangup Davis sequence in which she could go mad after berating Louis Napoleon for his neglect of her husband. On the brink of war in Europe, Warners had started to turn from subjects that would be of interest there, and had begun to look for material in neighbouring countries.

Paul Muni was the imperial head of the star list at Warners. Withdrawn, haughty, never a mixer, he was looked on with a mixture of awe and dislike by the crews. Very few dared address him as anything but 'Mr Muni'. A note from Hal Wallis to Muni dated 22 October indicates that even the head of production did not approach this monarch with impunity: 'Mike Levee has informed us of your willingness to permit us to co-star Bette Davis with you in *Juarez*. I want you to know that we appreciate very much your graciousness in acceding to this request.'

Even on the first day of work, Bette's behaviour was erratic. She had had several days in La Quinta to accustom herself to the script, but when she actually came on to the set of the Emperor Maximilian study on 13 December, two weeks into production, she suddenly froze and ran out, telling Al Alleborn that she could not continue, that she did not know the scene well enough to do it sufficient justice. Fellow actor Brian Aherne pleaded with her; but she was adamant. For the first time in her life, she told the director she would not proceed with the sequence in hand, she turned around, changed out of her starched dress, and drove home in tears.

The picture had to close down at great expense for several days. Tuesday, Wednesday went by, and she refused to work. No sooner was she back on the set than the weather turned rainy and threatening and she became more fretful and nervous than ever. By Christmas, she was yet again close to a nervous breakdown. Shooting one sequence on Christmas Eve, she slumped to the floor, announcing that her costume called for 'a stunt woman, not an actress'. The company looked at her dumbfounded and at last she pulled herself together.

Just after Christmas, she had sharp stabbing pains in the side of her chest, pains that were acutely aggravated by violent attacks of coughing and a feeling of constriction in her lungs. She thought she must be dying. She rushed to the doctor who told her she had a severe case of pleurisy. Almost everyone else on the picture had colds. She stayed in bed until three P.M. for several days and came in to play major dramatic scenes with a temperature raging over 100 degrees. When she had to do a complicated wardrobe change to play two scenes, in a Paris hotel and a coach in Mexico on the same day, she collapsed in the dressing-room and had to be taken home.

When she reached the big scene in which she confronted Napoleon III, played by Claude Rains, in the council room of the Tuileries, she simply announced she could not come in to work. The scene was held for her for two days until at last she struggled out of bed in mid-afternoon and drove through violent rain and wind over Coldwater Canyon, a perilous drive at best, all the way to Burbank, wrapped heavily in furs. It says much for her courage that she gave one of her finest dramatic performances in that particular scene, with the rain beating savagely on the studio walls.

Sick as she was, Bette used all of her skill to attract attention to herself in the sequence. She wore a black wig, tightened into a severe bun at the back of her neck, and dramatic dark clothes skilfully designed by Orry-Kelly, popping her eyes and tightening her mouth, and in two scenes playing with characteristic attack: in her furious descent on Louis Napoleon, played with icy effeteness by Claude Rains, and in her mad scene towards the end.

The shooting, which continued throughout the winter of 1938/9, proved to be heavy and boring. She had never particularly warmed to Dieterle, finding him pompous and pedantic, and devoid of the electric drive of Wyler or the subtle intelligence of Goulding.

In her memoirs, Bette accused Paul Muni of adding fifty pages to enhance his own part of Juarez, but the studio records show that no such enlargement took place. This is a natural error, a rationalisation of the fact that her part from the beginning was comparatively minor. No actor, even Muni, Hal Wallis confirms could possibly order fifty extra pages of any script. Nor could Bette herself have the power to alter scripts, or write dialogue as she so often has claimed she did; at best, she could ask for changes, and a writer could be brought on to the set to discuss them with her and the director. And this, too, was rare.

The truth is that as early as August, 1937, even before *The Phantom Crown* had been bought, Aeneas MacKenzie, a favourite writer of Hal Wallis, was brought in to build up the part of Juarez. It is also true that Muni's performance, glowering and obsessed, dominates the film. Aside from her own and Muni's acting, it is not a very good movie; the preview was a disaster. The picture had to be recut in its entirety, whole sequences cut and transposed, and even after it was rendered less cumbersome, the public was understandably indifferent.

It was during the shooting of *Juarez,* not *Jezebel* or *Dark Victory* as has so often been stated, that Bette and Ham were divorced – on 6 December 1938.

During the last year, Nelson uncontestedly claimed in court, Bette had been 'so engrossed in her profession that she had neglected and failed to perform her duties as a wife; that she had been inattentive, casual and distant to him to the point of rudeness and embarrassment; that during their times together she had insisted on occupying herself with reading to an unnecessary degree; and that when Ham asked her for "conjugal friendliness and affection" she had become enraged and rude and indulged in "a blatant array of epithets and derision".' He went on to say that she would upset the entire household and unnerve and humiliate him.

He charged that she wouldn't go out with his friends, that when he did bring friends to the house she would read intently in their presence and ignore them and make them feel uncomfortable and unwelcome to his extreme embarrassment and humiliation, and that this in effect upset those friendships and, he implied, affected his possible gain from them.

He said that she was not present at mealtimes, vanishing without explanation, that she would not go on her vacation with him but rather with her mother or sister, and that after he had chosen one location for a vacation and she had agreed to go there, she suddenly departed with her sister to another. This, he claimed, was widely gossiped about in Hollywood. He also said that she spoke embarrassingly in front of friends and business associates about the instability of her marriage, that she had said she did not want to go on living with him and asked him to leave her alone with her work and her family. Finally she spoke to him so bitingly and caustically, her comments were so cruel, that he left Coldwater Canyon and her life for good.

The divorce was finalised quickly, and Bette did not contest it. As she grew as a star, Bette could no longer cope with a man inferior to her professionally and intellectually. She had changed utterly; he had not.

Financially, he was the victor. Their property was divided down the middle, and hers was far greater than his. There was no real estate, stocks, or bonds. They had accounts in various banks, insurance policies, and three cars between them; nothing else. Ham had only one thought: to get out of California as fast as he could. He resigned his job with a local advertising agency and obtained a position with Young and Rubicam in New York.

Bette failed to respond to the two summonses to appear to settle the matter and Ham begged the court to rush the divorce through or he would lose the New York job. The divorce was finalised on 6 December, and he left at once for the Eastern states.

Bette continued *Juarez* in an acute state of depression. Her affair with George Brent didn't work out.

She finished *Juarez* after two long drawn-out months of hard work in February, 1939. Still weak from pleurisy, she had to lie down in her dressing-room between shots, and because the soundstage was so cold and damp she feared a recurrence of the sickness and arranged for a private bathroom with tub and furnace and toilet to be installed in her dressing-room. Jack Warner, ungenerous to his great star, failed to pick up the tab of $702.05, and she had to pay the amount out of her own purse. It was worth it to her to have this convenience: not to have to make her way to a seedy, draughty ladies' room when she felt ill.

She went to her beloved La Quinta Hotel to rest and try and repair her increasingly poor health. Hal Wallis decided to add a final scene in which she returned to visit her husband's grave and knelt before a shrine erected in his memory, a scene that disappeared from many release prints of the picture. She was slow in returning from La Quinta, begging for some grace so that she could look reasonably presentable at the Academy Awards dinner on 15 February, at which she was given the Oscar for *Jezebel*.

She was rushed headlong into *The Old Maid* in early March. Most of February was spent recovering from her influenza in La Quinta and fussing over the installation of her tub and furnace in her dressing-room; Ruthie took over when she was too exhausted to come to Hollywood for the installation arrangements. She began reading her part in her next movie, *The Old Maid*, and confronting everyone at the studio with a series of complaints about her billing in *Juarez*: she was adamant that she must not receive first billing as the picture had the title of a man's name; she claimed that the fans would think her vain for assuming such billing. Actually, she was fuming over the fact that the picture really belonged to Muni.

The Old Maid was certainly a dangerous undertaking. In this soap opera of the ante-bellum period, based on a novel by Edith Wharton, two women spend their lives locked in a struggle over a child. Hal Wallis cast Miriam Hopkins as Bette's rival: amusing, since Hopkins was so violently convinced Bette was in love with Anatole Litvak, and hated her most intensely. The director, Edmund Goulding, certainly wanted fireworks on the set; and fireworks he got. Every day, both actresses argued over their scenes with Goulding, and there was a further problem: Humphrey Bogart was cast as the romantic hero, and after two days of work, he was so hopeless in a scene at a railroad station in which he left for the Civil War, looking so thin and pathetic in his uniform and so unromantic in his last wave goodbye, that Warner demanded he be fired and Goulding and Wallis were forced to tell him he was dismissed forthwith. He stalked off in a rage.

At Bette's urgent recommendation, George Brent sportingly took over, despite the fact that the part was small for a star of his stature. All through March, Bette and Miriam indulged in a battle of champions. But Miriam did something deadly: instead of fighting Bette in the actual performance of the picture, she played her part on a note of sweetness and consideration that went entirely against the grain of her character. Bette, who wanted her to be unsympathetic, as the part called for, soon realised that Miriam was lusting for the audience to care for her. She would be vindictive and sharp in rehearsal, and then, once the scenes began, she would be all marshmallow softness and easy Southern charm. She also used her authentic Georgia voice to show up Bette's less convincing accent. In desperation, Bette said to the writer Casey Robinson one day, 'Casey, throwing a cue at this woman is like throwing a tennis ball in a blanket!'. Whenever Bette would make such complaints, Miriam underplayed so drastically that Bette was forced to do all the work. Miriam upstaged her at every opportunity. She was being supersweet, but without the strength of sweetness: just retiring and prissing meaninglessly around.

As if this behaviour were not enough, she argued over her dialogue constantly, and Robinson had to come back from a desert vacation and rewrite it. Miriam vanished off the set for days because she claimed her eyes were swollen from a sickness and she felt very low. She refused to do closeups. Bette took ill, perhaps in competition, and both ladies were away from the set so often the picture fell eleven days behind and ran well over schedule.

Bette was drastically concerned, that late winter and early spring, with the title of the film about Queen Elizabeth. She wrote to Jack Warner on 28 April that she was angry and frustrated because every effort to reach him through her lawyer Oscar Cummins had failed. She rejected *Essex and Elizabeth* and *The Knight and the Lady* as these would place her second billing, and, as on *Juarez,* she would not claim first billing against the order of the title, or her fans would think her vain. She wrote demanding, not asking, for first billing; the present title favoured Errol Flynn, whom Hal Wallis had cast as Essex. She went on, 'You force me to refuse the picture unless the billing is mine. If you'd be willing to discuss it with me I'd be more than willing.'

Warner was not willing. Nevertheless, in order to placate her, he changed the title to *The Private Lives of Elizabeth and Essex* at the end of April. Robert Lord, the associate producer on the picture, was agonising over her appalling state of anxiety. He sent a memo to Warner, reading, 'How about health insurance on Davis? Once she starts shooting we have no work without her. If she folds up, we stop shooting. I have been studying the lady and in my opinion she is in a rather serious condition of nerves. At most she is frail and she is going into a very tough picture when she is a long way from her best.'

Warner refused to pay for any such insurance, convinced that Bette was 'play acting' sickness to get more money and more power. Yet the same day as he was dismissing her as a 'hungry climber' he also granted her permission to have first billing and first place in the title.

During the row over *Elizabeth and Essex* – her mere week of rest after *The Old Maid,* her anger over the title and over Flynn's casting (she wanted Olivier) – Warner secretly tested Geraldine Fitzgerald for the part of Elizabeth, and even tried to get Hal Wallis to approve the casting. Wallis utterly refused to hear of it. Only Bette could play the part, and he was right.

Bette spent many hours working out a correct make-up with Perc Westmore. But at last it was clear that she would have to shave off much of her hair in order to obtain the correct bald look; and in her fanatical pursuit of realism, she even had her eyebrows shorn. She went over the clothes with Orry-Kelly, comparing them stitch by stitch, paste jewel by paste jewel, with the various royal portraits dug out of the files by the research chief Herman Lissauer. Much of her incredibly brief 'vacation' was absorbed in the work and she had to arrive even earlier than usual, about 5:30 A.M. every day, to spend two or three hours being made up and dressed and stitched into the cumbersome clothes. She blew up again when Hal Wallis rejected a costume to be used in a courtroom scene because he thought it was too elaborate. She memoed Wallis that the costume was startlingly authentic and she must have it regardless. Wallis agreed.

Bette attacked the problems of the part with her customary vigour and enterprise. Studying the Hilliard portraits, she realised that historical references to Queen Elizabeth's baldness were not exaggerated.

She read book after book on the Queen, determining

that Elizabeth's character was flinty, overbearing, and harsh. Yet she also determined that Elizabeth had tender feelings too: that she was capable of affection, even love. The script's writers took the line that Elizabeth's one abiding hunger in life was to keep England great, that this patriotism and sense of duty to the throne was the passion that devoured all others. Bette found this interpretation to her liking. And she welcomed the chance to play someone far removed from the fragile nervous women she had acted hitherto.

The chief problem with the picture was Errol Flynn as the Earl of Essex. She was furious at his casting, and futilely demanded his removal from the picture. He was then at the peak of his career, but he had never learned to take movies seriously: he secretly yearned to be a stage actor, playing Shakespeare in London and New York. Yet – so contradictory was his nature – he refused to provide the time and energy that would improve his acting: he thought more of his dog, his sailing, his amorous adventures, how he could force the studio to pay him more money, than he did of working on his scenes. He relied on his glamorous face and figure to get him through the picture, and Bette longed for a 'real' actor she could pit her strength against.

She became fretful and irritable, her scripted arguments with Essex acquiring a disturbingly realistic edge that suggested she was going beyond the point of merely acting them. Flynn's behaviour – forgetting lines, yawning off camera at her when she played hers, tweaking her bottom whenever the opportunity arose, making rude gestures at her – drove her into paroxysms of fury. He laughed uproariously at her discomfort. The summer heat in those days before air conditioning proved more insufferable than ever, especially in the heavy stifling period clothes; she paid a heavy price for her sense of accuracy – wearing layer over layer of stiff brocade, high starched lace collars, masses of jewellery.

167

One trouble followed another. The first weeks were consumed in quarrels with Orry-Kelly, Curtiz and the studio executives over flaws in her costumes. On 20 June, Flynn and his wife Lili Damita were driving down a street off Sunset Boulevard when they slammed hard into a truck. Flynn was away from work for several days, nursing cuts and abrasions to his head, fending off reporters who were convinced the injury was caused by Mrs Flynn's powerful blows with a champagne bottle.

Next day, Bette took to her bed also, announcing to the world at large that she had ruptured several blood vessels in her throat. She was told to rest and not to talk: a very tall order in her case. She sent a note to Hal Wallis: 'I feel bad about leaving the set . . . this was one picture I wanted to do . . . I will do nothing to interfere with it.' Her lawyer Oscar Cummins went to see her and found her coughing badly, wheezing disappointment that she had to cancel a Lux radio broadcast. Asked by Roy Obringer of the studio legal department whether Warners' Dr Conn could check her over to see if she was all right, Cummins said, 'No dice. She'll know you're wanting to see if she's lying. It will annoy her terribly.'

She began to lose weight – and realised as the picture went on that yet again her health was starting to fail. When Flynn bounced back on the set without a trace of his injury, bursting with vigour and vitality, she was more furious with him than ever. At one stage, she threatened to box his ears. She was amazed to see him turn pale and walk quickly from her dressing-room. She never found out the truth: that he had had double mastoid operations and a severe blow of her beringed hand could have deafened him or even killed him. Nor did she know that this famous male beauty was a victim of tuberculosis: a hypochondriac who spent much of his life flat on his back in a sickbed.

Probably because of her discomfort and anger, which gave her playing too strident and coarse an edge, and because of Flynn's indifference, which made his Essex weak, soft, and self-indulgent, *The Private Lives of Elizabeth and Essex* emerged as a stiff and awkward movie, dead under its lavish trappings and dull despite the rousing score of Max Steiner. Once it was over, Bette called a halt to work. She packed her bags and fled back East for a long and much-needed rambling vacation in New England.

The studio begged her to start preparations for yet another picture, but she was adamant she would do nothing. She wrote to Jack Warner from New York on 31 August: 'After making five pictures in twelve months with one week in between three of them, I am ordered to be on the lot. I am sure if I were in my coffin you would be finally convinced I am really exhausted and that I cannot turn them out like a machine any more . . .' She added that she knew it would be better for Warners if she could do just that, and she said she was 'truly sorry' there was such a lack in her; that some agreement would have to be reached about the future, 'for your sake and mine'.

She gave countless interviews in that difficult time, supplying a stream of radical opinions on marriage, men and women. One observation, to a writer for *Photoplay*, ran as follows:

Men continually work and fret themselves into bad tempers over their sex resentment of women's new-found independence in their careers. And what they don't know is the Great Fuss is in vain. Women never have, never will, never can be independent of the men they love – and be happy! All women know this. Only men are blind to it. And because it has made them so unhappy in general, this, to my mind, is the most important thing men do not know about themselves.

She added:

Men should boss women more! This is particularly true of American men. Women adore feeling they are possessed, that they belong to a dominant male. As I see it, the great danger in woman's new place in the scheme of things, is not nearly so menacing to women in that they will upset the apple cart by wearing the pants – as it is that men are going to let them get away with it! All men need to do is quit pouting over their lack of dominance, and begin to assert it more. The women won't mind. They'll love it.

While she welcomed women's independence, she insisted they be dominated at home: scarcely a point of view most women today would readily accept. Yet it was a point of view she retained against her own nature for years. She overlooked the fact that any man who tried to dominate and overpower her in or out of her own home would certainly not last long. One probable cause of her constant irritation and edginess was that her theories utterly failed to connect with her personal behaviour.

Eight

BETTE WAS now at the height of her career. Yet her life was still scaled-down, simple, devoid of glamour, dogged by sickness, exhaustion and depression. With two Oscars behind her, an extraordinary number of flattering reviews that called her the greatest actress on the screen, countless fan magazine articles, the adulation of millions of people, she was, in this period just before the outbreak of the Second World War, obsessed with the problems of the future. How, her letters to Jack Warner repeat over and over again, could she maintain her standards? How could she continue to work at a frantic pace and still give good performances? How – in brief – could she live? Her career had affected her personal happiness: her intelligence, her stabbing flow of speech, her streams of opinions upon everything, her sharp temper, her electric bursts of humour, her chain-smoking, her feverish movements round rooms, her compulsion to dig into the heart of a character to expose herself nakedly in her playing, her exhilaration followed by depression and exhaustion, all wore out her men, who were conditioned to dealing with subservient sexpots. Hers was the tragedy of a woman whose brilliance and aggression prevented her from achieving fulfilment in a relationship.

Her life, even in a period of convalescence, was not devoid of pleasure. Back in her beloved New England after *Elizabeth and Essex,* she was able to throw herself into leisure almost as wholeheartedly as she threw herself into her work. She strode briskly down country roads with her dogs, she dug into clam and lobster dishes, she sat by night fires and told Hollywood anecdotes to friends with loud bursts of raucous laughter, she gathered flowers and thrust them expertly into vases, she drove about in unpretentious automobiles, took in neighbourhood movies and plays, and roamed the country picking up or dropping old acquaintances. It was good to be back in the real world after the airless soundstages and klieg-glare sunlight of Hollywood.

While she wandered about on a free and unemotionally pleasuring ramble through several New England states, Jack Warner was doggedly determined to have her back. He flew to New York, checked into the Waldorf Towers and wrote or called her at various addresses trying to locate her. His visit was a secret: the public mustn't find out that this all-powerful studio chief had so humiliated himself he would chase after a reluctant star. But that is in fact what he did.

He was anxious to have Bette appear in *'Til We Meet Again*, a remake of the famous old weepie *One-Way Passage,* in which Kay Francis and William Powell had previously starred. It was the story of a woman stricken with a mysterious terminal illness who takes a last pleasure cruise and falls in love with a condemned criminal not knowing that his life is also doomed. Bette was not drawn to the subject; the experience of making *Dark Victory* remained a harrowing memory; the script was dumb and sentimental; and she was discouraging to Jack Warner when he called her from the Waldorf about it.

Her lawyer Oscar Cummins was in New York and Jack Warner at first considered going to see Bette with Cummins. But he finally decided it would be more flattering and appropriate to make the journey alone.

Warner cabled Hal Wallis in Hollywood that he was

making arrangements to see 'our young lady' and that Vivien Leigh was not to be offered *'Til We Meet Again* until the Davis matter was resolved. Then somebody at Warners made the mistake of announcing that George Brent and Vivien Leigh would co-star in *'Til We Meet Again*. Bette saw the item in the paper. She sent a telegram to Warner saying that it was clear he had no problem replacing her in *'Til We Meet Again;* she was shocked to learn that Vernon and C.J. Wood had been barred from the Warner lot; that all this proved that Warner had no interest in coming to terms with her; that if this was the case she would like to know as she wanted to make plans for the winter.

Jack Warner took this latest storm with weathered assurance. He simply proceeded to make arrangements to drive out to see Bette on Sunday, 25 October. She decided not to have him up to Peckett's Inn, Franconia, New Hampshire, where she was then staying, because their meeting would be widely commented on locally and perhaps picked up by the press; they were both determined to keep their discussion a secret and in one telegram to Hollywood, Jack Warner opened with a warning that sounded like an instruction to a plumber: THERE MUST BE NO LEAK.

Instead, the Summit Meeting was to be at the Ogden Farm, a magnificently luxurious place owned by a metal parts manufacturer. It was a reconstructed Dutch farmhouse, with elaborate guest quarters where the barn had been, pegged floors, and an office in a converted stable. The farm was a difficult place to find and Bette called Warner with instructions which still, in Jack Warner's scrawling pencilled hand, are to be found in the studio files. Warner drove down dirt roads with elms forming canopies overhead, in exquisite autumn weather, unobserved by the press, to talk for hours with his hip-swinging, uptight, cigarette-puffing, far-from-happy star.

173

This was unheard of: the head of a studio making a lengthy and difficult journey to persuade a major actress to appear in a soap opera remake. Unheard of and a failure – because for all his charm, Warner failed to persuade Bette to make *'Til We Meet Again*. However, he did succeed in calming her to the point that she agreed to come back to work at Christmas, after what amounted to a five-month leave. They discussed several properties: she expressed a preference for Maugham's *Up at a Villa* or an obscure property called *That Woman Brown*. She agreed also to do *Anna Christie* with James Cagney if the right script would be written; it was thrilling for her to think she might challenge Garbo, who had made such a hit in the same part at the outset of the talkie period. If none of these projects worked out, she agreed she would consider Rachel Field's currently successful *All This and Heaven, Too,* about a governess caught up in a French murder case. Oddly, the film's producer, David Lewis, had been trying unsuccessfully to persuade Garbo to play the part of the governess for over a year.

In those weeks, Bette became fascinated by the young man who worked as night clerk at Peckett's Inn. His name was Arthur Farnsworth. He was as weak as Ham in personality, though quite unlike him in appearance: stocky, broad shouldered and muscular, with a flashing smile and an aura of fake self-confidence, masculine security, strength that disguised a fawning servile weakness. He also came of a socially prominent family that had fallen on hard times. He suffered from epilepsy following an accident in a Piper Cub aeroplane. Bette's friends, Geraldine ('Fitzie') Fitzgerald and Jane Bryan (who was soon to fall in love herself, with the attractive and wealthy Justin Dart), her sister and mother all gave Farney the stamp of approval, overlooking his valet-ish

174

parasitism. There was rejoicing in the Davis camp that summer. She and Farney could enjoy the life of New Hampshire together: New Englanders both, they revelled in harness races, country walks, cookouts, picnics, riding on bridle trails. Passionately addicted though she was to her career, Bette was happier in this life than in any other.

Under Farney's slavish care, she at least grew stronger and put on a few much needed pounds. She began to laugh again: that deep, contagious, loud laugh that seemed to start at her feet and rose like a gush of water through her being until it exploded into the room. She read endless books and magazines, chain-smoking defiantly. She was starting to live again.

Bette bought a house at Sugar Hill with the surrounding acreage and reconstructed and remodelled it, with Farney's help; as a result, they became closer and closer; and at last she knew she was falling deeply in love once more.

She enjoyed the pleasures Butternut could bring her: the rich smell of a barn full of hay; joining in the local choir for hymn-singing; finding antiques in out-of-the-way places and cutting the pages of finely bound books on winter mornings; seeing snow swirl around Butternut when she was safe and snug inside with friends or Farney; going for sleigh rides; listening to the New York Philharmonic broadcasting on a Sunday; and receiving the *New York Times* on her doorstep every morning (the *Los Angeles Times* could never be a substitute for that). Life at Butternut was informal, but she made the house beautiful with her perfect New England housekeeping. She pressed and laid out her linen: she always bought dozens of handkerchiefs at a time, especially lace ones; and the beds were aired, the sheets and blankets shaken, the pillows plumped, with joyful expertise. She loved the ease, the relaxation of Butternut, far from the pressures of the soundstages. Photographs show her, wide-hipped

175

in riding breeches or slacks, striding down the long path that led to Butternut, attacking the problems of gardening or making preserves, smoking and laughing and running to greet the postman with all of the electricity she brought to her major roles on the screen.

A problem of that time was that Oscar Cummins, whom she had fired as her lawyer, arrived one night at Peckett's Inn without warning, insisting on being paid the $69,500 he said she owed him. Alerted by Farney, she ducked out the back door – and Cummins went home and sued her. The case was settled out of court. She had no lawyer now, but at least she was getting into property. Aside from the many rolling acres of New Hampshire, C.J. Wood bought her a house in Glendale near Los Angeles to come back to: the romantically beautiful, Grimm's fairy tale house known as Riverbottom, on Rancho Drive. Perfect to this day, with trees growing wildly in the garden, Riverbottom stands very close to the still unspoilt greenery and bridle trails and oak trees of Griffith Park. It was peaceful there then, the quiet disturbed only by the gentle sound of hooves, the murmuring voices of riders, wings of birds brushing through leaves, the gentle movement of a stream.

Riverbottom had been built by hand by its original owner Earl Callam; he had bought scorched tile for the roof and tiled it himself; he had fashioned bold timber beams for the open-beamed ceilings of the living-room; he had a great fireplace and a wonderful sense of space. Bette returned happily to preoccupy herself with furnishing the house, using many of her beloved New England things. And soon she furnished Butternut on her New Hampshire property, importing studio carpenters and builders to work on the house in their vacations. It was very similar to Ogden Farm, reconstituted Dutch in mood, with pegged floors and lofty ceilings and a storm cellar. Like Ogden, it had richly planted paths, elms that met overhead, a feeling of comfort and ease rather than ostentatious luxury. Bobby and Bette's mother fell in love with both houses at once, and for years Riverbottom and Butternut became Bette's havens against the world.

At the beginning of 1940, Bette arrived at Warners ready for work. But she had a kind of relapse as soon as she moved into Riverbottom and completed the task of furnishing it in a New England mode; she had the next picture postponed until February, wresting a promise that she would be able to travel to Honolulu right afterwards.

The movie ideas for *That Woman Brown* and *Anna Christie* had failed to jell. So *All This and Heaven, Too* was chosen for Bette's 'comeback', despite her misgivings about another period drama. The novel was overdone but had an interesting plot. Henriette Déluzy-Desportes was a governess (related to an ancestor of the novel's author) attached to the family of the Duc de Praslin in Paris in the 1840s. When the Duc murdered his wife, this innocent, mousy little woman became caught up in a major political and social scandal.

David Lewis, the producer, recalls that Bette was totally uninterested in the part of Henriette Déluzy-Desportes: she wanted instead to play the part of the vicious and sullen Duchesse de Praslin. She had a theory that the Duchess should be slatternly and unpleasant, whereas in historical fact the Duchess was immensely rich and distinguished and of a refined if somewhat neurotic character. She asked Lewis confidentially, 'If I didn't play Henriette, whom would you have do the part?' and he replied, 'Garbo.' 'That would be divine!' she exclaimed happily. But there was a problem: Lewis had recently asked Garbo to appear in a version of the trashy novel *Quietly, My Captain Waits*, and Garbo's friend, Salka Viertel, had conveyed the news. Garbo had rejected the part because it involved acting with a child; and now the same difficulty arose over *All This and Heaven, Too:* the part called for her to be the governess to four children and she hated them. 'That horrible monster Freddie Bartholomew!' Garbo said to Lewis. 'How boring he was in *Anna Karenina*! How I hated acting with him! No! No! I will never work with children again!' And Garbo was superstitious: she would never work away from MGM, or away from her dressing-room. So the idea was abandoned, and Bette agreed to act as Henriette, with Barbara O'Neil as the Duchess and Charles Boyer as the Duke.

Boyer fascinated everyone. He was secretive, withdrawn, private, monastically dedicated to his art. He was small, pot-bellied and balding; but by heroic acts of artifice he changed himself, with toupee, corset, make-up and lifts into a glamorous heroic figure. Bette told her stand-in, Sally Sage, she would never forget the moment when she saw him, prematurely aged, wigless, fat, for the first time; she didn't recognise him at first; she almost cried out with the shock and astonishment when she realised who he was. He was ideal as the Duke: his pale, oval face, his heavy-lidded, dreamily reflective, deeply melancholy eyes, his aristocratic manner, his incredible skill in wearing clothes, especially a superb, long, black-and-silver striped robe he wore towards the end of the picture – all were ideal for the part. Barbara O'Neil, moody and sulky, made a perfect foil. She disliked Hollywood, the part, the picture, working in pictures; she was just over a bad relationship with Joshua Logan that had resulted in a disastrous marriage; her look of ponderous despondency was perfect, and Anatole Litvak used it well.

Bette's situation with Litvak was extremely uncomfortable. She was over her impossible relationship with him and was apparently embarrassed by it. She did not like his directorial approach which she found solemn, heavy and obvious.

The biggest problem arose in the trial scene, when Henriette fell to her knees and pleaded to the judge that she was innocent. Litvak told her the scene was horrible. He told her to stand up straight and face her accusers. She stormed into David Lewis's office. 'That son-of-a-bitch!' she screamed. 'He won't let me play that scene the way I want!' Lewis came to the set and watched her play it both ways. There was no comparison to the warmth and passion with which she played it as she knelt, and Litvak had to give in.

Today the movie seems excessively long and overstuffed; turgid and too faithful to the book, too mired in the novel's stolid construction. But there are very good things in it: the children's Hallowe'en party, not in the novel and drawn by Casey Robinson from a variety of sources; the schoolroom scenes in America, when Henriette cows a vicious schoolgirl who has come to bait her; the murder of the Duchess, and the extraordinary death scene, played to perfection by Boyer.

Bette's performance is among her most controlled and subdued. Her health still not fully recovered after the experiences of the previous year; fretting over the countless ways in which Litvak had frustrated her, sick (according to David Lewis) about not having played the Duchesse de Praslin, Bette had to wrangle to obtain the promised one month's vacation.

As part of her deal she had to rush through costume tests for her next picture, *The Letter*, to be directed by her beloved William Wyler, in order to be free to make the voyage. Farney was back East, their romantic interest in each other thwarted temporarily by distance.

She had a pleasant stay in Honolulu and on the voyage back became very friendly with a nice Warners publicity man, Bob Taplinger, whose name was linked to hers romantically in gossip columns for several months thereafter. But she was preoccupied with Farney – and soon she would be engaged to him.

Refreshed by the sun and surf of Hawaii and the leisurely, week-long sea voyage each way, Bette was healthier and stronger than she had been in years when she attacked the part of Leslie Crosbie in Somerset Maugham's *The Letter* that spring of 1940. It was a marvellous crocodile's feast of a role about an adulterous planter's wife in Malaya who shoots her lover, stands trial, and forces her lawyer to deceive the jury in order to escape the hangman. Jeanne Eagels had made a great success in the part in an early talkie, and Katharine Cornell in New York and Gladys Cooper in London had also made vivid impressions. Bette had been fascinated by Jeanne Eagels since girlhood; it was flattering and exciting to be creating a new interpretation of a murderess.

It was a daring theme for the time – a killer as a protagonist who does not even try to elicit the audience's sympathy – and few actresses would have dared to play such a part. They feared identification more than anything else, but Bette, bold, fierce and at the height of her career, was enthralled by the chance. Together with Howard Koch, the writer, Wyler worked out an ingenious idea to illustrate the character she would play, Leslie Crosbie.

He would have Mrs Crosbie work away grimly at a lace shawl, stitching it piece by tiny piece as a symbol of her complex pattern of deceit. She would apply the needle on the small, white, oval parts of the whole with a fanatical concentration not altered even by the tension of waiting for the verdict. Everyone applauded the idea: Bette herself liked to do needlework in real life to keep her hands controlled, her nerves steady: Wyler, as her lover, knew this better than anyone, and here gave it a brilliant melodramatic application.

Koch worked out another device for her, enhanced beautifully by Tony Gaudio's lacquered photography. She would be obsessed by the moon: it would seem to control her fate. She would look up at it after she shot her lover on the bungalow steps; she would look up at it again when after her acquittal she walked to her death in the tropical garden. When a knife was left by her intending killers on the rattan floor of her room, she would again glance up, the white intense light shining in her eyes.

The two devices, the lace and the moon, gave the movie an extraordinary poetic intensity that raised it above the level of melodrama, and the picture contained perhaps her finest performance on the screen. Her interpretation most intriguingly differed from Jeanne Eagels's: whereas Eagels had been brilliantly fluttery, nervous, insecure, Bette was cold and implacable. Eagels plays the scene in which she learns she may be hanged with a hand clutching her throat, as though she is already anticipating the hangman. Bette becomes more and more taut, until at last her will suddenly gives out and she falls fainting to the floor.

After the tough but rewarding experience of making *The Letter* was over, Bette gratefully returned to Butternut for a brief vacation. She completed the remodelling of the house, which was by now her pride and joy. Farney was there whenever he could be. Now that war had broken out in Europe he was, because of his considerable experience in aeronautics, being asked to take part in some very secret investigations into aircraft construction, and soon he would go to Minneapolis, to the very important Honeywell plant.

Their relationship developed easily and comfortably. Because Farney had a good family and money of his own there were few of the miserable imbalances of Bette's relationship with Ham. They planned to be married at the New Year. They were happy working on the house

181

together: the house that would be their home together for a time.

Back to the grindstone at Burbank, Bette found herself confronted with a wretched script, *The Great Lie*. It was the story of two women: Sandra, a famous pianist, and Maggie, an ordinary middle-class housewife. The hero, with whom both women are in love, is a flier of the Farney mould, and even more oddly, he is involved in important pre-war work in aeronautics. Amusingly too, he was played by Bette's previous flame, George Brent. The story is an absurdity: Sandra marries the flier in a hurry, becomes pregnant, and no longer wants the baby. But she is too selfish to part with it to Maggie, who wants to have her flier's child. Finally, Maggie gives Sandra a life income so that she can have the baby in return. Soap opera had seldom been sudsier, or situations more wildly improbable.

Casting Sandra, the pianist, proved to be a major headache. Miriam Hopkins, who might have been used, was not even considered: nobody could face her tantrums any more. Anna Sten, a fine actress in European films who had been ruined by Goldwyn, was offered the part, but the executives were unhappy with her test. Sylvia Sidney was also tested, then Mary Astor, then Muriel Angelus and Katherine Locke.

Bette never liked to look at her own rushes, hating virtually everything about herself except her hair, but she did enjoy seeing these tests and giving her opinions loudly and clearly to anyone who would listen. She was shocked that Mary Astor, who was by far the most striking of the contestants, had simply been passed over, and demanded that Hal Wallis and Jack Warner arrange another test, this time with Mary banging away at a piano. Mary, with her dark hair, mysterious dark eyes, delicate features and look of infinite melancholy, would undoubtedly bring glamour and allure to an intolerably ill-written role. She would be a worthy contestant: Bette loved playing against powerful actresses who worked hard at trying to outmatch her in scenes.

The executives hung fire, and Bette was furious. She had to start the picture without the part of Sandra firmly cast. Goulding was to direct, which was nice; but he was not in a good mood; there were many quarrels. Bette got a sore throat from shouting at him and grumbling loudly over the lines. The picture was closed down – on 6 and 7 November 1940. When Bette returned, she insisted Goulding, the producer Henry Blanke, and the writer Lenore Coffee came in and produce words she could speak and situations she could play.

Mary Astor walked into the midst of this highly charged situation. She was cast on 8 November – on Bette's further and angrier insistence. Bette was so irritable at the delays and problems she sat in her chair on the sidelines smoking furiously, with one leg tucked under her and the other swinging dangerously, when Astor walked on to the set for the first time. But they were friends at once.

Bette's unselfishness towards other actors was always one of her most attractive features. She had befriended Geraldine Fitzgerald on *Dark Victory* when Geraldine wrongly feared that Bette would upstage her, force her into corners; and now she eased Mary Astor's insecurity, lulling her, telling her they must work together to improve the story. Lenore Coffee was on the set day after day reworking scenes to enhance the conflict between the two women in the story, to shear away the laughable triangle that threatened to sink it at the outset.

Bette was responsible for the simple, close cut, short bob, almost masculine and very daring for the time, that Mary wore in the picture. The style instantly became a fashion. Despite differences between them, Bette again found Goulding a delight. His homosexuality was a constant cause of ribbing, as he first played out Bette's part – all swinging hips and clipped nervous speeches and sudden highfalutin' 'Hepburn' imitations, then Mary's – all sombre stares and glares and murky exhausted side glances and a look of having been at several funerals successively. Bette and Mary broke up ecstatically at these witty mimicries.

They all had fun throughout the shooting. In a scene in which Mary had a baby in a remote desert cabin, Bette insisted on striding up and down outside the room in riding breeches in an imitation of 'waiting for the baby' that had everyone in stitches. There is a scene in which Mary is asking for a brandy (Goulding summed up her part as 'a piano, brandy, and men'). Bette tells her, 'The doctor says you can have an *ounce*.' After a hasty conference, Bette, Mary and Lenore Coffee came up with the line, 'Whoever heard of an *ounce* of brandy!' Everyone laughed and Edmund Goulding said, 'Why don't you two gals take over the studio. And Coffee, how about another brandy?'

There were uncomfortable problems on the picture. Because Mary had come on to the set so late, the entire schedule had to be redrawn from top to bottom. The baby that was supposed to be Mary's was ill for much of the shooting, and then a nurse dropped it and and injured it so badly it had to be replaced. There was a major lawsuit over this. Mary was having trouble with her husband and insisted he accompany her on location to Victorville in the desert where the childbirth scene was to be shot. No sooner had she secured permission than he refused to go. Bette again suffered from a 'charley horse' and had to cut down work. George Brent and Mary were ill during so many days that the picture had to be shut down. The desert dust and glare again played havoc with Bette's eyes and throat. Sometimes, scenes were so bad that, when the front office refused to tolerate rewrites, Bette, Mary and Goulding would shoot two versions, the original scene and the revised one, and then Goulding would act as referee.

As Christmas approached, everyone was heartily sick of *The Great Lie*. Even in its rewritten form it was 24-carat soap: just a series of quarrels and financial arrangements, partings and reunions, without a grain of realism. Bette just virtually played herself: her healthier, more vibrant, outgoing self, not the nervous, vulnerable, breakdown-prone self hidden from the public. Mary didn't steal the picture: she was given it. It wasn't worth having, but she won an Oscar for it.

Bette was determined to finish by Christmas Eve. Goulding was slow, but, in the words of the assistant director, Al Alleborn:

> Miss Davis insisted we must finish before the holidays. She was determined the crew would enjoy the season with their families, and that she and Brent and Astor would too. She literally pulled the whole troupe with her so we could have a great Christmas. She was the trouper of all time.

In a break following a particularly overwrought dramatic scene in *The Great Lie,* Bette received a comedy script from Hal Wallis entitled *The Bride Came C.O.D.* She laughed at the title: she and Farney, who was visiting from the East, would surely be married right after the holidays. She said she would love to make the picture without seriously considering its essential stupidity.

She had managed, with remarkable skill, to keep her marriage a secret from the press. She announced it only on 30 December, when most newspapers were operating on minimum staffs for the holidays and when photographers were at a premium. She even failed to advise the studio publicity department, which infuriated several members who had hoped to capitalise on the wedding to publicise *The Bride Came C.O.D.*

She decided to hold the ceremony on New Year's Eve at the home of her beloved Jane Bryan and Justin Dart in Arizona. A Methodist minister was chosen because of Farney's faith: the Reverend Price, of Clarksburg. Bette chose a long white jersey evening dress with long sleeves as her wedding gown, and lilies of the valley. Bobby's husband Robert Pelgram was best man and Jane Bryan was matron of honour. Among those present were Ruthie and Bobby, Bette's cousin John Favor, and make-up man Perc Westmore and his girlfriend and later wife, Bette's beloved hairdresser Margaret Donovan. The marriage took place in the magnificent living-room of the Spanish-style ranch house in the 15,000-acre tract. It was Farney's second marriage: he had formerly been married to an aviatrix who had joined him in several of his heroic pioneer flights.

It was an extremely joyous occasion. The Darts were certainly Bette's closest friends, and she would not have tolerated the absence of Westmore, to whom she felt she owed everything: for making her 'beautiful' on the world's screens.

She was delighted to see once more Farney's parents and sisters. The honeymoon was extremely brief. Bette had to report for work at the studio almost immediately.

Perhaps because of the excitement of her second and far more promising marriage, Bette almost immediately lost enthusiasm for *The Bride Came C.O.D.* On 7 January 1941, Al Alleborn, assistant director on the picture, called her and asked her when she would be coming in for her wardrobe tests. This was a mistake: because of the rushed schedule, Hal Wallis had ordered Bette not to have a special wardrobe made for the picture, but instead, and astonishingly, to buy all her clothes for the picture at I. Magnin's store. Therefore, Alleborn's call was distinctly misjudged. She snapped testily: 'I've already got my wardrobe from some store or other. I won't have to test, thank God.' Alleborn stammered, 'There seems to be some question about your wardrobe.' 'THERE IS NO QUESTION!' she shouted and hung up.

Alleborn took a deep breath, counted up to ten, and called her back. He said, 'We're leaving for Death Valley on Sunday.' 'Oh my *God!*' she replied and hung up again.

Leave for Death Valley she did. After the long and complicated journey back from Arizona, it was not pleasing to have to leave her husband and set off again. Even in January, the heat in Death Valley was well over 100 degrees in the daytime and dropped alarmingly to chilly conditions at night. A consolation was that the cocky, high-strung, aggressively humorous James Cagney was her co-star. They both despised the script and laughed nightly over the crazy lines and situations.

One afternoon, the script included a sequence in which an aeroplane piloted by Cagney made a forced landing, with its tail in the air. Bette was supposed to open a door and jump into a sandhill. She obeyed, when the director William Keighley shouted a command, only to plunge into a cactus patch. She screamed and was carried in agony, bristling with forty-five spines in her rear, to a local hotel where a doctor painfully removed the spines one by one. Recovering bravely, she picked up a new page for the script for the following day. It announced that she was to receive a slingshot in her behind, aimed by Cagney. The scene was postponed – and her fall in the cactus patch included in the picture. A photograph was run in the papers, leading many to suspect that the entire episode was invented for publicity purposes. The caption read: 'Forty-five point landing; fundamentally speaking, a patch of cactus is no bed of roses.'

The picture was as nonsensical as Bette had feared. Yet it contained many sequences in which her little-known flair for comedy was agreeably exploited. Her mood, despite her impatience with the material, was good; she only wished she and Farney had not had to yield, so soon after their wedding, to the pitiless studio schedules.

After *The Bride Came C.O.D.* ground tiresomely to its conclusion, Bette was confronted with a very different project. She had been pestered for some considerable time by William Wyler to make a screen version of Lillian Hellman's savage play about greed and cruelty in the deep South, *The Little Foxes*. Wyler was convinced she would be ideal in the part of Regina Giddens, a former Southern belle warped by frustration and repression into becoming a monster obsessed by money. Regina recalls her husband after a long absence in order to make sure that he leaves her his inheritance which will give her power equal to that of her brothers. She allows her husband to die of a heart attack, discovering at the end of the play that her new financial status has left her utterly alone.

Tallulah Bankhead had been supremely successful as Regina on the stage. She had played the part with great boldness, warmth and authority, forcing the audience to sympathise with her as a woman, making them understand why she had been turned into a demoniacal force by the contempt with which her family had treated her. Bette, very much against her own judgement, yielded to Wyler when he insisted she see Miss Bankhead in the play. It was a fatal mistake. She was so overawed by Tallulah's performance that she overcompensated by working out a completely different interpretation of the part. Once Wyler talked her into playing Regina, she decided to emphasise the coldness, the calculation of the character. Instead of Tallulah's sexuality, her full-blown thwarted voluptuousness, Bette decided to portray a woman whose sexuality had been destroyed by competition with men. She had grown frigid, so that when she made up her face to greet her husband and try to seduce him into following the purpose of her will, she simply produced a deathmask of white powder. Bette worked out her own make-up with the aid of Perc Westmore, an icy resistant appearance that suggested the sterility of Regina's spirit but at the same time greatly reduced the range of the actress's expression.

No sooner had Bette reluctantly yielded to pressure to play the part than Jack Warner refused to loan her to Sam Goldwyn, who owned the rights. It seemed that Tallulah might be hired after all when suddenly Goldwyn decided to use Miriam Hopkins. Miss Hopkins was gleeful that she would replace her hated rival in so important a vehicle, and indeed she would probably have been brilliant in a part that was very close to her own character. Wyler refused to proceed with her and Goldwyn was forced to try to make a deal with Warners.

He had a stroke of luck. Jack Warner and Hal Wallis ran into casting problems on the picture *Sergeant York,* a story of the First World War hero, and they needed an actor immediately for the title role. Gary Cooper was the perfect choice. They had to have him. Goldwyn was eager for the money that a loan-out of Cooper would bring. He traded: Cooper for Davis. Bette was freed at a price of $150,000 to Jack Warner while still paid her usual $3,000 a week for twelve weeks. Thus, Warner made a profit of $114,000 on the deal.

Bette was annoyed about this, but soon other problems consumed her. Farney, so soon after their marriage, had to return to Minneapolis for secret work on planes, and the separation was extremely painful to her. She was lonely and desperately needed affection from Wyler at the time. Sally Sage, her stand-in, says she even sought a resumption of her earlier romance with Wyler, but this is unlikely since she was friendly with Wyler and his wife, Margaret, and Bette was deeply in love with Farney. She did need warmth, consideration and support at this time. But from the beginning, Wyler was annoyed with her because she would not play the part with the warmth and womanliness he wanted.

She insisted that the house occupied by her clan, the Hubbards, was absurdly too opulent; that it should have a frayed, run-down look to indicate the family's desperate need for cash which consumed their lives. She also felt that if she exuded sexual charm it would be incomprehensible to the viewer that there was no man in her life. In this, she was entirely logical but Wyler obstinately refused to see the point. Worse, Goldwyn changed his mind from day to day over her costumes. He also kept shifting her hairstyles and make-up from one day to another. This indecision drove her nearly mad. The cold rage with which she played the part extended into her behaviour off the set. Much as she criticised Warners, she hated being away from 'home', her own studio. Both Wyler and Goldwyn criticised her appearance: they hated the almost 'Japanese' quality of her white make-up. A big explosion came just before the big scene in which Regina, seated in the foreground, lets her husband die of a heart attack by failing to bring him a medicine bottle. Bette pointed out that if the audience was sympathetic to Regina at this stage then surely they would not tolerate what amounted to a form of murder. Surely this, more than anything else, proved her to be correct in her interpretation. Wyler said that he wanted a shock to the audience: by making her monstrous from the beginning Bette had provided no illuminating change in character at a moment of crisis.

The arguments went on and on, screaming match after screaming match with no resolution. Wyler, despite his dislike of the interpretation, gave Bette the full star treatment, placing her at the exact centre of every shot, forming the cast around her in geometric patterns. He allowed her to reflect her character in her clothing, her hair tightly and forbiddingly wound up *à la concierge,* her dresses tight fitting and corseted and made of intricate handmade lace. Nevertheless, she was not consoled. One evening, following a particularly bad

190

argument, she literally ran from Wyler's office. She had scarcely slept for the past week, and, her nerves tight, drove to a pharmacist who had prepared a sedative for her on a doctor's prescription. By accident, she was given household ammonia in the bottle. She swallowed the poisonous substance and became seized by wracking convulsions. She collapsed and her maid rushed her to the hospital where the application of a stomach pump just saved her life.

This horrifying episode unsettled her drastically. Wyler continued to announce as she came on the set that a particular costume was lousy and the designer would say the opposite. She would stand there fuming while the argument raged around her, and finally joined in enthusiastically herself. The real crisis came during a big dinner party scene at the Hubbard house. She played it with a neurotic edge whereas Wyler wanted a glow of hospitality barely concealing an inner bitterness. She could not come to grips with the part as Wyler wanted it; she could not, in the parlance of the industry, get 'into' it. Wyler let the sequence play out and then said to everyone on the set, 'That's the lousiest goddamn dinner scene I ever saw.' He added the cruellest cut of all, 'Maybe we'd better get Bankhead.' To be insulted like this by the man she most admired and perhaps still loved was unbearable. Bette went off to the beach for a week and the picture was shot 'around' her.

Wyler and Goldwyn seriously considered scrapping the footage and bringing in Hopkins, who was waiting gleefully in the wings, but they realised this was insanity: they had to complete the picture with Bette. They rudely tried to prove she was faking (when her doctor reported she was having a nervous breakdown) but failed to make the case stick. Unsmilingly, very far from feeling like a happy newlywed and desperately needing Farney, she fought her way back to work on 7 June 1941.

No sooner had she started than a script arrived from

Hal Wallis entitled *The Gay Sisters*. It was the story of three heiresses to a fortune whose father goes down on the *Lusitania:* most of the action was taken up with quarrels in boardrooms. She found the script dull and laden with too much talk. She wrote to Wallis that she was tired of playing women older than she was; the part of the older sister seemed to be poorly written; the part should be played by an actress actually in her twenties; it called for someone who had a hard and bitter quality in her acting which did not have to be assumed; she was tired of pretending to be hard and bitter in her late thirties as she was in *Foxes;* that there was 'plenty of time for that later on'. (She was now thirty-three.) She said, 'I would be so grateful if you could give *The Gay Sisters* to someone else.' Wallis did: to Barbara Stanwyck.

She proceeded miserably with *The Little Foxes*. Wyler soon began to carp yet again about her sternness and grimness in playing the scenes. She yielded to his entreaties by playing some of the sequences with a bitter laugh, an antic savage humour.

The picture turned out to be, surprisingly, a major work. Seen today, Bette's performance is 'modern'. By removing all sentiment and softness from her character, by playing it on an even note of steely effrontery, she is entirely ahead of her time and undoubtedly made the right choices in almost every scene. The warmth and charm Wyler wanted would have been wrong in the context: Hellman wanted a symbolic story of American greed, and Bette showed by inference how a desire for money in many American women overcame a desire for sex. The reviews were mixed but she undoubtedly added to her stature by undertaking the picture. It has improved with time; its coldness and hardness now seem more acceptable than they may have seemed in a romantic and sentimental age.

Nine

AFTER *The Little Foxes*, Bette had another nervous breakdown, feeling so depressed that she lay crying all day long; when Hal Wallis and Jack Warner tried to reach her to discuss her playing in her next picture, *The Man Who Came to Dinner,* she refused to accept their calls and simply lay on her bed sobbing and sobbing. She longed for Farney, but he was tied up in Minneapolis. She finally did write to Wallis, thanking him for the flowers he sent, and saying 'When I cry all day long there really is something wrong,' and asking him to help a friend of hers, Dwight Fiske, obtain work as a writer. She was needed for the part of Maggie, secretary to the extravagantly boorish Sheridan Whiteside, a parody of Alexander Woolcott on whom the play was based. It was a nice part: Maggie was a super secretary, utterly efficient yet exasperated by Whiteside, and who improbably discovers love with a newspaper man in a small town. It was the one sentimental and ill-written part in the play, yet it offered chances to act somebody brisk, no-nonsense, efficient and tough – in other words, the image the public had of Bette in private, an image fostered by her own extraordinary command of her own publicity.

For the public knew nothing of the real Bette: of her distress, her shattered nerves, her outbursts of tears and fury, her sheer temperament; they knew her, from the fan magazine articles she vetted or wrote to be only a cheerful, outgoing, extroverted, warm, composed and assured human being – like Maggie. It is therefore ironical that, just as she was considering the script for *The Man Who Came to Dinner,* she was virtually bedridden, and crying miserably from morning to night.

And when at last she was able to pull herself together, she began turning herself for the picture into that brisk, cool character the public thought she was. And when she forced herself to accept Monty Woolley instead of John Barrymore whom she wanted for the part of Sheridan Whiteside – one of those weird inexplicable accidents that marred her life upset everything.

She was playing with a Scottie (some say her own dog, Tippy, some a friend's dog) when the dog bit her, this devoted, dog-loving President of the Tailwaggers, bit her on the most prominent public feature: her nose. She screamed at the pain; but, adoring her dogs, she did not punish the animal. She was terrified of blood poisoning, and summoned her doctor; she learned she had been saved from poisoning but might be disfigured; and that the deep and dangerous wound would take weeks to heal.

She was already involved in costume fittings for *Dinner* when this bizarre accident, as bizarre as that with the ammonia bottle, took place. Much to the distress of Jack Warner, Hal Wallis and everyone else at the studio, she announced the picture would have to be postponed while her nose healed up. She was doubly embarrassed by the fact that she had asked for the part of Maggie, which certainly wasn't a starring role. Now she acted with characteristic extremeness. Instead of staying in town, where at least she would have been handy for discussions, she suddenly and impetuously left for New Hampshire. She spent the entire journey on the train confined to her drawing-room, petrified that somebody would see her and leak the story that she was disfigured.

She rested and recuperated at the Farnsworth Farm in

Vermont and Farney got leave from Minneapolis to visit with her. Her telegrams to the studio became increasingly more bizarre, making as many references to her nose as Cyrano de Bergerac did to his in the famous play. Her nose seemed to loom larger in her life than the Statue of Liberty: now it was not as red as the day before; now the scab was about to fall off; now the swelling was down; now it would not be gross and disfiguring; now it was its small, unassuming self again; now it would be ready for church on Sunday; now she could even sniff flowers and, presumably, poke it into other people's business . . . the telegrams and letters have a surrealist black humour, an antic, frantic oddity, that make them irresistibly outlandish and comic today. And at last her world-famous proboscis did mend, and she came back to Hollywood with a large piece of sticking plaster attached to its now modest dimensions, to confront a helplessly giggling cast on her first day of work, playing her scenes with her back to the camera and snapping out her lines too acidly – beyond the demands of the script.

She was in a temper when she started *The Man Who Came to Dinner,* and the fact shows in her expert but too hard-edged and bitter playing of Maggie Cutler. Her dislike of Monty Woolley seems to go beyond the demands of the part, which calls for Maggie to show a wry, sceptical attitude towards the great man she is working for. She is skilful enough to pretend affection for the newspaperman in the story, but her 'love' scenes are notably brittle and artificial. Nevertheless, she brings great style – almost too much style – to a part that could easily have proved a liability: her long swooping rushes of greeting to Reginald Gardiner (as a parody of Noël Coward) and Jimmy Durante (improbably as a version of Harpo Marx) are in themselves marvels of simulated enthusiasm.

Most of all, it is fascinating to see how she triumphs over breakdown and dog bite to give a cheerful naturalistic performance. She worked barely two weeks. She began reading the script for *In This Our Life* almost at once: she had been denied, like a naughty schoolgirl, the right to her usual vacation between pictures because she had taken leave to go to Vermont over her dog bite. *In This Our Life*, based on a gloomy, repetitious and poorly written novel by Ellen Glasgow, about two sisters in conflict, was for some reason admired by her; she did not feel equally happy with the screenplay.

On 20 October, she was in costume and wig fittings for *In This Our Life* when she received a telegram saying that Farney had been stricken with a severe case of pneumonia and had been rushed to a hospital in Minneapolis. She completely lost control. Refusing to wait for a scheduled flight, which would involve changing planes several times, she called the famous stunt flier Paul Mantz and asked him to fly her to Minneapolis in person.

'Bette, I'd love to help,' that tough aviator replied. Referring to the great distance to Minnesota, which was already in the grip of foul autumn weather, he added: 'And my plane is only a single-motor job.'

'Is that bad?' Bette screamed down the line. 'What difference does it make? Doesn't it fly with one motor? What does it matter so long as it gets there?'

'It's one hell of a flight. We'd have to stop every hundred miles,' Mantz replied.

She told him she would go anyway and he promised to help. But Hal Wallis and Jack Warner were adamant she must take no such risk. She immediately called Howard Hughes and asked him to give her a plane.

'The weather's pretty thick,' he said. 'I wouldn't advise the trip, Bette.'

'Does that mean bad?' she asked.

'It does, Bette,' he told her. 'But if you want to chance it, I'll arrange a transport for you.'

While she waited, chain-smoking, for Hughes to call

her back, Farney managed to get to a telephone from his sick bed and call her. His voice sounded creaky and weak, and she was unable to sleep all night. She had to laugh when he told her his doctor's name was Jay Davis. 'Poor darling!' she told a friend. 'He just had to have a doctor whose name was Davis!'

When Dr Davis called her, she called everyone saying, 'Dr Davis says there's no fat on Farney. Is that good or bad? His white corpuscle count is up. Is that good or bad?'

At last Hughes fixed her up with a TWA plane. All others were grounded. She and her travelling companion, her new manager, Lester Linsk, and a friend, Elaine Byers, were half an hour late for the flight. They flew through fog and stormy weather. She was terrified the plane would crash, feeling such violent rocking that she feared she would have to sit in the middle in order to balance the plane. She constantly bugged the pilot for word on whether the conditions would improve.

She and her companions landed in Kansas City and were transferred to a specially chartered clipper in which they were the only passengers. Paul Richter, vice-president of TWA, and a close personal friend of Hughes's, piloted the plane. Fog was so bad that he had to make an unscheduled landing in Des Moines. Bette paced up and down the airport lounge, her nerves in shreds after a sleepless night. At last there was a clearance to fly via Rochester. A Warner representative in Chicago called Bette and lied to her on orders: 'Farney is well, his temperature is normal.' She decided to go ahead; her instinct told her Farney was still desperately ill and she was right. She knew the studio hated her undertaking the flight with so many planes grounded and weather conditions violent all along the route.

Fog delayed the plane again. She did not sleep the second night. She was unable to endure the constant

197

bumping, trembling and rocking of the plane. She wondered if she would ever make it to Farney. Lester Linsk and Elaine Byers tried to calm her. It says much for her courage and determination that despite her terror she pressed on, driven by her intense love, in an adventure that surpassed any she experienced in pictures.

The travellers arrived in Minnesota after a 2,000-mile flight on 22 October. Bette was so exhausted and helpless with long hours of crying and two nights without rest that at first Farney's Dr Jay Davis felt she would have to go into the hospital herself. She checked into the Curtis Hotel, dodging a mob of fans in the airport and hotel lobby, and against Lester Linsk's advice insisted on going to Farney at once. He was in intensive care, still on the critical list, and she sat with him all afternoon; he was too ill to recognise her.

She feared she might lose him; and she still could not stop crying. Her fans among the nurses and personnel constantly peeked through the door to catch a glimpse of her. Dr Jay Davis begged them to go away. She was so pale and weak by sundown that Dr Davis demanded she return to the hotel and go to bed. She did – but again lay awake through much of the night.

She had only been married for ten months. Surely Farney couldn't die now: that robust, vigorous former flier? That outdoorsman and athlete, trim and strong, who loved her so tenderly?

She told Dr Davis the next morning, 'If Farney isn't better by tomorrow, I want you to find a room near him and check me into it.' Davis explained that was against hospital policy, but she insisted the policy be overridden, and indeed she did move into the room.

Meanwhile, Jack Warner bombarded her with cables. He didn't send flowers, offers of the finest doctors, or insistences she return by train. Instead, he bugged her callously to return at once by plane for costume fittings on *In This Our Life*. The sheer ruthlessness of the messages in the Warner files is shocking; Bette's resolution to stick by her husband is beautiful and moving.

Bette was not too pleased by the merciless pressure. The same day, she cabled Warner that she had already received three wires from him and from Taplinger; that she was sorry to be such a nuisance but still had no intention of leaving until Farney was in no danger of relapse; that this was no vacation she was taking; that she would try to return by air, weather permitting; and why would she stay longer than necessary? She was usually, she added in conclusion, fairly honest about such things . . .

She sent the telegram in a state so drained of energy, so utterly exhausted, she thought she might die. Dr Davis forbade her outright to make the journey by plane beyond Chicago. He demanded she have a few days' rest before flying to Chicago for the Santa Fe Chief to Los Angeles. He was worried that Farney would be upset, and would become sick again, if he learned that Bette was going to fly through storms. He cabled Jack Warner that she was still worn out from her trip north and that the strain was so severe she might break down completely at any moment.

With her usual energy, she bounced suddenly back and greeted Mrs Farnsworth, Arthur's mother, and his brother, Dan, a musician who played with the Renaissance Quintet of Ancient Instruments. She made a tour of Farney's work place and even managed to play hostess to reporters at a conference. She won them over completely with her charm. Seemingly untouched by her experience, chipper and full of fun, she gave scarcely an inkling of her condition the day before. Curled up with her feet beneath her in a chair, wrinkling her forehead, cupping her chin in her hands, chortling or roaring with laughter, and talking ten-to-the-dozen, she seemed to be completely recovered.

It was a terrific performance, as good as any she had

given on screen, and marred only by the fact that her voracious hunger for a good dinner afterwards was suppressed because the doctor refused to allow her to eat a solid meal along with her in-laws at the Curtis Hotel dining-room.

On 27 October, she was thrilled to find Farney sitting up in bed with some colour in his cheeks. Propped up on pillows, he urged her weakly to go back to Hollywood and her new picture. He promised he would follow her soon. She insisted he come to California to recuperate. He must not risk catching pneumonia again. The work he was doing was tiring, with endless pressure and very long hours. There was much to do in California in aircraft plants, because of Roosevelt's defence schemes now that war was so far advanced in Europe.

So fierce was Jack Warner's determination to have Bette get to work that she had to go straight from the train to the studio for make-up and clothing tests. She was very thin, her eyes seemingly the only living features in a chalk-white face, her nerves more seriously stretched than ever before. She quarrelled violently with the producers over her hair style, insisting on a hideously unbecoming fringe that made her look ridiculous and caused laughs at the previews, and she made Orry-Kelly re-do her clothes, defying Hal Wallis to create a drastically unbecoming wardrobe.

She was angry about everything. She had wanted to play the good sister in the story of a corrosive clan, with Olivia de Havilland cast against type as the bad sister, but Olivia had refused to risk her public image. Hal Wallis thought it ridiculous that Bette's character should be given a man's name, Stanley; but she thought the name interesting ('Besides,' she told Wallis, 'it's in the novel.'). Olivia was exceptionally nervous herself: over-weight, she had been ordered to lose a pound a day and was only losing half a pound – by starving herself so much she felt weak, ill and uncomfortable. John Huston, who was directing, fell in love with Olivia and Bette was upset with him. She meant well, but the associate producer David Lewis recalls that this protectiveness caused severe friction between her and the director which upset the whole picture from the start. Night after night, Bette would visit Olivia and talk things over while Olivia soaked in a hot tub.

In that difficult period, Bette rashly took on the prestigious position of president of the Academy of Motion Picture Arts and Sciences. It was entirely a mistake. She had responded to the invitation before the crisis over Farney. Instead of cancelling and backing out, she resolutely pushed ahead. But she had no time to attend to Academy business. The fretting over Farney, the worry over the picture and her poor state of health conspired against her success in this important position. She clashed over policy with members of the Board and was surprised to find a grimly conservative and rear-guard atmosphere in the upper echelons. She was shocked to learn that the Academy intended cancelling the annual dinners for the duration of the war and insisted that it was essential for the industry's prestige and morale that the Oscars be retained. In this one point she was victorious and indeed her purpose was wise. She resigned only a few weeks after she took up her position, probably with relief.

On 1 December, Farney arrived in Hollywood, pale and weak but over the pneumonia, and Bette insisted on going to meet him off the train, thereby holding up production for the day. She was ill with worry during much of the time she was waiting for him; and Olivia, torn between her sisterly advice and Huston's *macho* fascination with her youthful prettiness and charm, was ill, too – on some days announcing she would not begin work until after lunch. Bette caused Hal Wallis to write a critical memorandum when she kept imitating Hepburn, leaning against a doorway and saying, exhaustedly, in a flat Hepburn voice, 'All I want to do is drive, drive, drive.' Then, to make matters worse, Olivia began to imitate Bette imitating Hepburn.

Once Farney was back, Bette obtained little sleep. She had Adele call twice to say she was so exhausted from insomnia she would not come to work. Six days later, news of Pearl Harbor came over the radio and again she was sleepless. Matters came to a head on 10 December. Huston had to leave town on a war department assignment. Raoul Walsh was brought in to direct a scene in which Stanley, played by Bette, goes to the house of her Uncle William, played by Charles Coburn, sees him, then gets into her car and drives off into the night. Police pick her up for speeding. The scene was supposed to be played stealthily, so that Stanley would not be seen entering the house. But Bette, disliking Walsh and in a rage with the whole picture, got out of her car, slammed the door, slammed into the house, slammed out again, got back in her car, slammed the door again – and Walsh screamed 'CUT!' He told her to do the scene as he wanted and she refused. She rushed home and wrote to Jack Warner that it was ridiculous to do the scene again. She also refused to do retakes of a scene in a shanty and a Baltimore apartment, citing, amusingly, the economy wave as a reason. Surely it would be a waste of money in a national emergency to do the scenes again as she didn't know how she could possibly play them any differently. Wallis cancelled the retakes but demanded she re-do the scene at Uncle William's house as he wanted it. She said – reluctantly – she would. A day later, she lost her voice and took to her bed, fuming inwardly, making it impossible for her to do the promised scene. The studio kept calling her house and getting Farney. She returned on Christmas Eve – when it was too late to set up the sequence.

She finally submitted to order on 1 January 1942. She was supposed not only to play the 'exit and entrance' scene at Uncle William's house but a further scene in which she argued with police. She refused to play any of the lines in the manner Walsh wanted. He told his assistant he was going to walk off the picture. Wallis called up and demanded to know what was going on. There was a major row on the telephone. Finally, Bette played the scene in a compromise between her interpretation and Walsh's. Wallis suddenly decided to reshoot the Baltimore apartment sequence after all. Bette refused to do it. Wallis insisted. She just stopped herself from walking off. She played the scene, but in a manner Wallis found unacceptable. And when he ran the 'exit and entrance' scene she was still slamming doors as before.

Between 8 and 10 January the sequences had to be redone yet again. Bette was at the end of her tether. So were Walsh and Wallis. Inevitably, Bette reached a new series of compromises. But she wrote the picture off in her mind and indeed gave her worst performance in what was perhaps her worst major picture and Huston's as well. Scene after scene bordered on the amateurish. The preview was a disaster. Comment cards attacked Bette's hairdo and make-up and clothing. She would have been mortified – if she had cared at that stage. She thanked God there was a better picture ahead: *Now, Voyager*, from the novel by Olive Higgins Prouty.

Hal Wallis had discovered Mrs Prouty's novel in the late summer of 1941: a soap opera in the tradition of her earlier *Stella Dallas*, it was a wish-fulfilment fantasy about a repressed unhappy Bostonian girl who escapes her dragon mother through the aid of a psychiatrist and emerges on a pleasure cruise with a new face and figure and the chance of a romance with a Continental charmer. Originally, the story was set in Europe; but because of the outbreak of war it had to be transferred to South America. This was equally improbable: following the sinking of the *Athenia*, few American ships dared make transit through the U-boat riddled waters of the Caribbean and Latin America. The story therefore took place in some unknown time; it achieved a kind of abstract quality, belonging to no particular era and dealing with a group of impossibly noble or ignoble characters who had little or no resemblance to living people. The author of the book wanted the picture to be made in rich colours, with the flashbacks shot silent, subtitled; apparently unaware that war was taking place, she wanted locations shot in Italy.

Hal Wallis wanted Irene Dunne for the central role: the Dunne-Boyer *Love Affair* had been a hit, and the reason the picture was bought was to cash in on the current public interest in romantic fantasies set aboard luxury liners. Originally, Edmund Goulding was to direct it; and he was asked to supply his own script. But he became involved with another picture. Meanwhile, Norma Shearer expressed a warm interest; Wallis sent her a copy of the book. Charles Feldman represented her as well as Irene Dunne. He refused to convey a firm offer to Miss Dunne because he was afraid Norma would be upset, and would accuse him of playing one client against another. When Norma finally decided not to go ahead, Irene Dunne was already committed elsewhere. Wallis sent the book to Ginger Rogers, who had enjoyed a great success in another soap opera, *Kitty Foyle*.

Bette heard about these negotiations while vacationing in New Hampshire and flew into a rage, demanding to know why she, a New Englander herself, had not been considered for the part. Nobody was rude enough to point out that Jack Warner did not think she could achieve a transition to great beauty from sheer ugliness; that audiences would find it impossible to accept the change. She made it clear that for Charlotte Vale, the ugly duckling in the story, to become Irene Dunne or Ginger Rogers would be laughable: Bette with her attractive plainness would be a far more likely figure.

She argued the point in letters. She sent telegrams. Ginger turned the part down. Bette, busy with Roosevelt's cause, attending a mass Democratic Convention at Madison Square Garden to support her idol, and joined by Farney, who was distantly related to the Roosevelts, pressed her cause still more firmly. And finally Jack Warner, influenced by Hal Wallis, agreed.

Why was Jack Warner so adamant at first that Bette should not play in *Now, Voyager*? Because he was drastically upset by her appearance in *In This Our Life* and by the fact that for the first time the comment cards, guides to mass audience taste as ratings are today, were damaging to her in that picture. Bette returned, refreshed after six weeks' leave and the exhilaration of the convention; thrilled that she would play Charlotte Vale starting 16 March. She was annoyed to hear that Michael Curtiz was supposed to direct after he finished the patriotic musical *Yankee Doodle Dandy*, but much to her relief he was replaced by Irving Rapper. She remembered the witty, intelligent Rapper with great pleasure from his job as assistant director on *Kid Galahad* and *Jezebel* – and he had allowed her as a gag to play a bit part as a nurse in his movie *Shining Victory*.

Bette left New York for Chicago on 12 March. She was on the train, looking forward to seeing Ethel Barrymore in *The Corn Is Green*, which she planned to make as a film. Suddenly, she was stricken with agonizing stomach pains and an attack of vomiting. There was no doctor on the train and she had to suffer miserably through the night until she arrived in Chicago, where she was carried off on a stretcher to the hospital. It seemed she had eaten something in New York which had given her ptomaine poisoning. She finally rallied, and managed to sit up in bed and check her luggage. She was horrified to discover that one of the pieces was missing. It was a cabin trunk containing a fur coat, suits, dresses, lingerie and silk stockings, all valued at a total of $3,150.

She was very upset, realising that some member of the train's staff had taken advantage of her serious condition to rob her of her possessions. She called police, who came to see her at the hotel.

In a bad mood, she attended Miss Barrymore's performance. She was electrified by it. Typically, she bounced back from sickness and gloom to high-powered enthusiasm and admiration. She rushed backstage and congratulated Miss Barrymore on her superb acting. Miss Barrymore burst into tears.

Bette was determined that she would play *The Corn Is Green* in pictures but meantime there was the business of making *Now, Voyager*. Given the fact that it was a soap opera, she knew she would have to have make the part of Charlotte Vale as realistic as possible. She consulted closely with Orry-Kelly on the matter of her wardrobe, which was to show the drastic transition from a miserable girl to an assured and attractive woman. She suggested an ugly Foulard dress with a heavy pattern for the early scenes and a stylish costume for the cruise. Orry-Kelly made the clothes deliberately timeless with an emphasis on hats which at first shadowed Bette's face, suggesting the character's extreme shyness and only gradual change.

Another matter which concerned Bette from the outset was the casting of the part of her mother, the formidable Mrs Vale.

Rapper came up with the idea of Gladys Cooper, who had played in *The Letter* in London. Bette, who had admired Gladys Cooper on Broadway, was delighted with the idea; and indeed, as the ferocious, pathetic matriarch, Cooper's performance provided powerful competition with Bette's own.

Shooting the picture was an intolerably slow and laborious business: it dragged on weeks over schedule. Rapper was an accomplished craftsman, but he was so deferent to Davis that every time he wanted her to interpret a scene in a particular manner, he had to wheedle and cajole her like a courtier: he dared not *command* her. She and Perc Westmore together worked out a make-up for the ugly duckling Boston girl that was horribly over-emphatic; the great beetling eyebrows and overstuffed figure made her laughable instead of tragic. And even though Rapper forced this preposterous disguise to be played down, it still seemed impossible, forced, in the final movie, just as the transition to good looks and a slim figure – and even the cure of an eyesight problem – seemed improbable: too much from the pages of fairy tale.

Both Jack Warner and Hal Wallis, whose 'independent' production this was, grumbled constantly over the slowness of the shooting, the excessive costs; but the results, seen in the screening room each night, were splendidly effective. It was a good picture, undoubtedly: well-made, polished, expert.

A tiny but potent controversy has swirled about the origin of the famous sequence in which Paul Henreid places two cigarettes in his mouth, lights them simultaneously, and passes one to Bette. Irving Rapper, unhesitatingly, states that he invented this particular bit of business, inspired by a similar passage in the novel. On countless public occasions, Henreid and Davis have denied Rapper's claim, stating that they cooked up the sequence together on the set while he, presumably, was out to lunch. Casey Robinson, who wrote the script, recalled including it long before the star was cast. The script prepared before shooting clearly indicates that he was right, but it is possible Bette may have influenced the precise direction of the scene. It had occurred much earlier, in *The Rich Are Always With Us:* no doubt Bette's envy of Ruth Chatterton while making the picture stemmed in part from the smoothness with which George Brent performed the same gesture in a bedroom scene.

Scripts in those days were explicitly tailored for stars, and Robinson included many touches which suggested Bette's New England background. Out of his long friendship with her, he drew the moment when the heroine takes from her handbag a photograph of aunts and uncles ranged before the camera in a sombre Boston living-room as though before a firing squad. We might as well be back in Lowell, with Bette's family similarly arranged for a wedding or a funeral. There is a waxen quality about the group, a sense of moral purpose and rectitude, that ideally reflects Bette's background. There is a good scene later on, in which the heroine has to confront her relatives after she has been transformed from an ugly duckling into a swan. The same formidable figures that appeared in the group portrait now appear in person, challenging her, threatening her with ancient shibboleths and customs.

Now, Voyager is, of course, a camp classic, a masterpiece of schmaltz. The movie provided a wish-fulfilment fantasy for millions of women during the war years: no matter how plain or badly done by a woman might be, she could, through the attention of a psychiatrist and a Continental lover in a white suit, achieve a sublime existence. But, so strict were the moral codes of the era, she must not go unpunished. Because she had an affair with a married man, she must be condemned to occupy a Back Street role, forever suffering in a remote compartment of her architect lover's life while he continued to devote most of the year to a humourless and unattractive spouse. 'Why ask for the moon? We have the stars!' uttered by Bette in a final transcendent moment, is supposed to keep the audience pleasantly uncomfortable as it goes home. After all, the public settled for second best in everything, so why shouldn't the figures in movie dramas?

As a dream, a shimmering fantasy, the movie still works. All the formidable resources of a major studio were brought to bear on an insubstantial plot. The throbbing music of Max Steiner with rich, sweet melodies lulls the audience into submission before the most rampant absurdities. But above all it is Davis's performance which sustains the work. Her atmosphere of brisk New England common sense, her uncanny ability to hold the eye overcomes many weak or soggy passages. She has a logic, energy, drive and charm that no dialogue can defeat. By seemingly believing in the plot, the star almost makes one accept it.

Now, Voyager was perhaps Bette's most successful picture to date. A pleased Jack Warner gratefully increased her salary to $2,500 a week. Girls sent her mail in shoals, many of them unhappy, plain or crippled, all of them burning with identification.

In 1942, while *Now, Voyager* was going on seemingly forever, Bette became involved in a project designed to give entertainment to servicemen on leave or stationed in and around Los Angeles. This was the Hollywood Canteen. The inspiration for it came from the actor John Garfield, who was determined to do something for the war effort when he was failed for the military service. He asked to have lunch with her one day in the Warner's commissary and outlined his concept: a canteen to be run by the stars. She was fascinated and delighted with the idea. When Garfield asked her to be chairwoman, she exploded with an uproarious cry of 'YES!' Electrified into action as only she could be, Bette began scouring Hollywood for the premises. She soon located one and flung herself into weekends of eighteen-hour work days to raise money and decorate the place.

She went to her agent, the tight-fisted Jules Stein, and pushed him into taking charge of the financial committee and even pouring money into it himself. Stein's wife, Doris, enormously charming and energetic, took charge of assigning the hostesses from the ranks of leading actresses. Most prominent among these, Marlene Dietrich gave herself unselfishly to scrubbing floors, washing dishes and cooking food.

During the shooting of *Now, Voyager,* Hal Wallis had closed a deal with Lillian Hellman to film *Watch on the Rhine,* from her famous stage play about an expatriate German family that arrives in a rich middle-class American home. The play, a telling exposure of American isolationism, would make an ideal propaganda picture in time of war.

There was no question of Bette being offered the part of Sara Muller, the tormented wife of an underground leader and patriot. She was tied up in *Now, Voyager,* which, in view of its countless delays, would not be finished until the summer of 1942. While Miss Hellman's lover, Dashiell Hammett, began work on the screenplay at his farm in Pleasantville, N.Y., Wallis began casting around for a suitable actress. He offered it to Irene Dunne, who liked the material but didn't think the part important enough for her. Her agent, Charles Feldman, agreed. Wallis thought of Margaret Sullavan but she proved so disinterested she didn't even bother to return his telephone calls. Wilful and mercurial, Miss Sullavan then suddenly announced she was interested, but when Wallis sent a New York representative to see her at her apartment, she wasn't at home. Wallis began to think about the British actress Edna Best, or possibly Rosemary de Camp. Meanwhile, the potential director, a friend of Lillian Hellman and Dashiell Hammett named Herman Shumlin, who had directed the play on the stage, suggested Helen Hayes. Wallis rejected the idea.

Paul Lukas was not at first considered as the patriotic Franz Muller. Charles Boyer was the first choice, but he became nervous about not having a German accent and backed out.

Finally, Hammett injured his back and work on the script was delayed to the point at which *Now, Voyager* was finished. In the last days of shooting, Wallis sent

Bette Dashiell Hammett's first few pages. She accepted at once: as ardent a supporter of Roosevelt as she had ever been, fiercely patriotic and a leader of anti-Nazism, she found a deep personal attraction in the play. Lillian Hellman was delighted with the choice and came to Hollywood in May to do a final polish of the script and to confer with Hal Wallis. On Wallis's advice, she created additional scenes to build the character for the basis of a star performance: in the opening scene, Bette would make a headlong run from the street into her family home and lovingly rediscover it room by room. Other scenes in which Bette was shown in Washington had to be cut because of wartime restrictions on the filming of government buildings.

As so often before, Bette was furious about her billing. She insisted she should be in second place to Paul Lukas, finally cast as her husband. She said people would think her ridiculous in assuming first position when her part was secondary. She quarrelled incessantly with Wallis over this. But the publicity department was adamant that the picture could not be sold on Lukas, only on her. It won the battle.

Bette had never worked with Herman Shumlin before. She was extremely superstitious. No one must whistle in her dressing-room or wear green socks. If anyone spilled salt, it had to be thrown over a shoulder immediately. She was constantly found touching wood. She would never walk under a ladder, or open an umbrella in the house. When Shumlin walked into her dressing-room for the first time, he removed his hat. She watched paralysed with horror as he placed it on the sofa she sometimes used as a bed.

It was a forewarning. She had waived her vacation to do *Watch on the Rhine*, which started on 15 June, only seven days after *Now, Voyager* finished. As a result, she was on edge, and Shumlin was lacking in the experience that would win her respect. Always at her most savage when confronted by uncertainty or incompetence, she began arguing with him almost from the beginning. She overacted several scenes disastrously, drawing attention to herself when she was supposed to be one of an ensemble. Wallis had to send a stream of notes to Shumlin warning him to 'hold Bette down' whenever the dialogue became strongly emotional in tone. Bette did not have a rapport with Lucile Watson as the dominating matriarch of the clan who shows a gradually eroded isolationism in the action. Miss Watson was an extreme Republican whose haughty manner and high-powered right-wing politics contrasted ironically with the part she played. Bette, a Democrat to the core, found her tiresome and made no bones about showing it.

Although stagey and heavy-handed, its political message too crudely spelled out, *Watch on the Rhine* was a valuable contribution to the war effort. Unfortunately, Bette's performance, though sincere and deeply felt, was altogether too strong for the film. Her crisp theatrical delivery and great command of action made her too dominant in scenes that called for subdued underplaying. Paul Lukas, a stolid, boring actor who exuded little sympathy or warmth, was so clearly outacted by her that the focus of the story became blurred.

A pleasant experience of the picture was meeting Geraldine Fitzgerald again; Miss Fitzgerald played the part of the unhappy wife of a Nazi agent. She had kept in touch with Bette in the years since *Dark Victory;* they had many evenings together after the day's work.

Arthur Farnsworth was in Hollywood now, on secret war work connected with Honeywell. The marriage bumped along fairly comfortably, only occasionally interrupted by strenuous arguments. There was much to do on weekends improving Riverbottom, their lovely house in Glendale. They continued to have an intense personal affection for each other, based on shared backgrounds, interests and friends. Justin and Jane

Bryan Dart and Perc Westmore and Margaret Donovan remained their closest and dearest friends. Bobby was much recovered from her years of mental disturbances and had married. Ruthie was enjoying the relaxation of relishing her daughter's enormous success. The family was closer than ever, Bette's circle deliberately restricted, her work on the Hollywood Canteen occupying her pleasurably in every moment she could spare.

This, undoubtedly, was the best period of Bette's life: perhaps the only time in which she achieved complete fulfilment and happiness on a personal and professional level. The summer of 1942 was her apex: she was thirty-four years old – a perfect age for a woman, she was happily married to a man she respected, she had made a huge box-office hit followed by a valuable patriotic film, she was personally involved in the war effort through the Canteen, her health was markedly improved from previous years, and her difficult contentious nature was almost serene. But it was a summer that was quickly doomed.

Ten

As EARLY as 1940, Hal Wallis had planned to make a film of John Van Druten's stageplay *Old Acquaintance*, which starred Peggy Wood and Jane Cowl on Broadway. It was the story of two girlhood friends, one ruthless and selfish, the other cheerfully down to earth and outgoing, who, rivals from the outset, become novelists in competition. It was a thin mechanical contrivance enlivened by witty dialogue and skilful touches of characterisation.

In the period just before and during the first months of America's entry to the Second World War, the play provided ideal escapist entertainment. Edmund Goulding, fascinated as always by the bitchy quarrels of neurotic women, very much wanted to direct it on the screen but right away the project seemed an impossibility. When Wallis sent it to one of his favourite producers, the German expatriate Henry Blanke, Blanke saw major problems in its thinness and poor construction. When he sent it to Joseph Breen of the Hays Office, Breen rejected it outright, saying that since it showed a middle-aged woman with a young lover it would be totally unacceptable; that it displayed gross illicit sex; that it showed the heroine as having had numerous sexual affairs; that the characters were frequently drinking alcohol; and that the entire work was damaging to the image of the industry.

Wallis decided to go ahead, but work was very slow. He put the writer, Lenore Coffee, on to it but she was distracted by other work on *In This Our Life* and the Errol Flynn vehicle *They Died with Their Boots On*. She had to fill out the plot with particulars of the early lives of the two women. Finally, she gave up in despair; she was unable to lick the material. Wallis brought Howard Koch, who had written the adaptation of *The Letter*, into the production, and he struggled with the script for several months, followed by a writer named Ann Frolick.

By March, 1942, there was still no satisfactory screenplay. Rosalind Russell was determined to play the part of Kit, the more decent of the two female characters; and she would have been ideal for it. But she was delayed by a commitment to *My Sister Eileen*, and Hal Wallis was greatly disappointed to find that even for $150,000 for the picture she could not be released in time to begin work. Wallis then offered the part to Irene Dunne but she couldn't make up her mind and negotiations dragged on for months.

In June, 1942, John Van Druten began working with Edmund Goulding on the script at the Hotel Pierre in New York. Basing their work on Lenore Coffee's original draft, they filled the action with many entertaining 'in' New York jokes and references and more clearly defined the contrast between the two women. Finally, Irene Dunne decided not to go ahead.

It was not until late June that Bette, last as usual, was added to the cast. And even then it wasn't sure whether she would play the nice, no-nonsense Kit or the ferocious self-pitying Millie. She told everyone she would be perfectly happy in either part.

In New York, the witty Goulding sent a stream of letters on Hotel Pierre stationery to the associate producer Henry Blanke beginning, 'Darling Heinz'. At first, the letters were filled with enthusiasm, but soon Goulding, who was British, became weighed down with the triviality of what he was doing in the face of his country's peril in time of war. He wrote to Blanke on 23 July: 'Alas, when you come down to it, it is a very light cream puff with no cream. And in the light of the furious things that are going on in the world, the petty quarrels of a couple of bitches seem fragile and inconsequential.' Jack Warner read the letter and said to Blanke, 'The only cream puff in this matter is Eddie Goulding. Tell him to get back to the pastry kitchen and produce something that will keep the public's mind off this goddamn war.'

Goulding suggested Miriam Hopkins as the villainous Mildred. Warner responded: 'Yes, a bitch she is!' Miriam was cast. Bette groaned, but agreed Hopkins would be ideal – as the bitch.

Fuming that she had been last choice for Kit, dreading Hopkins, Bette was in a very poor state of mind that summer. Suddenly, Miss Hopkins proved difficult again: she wanted an enormous amount of money to play the part, twice as much as Bette, and insisted she be allowed to supervise her wardrobe, make-up and hairdress without the slightest interference from anyone. As a result, she was put on hold while everyone began looking for an alternative. Goulding and Van Druten, who had been concocting numerous vicious lines which they knew Hopkins would spit out to the manner born, suddenly had to pause, wondering if the entire screenplay would have to be rewritten.

Wallis offered the part of Mildred to Margaret Sullavan, who declined once more even to see the studio representatives and announced that she found it insulting that she would be asked to play a bitch. Instead of saying this in private, she said it in a radio interview which annoyed everyone intensely. Henry Blanke came up with the crazy idea of casting Janet Gaynor, the saccharine heroine of numerous romantic novelettes, and of having the authors rewrite the part to resemble a kind of Billie Burke character. John Van Druten and Goulding were adamant that Gaynor's sweetness would be impossible: 'I do not feel' (Van Druten wrote to Wallis) 'Gaynor can play it . . . The actress needs great physical force and strength for her outbursts and attacks of hysterics . . . This would be swell for Hopkins . . . This is *pure* Hopkins stuff . . .'

Jack Warner suggested Constance Bennett but at last everyone groaned, shrugged, and decided to put up with Miriam's predictable tantrums on and off the set.

A tremendous row blew up over the cameraman. In August, 1942, Bette refused to tolerate any photographer except Sol Polito. She flatly refused to work with Tony Gaudio, who had shot *The Letter*. Edmund Goulding was furious. He sent a cable to Wallis from New York: I AM EITHER WORKING FOR WARNER BROTHERS OR MISS DAVIS AND THERE IS A DIFFERENCE. URGE YOU NOT TO COMMIT YOURSELF TO ANY PROMISE ON CAMERAMAN UNTIL AFTER TALK WITH ME. THAT WOULD PUT ME IN A POSITION OF DAVIS, HOPKINS, MOODS, FADS, AND NONSENSE. Needless to say, Bette won: Polito, not Gaudio, photographed the picture.

The arguments dragged on. Miriam Hopkins came to Hollywood in October only to find nobody to meet her at the depot or at the hotel. No one was interested in speaking to her until it became essential. She received no invitations to dinner and sat alone in her suite in the Beverly Wilshire in a state of seemingly permanent fury, threatening to return at once to New York.

Goulding received several phone calls from her filled with violent complaint. He became so exhausted from the endless hours of work with Van Druten, often extending through the night, and from Miss Hopkins's uninterrupted stream of hour-long calls that he had a heart attack the day after he arrived in Hollywood and was carried off to the Good Samaritan Hospital. The director Julien Duvivier was offered the picture but

217

declined it, and Vincent Sherman was signed. Nobody, in those ruthless days of Hollywood, considered waiting until Goulding recovered. All of his long months of work were wasted, months which resulted in his almost losing his life, and his name was not even included in the script credits.

Sherman was very worried about the script, even in its final draft. Work began in the rainy November of 1942. Bette was in Palm Springs with a severe throat condition when shooting began. She was very uneasy about working with a new director; she was unfamiliar with Sherman's work and wasn't sure if she would get along with him. After five days, she walked into the studio with her agent Jules Stein's partner, Lew Wasserman. She asked Sherman in her dressing-room, 'How are things going?' 'Very well,' he replied. 'How is Miriam behaving?' 'Fine,' he told her. She looked amazed. Sherman asked her, 'Why don't you look at the rushes?' She was delighted because she knew from looking at Sherman's work she would be able to tell how he was handling the picture. She went to the projection room and sat enthralled. Merciless with incompetence, she instantly recognised quality. Sherman had done wonders with Miriam: he had used her harshness, her vicious edge effectively to illustrate the self-destructive nastiness of the character. Sherman came in a little uneasily to determine her reaction. Snapping her cigarette lighter open and lighting up a cigarette she said, 'It's fantastic. All I want to know is, when do I report for work?' Smiling, Sherman replied, 'Nine o'clock tomorrow morning.' Bette thrust the lighter into her handbag with a brisk touch of finality. 'I'll be there,' she said. 'You're doing wonderful things with Miriam.'

The first day on the set, Miriam turned up wearing a copy of a Bette Davis costume in *Jezebel* to infuriate Bette. Even though Miriam was better paid than Bette, she regarded herself as a visitor on the picture, forced to overcompensate for the fact that Bette was the reigning queen of the studio. Every time there was an over-the-shoulder shot from Miriam to Bette, Miriam would bring up a cigarette lighter across Bette's face and light a cigarette with it, blowing the smoke slowly and deliberately into Bette's eyes. Whenever Bette went into a speech that demanded Miriam's complete attention, Miriam would discover that one flower in a vase was set unevenly with the others and painstakingly fix it into position. On one occasion, when the scene called for Miriam to hang on every word Bette uttered, she went to a clock and reset the hands. She would drop a handkerchief and go to extensive business to retrieve it or straighten a painting on a wall or even tinkle the keys of a piano. Bette exploded again and again, and Miriam would smile sweetly, saying, 'But nobody was looking at me.'

One afternoon, Bette was dressing down Miriam in a sequence, attacking her for her jealousy and hatred of her character's superior writing. During Bette's speech, Miriam circled the room, straightening chair covers, putting paintings into position, rearranging ferns in a vase and picking up an imaginary hairpin from the carpet. Finally, Bette turned on her and screamed. Miriam said, once again, 'But nobody will take any notice of me. They're all going to be looking at you!' Bette stood for a moment in silence. She looked Miriam square in the eye and said, 'Only if I pop corn!'

On 11 January 1943, Vincent Sherman blew up, saying to Miriam, 'I'm going to have a showdown. Either she directs the picture or I do. I'm not going on in this way.' Bette had been giving him extended advice on handling Miriam for several days, and in desperation he had turned to his worst enemy for consolation. Miriam's reaction was typical. She said, 'Vince, don't talk it over with me. She's been riding roughshod over me from the beginning. I'm better out of it. I'm an innocent in this matter. I never did any harm to her. I don't know what she's talking about.' Sherman shrugged. He realised that he was having little support from that quarter.

A letter from Miriam Hopkins to Henry Blanke, associate producer, gives a clear picture of Miriam's side of the story. Because of its great interest, its rare insight into an actress' mind, it appears here in full.

Monday Night (Jan. 11, 1943)

Dear Heinz,

I was lying in bed talking to myself and as I don't work until one tomorrow, I thought perhaps I was saner to get up and write it all to you. Up until now I haven't called you ever to complain about anything, only maybe suggestions about the clothes, which I thought might be helpful, because it isn't the easiest wardrobe in the world to arrange. On *The Old Maid*, if things seemed very difficult I called your office or had my hairdresser Billie do it, if you remember; none of that has happened on this picture, but there has been even more to choke down inside me. I figured it was up to me to take it because I was so damn grateful for the part. Even with a sense of gratitude your human feelings and sensitivity don't cease to exist.

I want to go back just a little: during the first two weeks of the picture Vincent came to me at least four times starting a conversation with – 'I'm going to have a showdown. Either SHE* directs the picture or I do. I'm not going on this way.' I said each time – 'Vince, don't talk it over with me, I'm better out of it, I'm in an awkward spot.' Then one day he said to me that it was all going too far: he was going to have things settled once and for all. I said, please not when I'm around. The Wednesday

*Bette Davis

220

before I was called into Trilling's* office I was doing the scene in the hall where I looked after Preston when he went down in the elevator after talking to Millie. When it was finished I said to Vincent – can't we talk over the scene for tomorrow and if there are any changes or anything you want me to do different from the script tell me now so there won't be any confusion when Bette comes in. He said – there isn't going to be any more confusion – I've taken care of that – don't worry about it – I've stood all I'm going to. Again I said not to tell me about it – I'd rather not know, and walked away. It was the next day when Bette came in and Vince had said over the early morning coffee he wondered how the scene should be played – it didn't seem like a fight but what were we going to do with it? I said I had been thinking too the night before and I remembered conversations with a friend of mine, Libbie, in New York. We've known each other for about fifteen years and talked completely honestly. I remembered things she had said like – 'Miriam, why don't you go on wearing your hair in bangs, when you pull it back from your forehead you look ten years older' – then she would go right on chatting about some play she had seen or her newest beau. And I might criticise her the same way, but it was never in temper. It was during the end of the discussion Bette walked up and said, 'Well, if you are going to play the scene that way I'll have to rewrite it.' I pretended not to hear.

That is one of fifty such remarks that have never been answered – nor has there been one quarrel between us since the picture started, that is purely because I've pretended not to hear the things she has said to me and about me on the set.

There are two more weeks to go. I intend to keep the 'turning your other cheek' attitude up, but

*Steve Trilling, head of production

221

I must feel that someone sees and understands my side. Otherwise, and lately I've felt as if I were in a concentration camp. Vincent has decided it is wiser to side with one of us and I can, and possibly would if I were in his position, take Bette's. They now go into her dressing-room between takes, she calling, 'Vince darling, bring the script and we'll finish rewriting that other scene.' So then the pink pages are rewritten and I'm given new white ones, and OK then the white ones are rewritten on the set. Bette not wanting to say anything that isn't noble, even if in a normally human reaction between two women. I was very relieved you said you liked the crying scene in the bedroom, because her comments on the set about the way I was playing it were almost unbearable – that's why it was very easy to cry for each take, and the crew couldn't understand how I could turn [the tears] on so easily. It wasn't good for me to say the line – 'Why are you being unkind to me?' so that went, also, her line – 'Men don't walk out like this, even on women like you.' Was changed to – 'Even after the way you've acted.' Then it was taken out all together. As well as the line, – 'Mildred Watson Drake loses husband, reward offered, etc.' So my speeches were just blended, I said nothing, but couldn't help thinking, how stupid to try and be more noble than human. But I was glad today when you said I had played it all right. I'll go on to the end with any changes and rewrites they want to make until the end but I beg you don't have me clawed to death over every tiny detail of hair, clothes, face. I want so to give a good performance for you and please you, work these things out with me and I'll completely cooperate with you a hundred per cent. But when Vincent comes over, criticises pompadour he sat in a projection with me

before the picture started and told me how much
he liked it, but to break it with a curl or two if I
could – that he had just seen *The Old Maid* and the
pompadour hair at the end of that he loved. I told
him I would. I knew it was a little severe but it was
the original piece and it was better to test that and
see where to go from there. Today the test was only
called at nine-thirty. Ida, my hairdresser hadn't
had time to pick out curls that would match my hair
and set them right, so we used what we could of the
ends of mine and I thought I could explain to you.
Which I always have been able to and would have
clearly today and you would have understood.
Then Vincent appeared and produced that absurd
picture of Peggy Wood. All I could think of was the
way Jane Cowl looked too and how far Bette has
deviated from that. On the stage we all know, and
Vincent from the theatre certainly should, there is
a great exaggeration necessary. The eyelashes are
beaded way up with cosmetic, larger and redder
lips are put on, clothes and hair must be exaggerated too to carry to the back of the audience and
the balcony. You are so much further removed
from the public than with a camera. And two
different people playing the same part must look
according to their build, hair and temperament.
The pompadour, I would never have thought of – it
was Goulding's idea. He said he and Van Druten
saw me that way with the phoney exaggeration it
gives you, and then too the play was done two
years ago and we do want something slightly modern of 1942 in the styles of clothes and hair. As for
the clothes – I've tried when there was a jam, like
with the black velvet coat for the hotel, to produce
anything I had, any possible suggestions for the
end, anything I can do. But now tomorrow, when I
appear with the hat with the plume, if Vince says,

'That isn't the hat I saw in the test,' I haven't the vitality to argue. I will just say it is the one you OKed please to call you. I don't want to have a clothes controversy when I want to remember my lines and not be with a gulp in my throat, when I'm supposed to be the up and sparkly type. I've tried so for the hostess gown. The black under any condition you were so right wouldn't do, she was sealed up. This brocade was too chic with the tailored tie at the neck, but with the lace, oh, I thought that was just what the doctor ordered, and I swear to you I don't think we can do better. You can pile yards of chiffon on me, I'll look like a barrel with a small face. I won't be able to get comedy laughs tripping over it as Peggy did on the stage, because everything she did was in long shot and she had to, but I can guarantee you, my little feathered friend that I love very much – I shall get many laughs that Miss Wood didn't! That I say with arrogance, conceit and a consciousness of the knowledge of a trade learned over a period of eighteen years. Trust me – just a little, someone has to or I can't stand it.

One other think I want to talk about – there has been no self-consciousness, or an acknowledgement of the existence between Sherman and me that there was ever a scene in Trilling's office. The next time I saw him on the set it was just, 'Hello, Vince.' etc . . . I had bought when I got the dolls for Naomi and Michele, a silly big rag doll about three feet tall for his little girl. I had planned we would have a great deal of fun bringing it on the set Christmas Eve. The afternoon I went shopping was after that scene in the hall that I told you about, and the only afternoon I had a chance to go down town. Somehow after the confusion in Trilling's office, it seemed cheap not to give the doll to his little girl and when Georgia took the things over to the studio she gave it to Cora my wardrobe woman to give to him when he left the studio. She went out and put it in his car when no one was around and he was leaving. She told me it was rather pathetic, she had been with him on *The Hard Way*. He said to her, 'Do you know I hauled her up to Trilling's office, I was behind and they wanted to know the reason. Oh, God, Cora, do you know now I feel so awful for what I've done.' When he called me on the phone we had such a nice chat. I said that these were hard times but just know some day when this picture was finished we would be very great friends. I've tried to be as he asked – never to speak on the set. I didn't but two days after it amused me and my niece Georgia who goes to the studio with me and the people around me when he came up, as any number of times before, and asked me to go in my dressing-rom with him. He needed some additional dialogue for my exit and entrance out of the living-room in the scene where I had to go in the bedroom for the jewellery. We got it in a couple of minutes. That has happened any number of times – you know the pink pages and you see the rushes – the scene at the beginning during the party when I take her up to bed, all the dialogue up the stairs, again going down the stairs he said help me out – when she came up to get me out of the bathroom and we go down to Preston at lunch. Also if you refer to the pink pages on the scene in the hotel where I go to meet Preston and Kit says he won't see me and compare those with what was shot – I can show you how I worked until one o'clock one morning, put part of the scene with the clerk back in, then all the speeches about he's ruined my life – there's nothing left to live for, etc. I'll never write another line, etc., all I took in very apologetically to him. He said that it was very funny, thanked me, folded the page in his script and the new stuff came out the next day. No one knew now, even you, but to have that man say just a few days later to Trilling I was being difficult for him, somehow wasn't sporting. Well, now I feel better – it's off my chest. I've forgotten it – now that I've told you, you do. I write this so I can feel, although you'll never mention it you will know my effort and interest and if I have someone who knows, I can go on stomaching the insults. Also, I swear to you on everything that is decent in me that everything in this is true. Thank you for wading through these words, they've probably bored the hell out of you but they've helped me a lot.

Miriam

P.S. I guess you knew what you were doing casting me for Millie – as far as being a wordy wench. I've never been able to write a ten-word telegram – always night letters.

Miriam complained constantly that she was having fewer close-ups than Bette. Sherman sent a note to her reading, 'Miriam, if I had my own mother in the film I wouldn't favour her over any other actress because I do what I think is best for the film and not what I think is best for any individual . . . There's no such thing as giving a person a close-up more often than another in a position of equal strength in the cast . . .' Miriam developed a habit about halfway through the shooting of pretending to be suffering from an attack of temporary deafness whenever Bette spoke to her off the set. She would take an elaborate hearing aid from her purse and fix it in her ear while Bette was going into a tirade and then discover to her pretended distress that it was failing to function. When Bette came at her as though about to strike one cheek, she turned the other. Every time Bette would order a 'blue page' or revised passage in the script, Miriam would bring in a pink one. On one occasion, when Bette said that Miriam had played a scene like a dead person, Miriam appeared on the set in black. When Miriam played a lengthy crying scene, Bette stood on the sidelines commenting on it as though it were a horse race at Santa Anita. In revenge, Miriam gave the crew small radios encouraging them to listen to the races the following day when Bette was playing a love scene with a younger man. She was delighted when the announcer rapidly described the neck-and-neck finish, just as Bette passionately kissed her boyfriend.

Miriam became so nervous as she was leaving the shower one morning, she skidded on a piece of soap and fell on a steel fixture which split her ear and cracked her head. She swore Bette had put the soap there. She lay in bed for a week grumbling incessantly, and Bette, perhaps in competition, was also absent from illness for a period. During the shooting, both women were absent, often on alternate days; Bette's old problem of laryngitis was flaring up.

Bette's biggest scene was one in which she learned that her lover had abandoned her and was going to marry her rival's daughter. She insisted Miriam be kept off the set and played the scene with great skill. But it proved impossible to get the close-up Vincent Sherman wanted of her face crumpling when she receives the news. Sherman deliberately waited until two o'clock on a Sunday morning after many hours of difficult shooting to retake the close-up. Bette was exhausted and her face was drawn and pale when he made the shot. At the preview, the producer Jesse Lasky said to Sherman, 'That woman is the most remarkable actress I've ever seen in my life. In that scene where she hears she had lost her lover to the daughter, she aged in one shot.'

'That's not surprising,' Sherman replied. 'I took that last close-up three months after the rest of the scene.'

Perhaps the most famous sequence in *Old Acquaintance* was that in which Bette shook Miriam and threw her on to a couch. Everyone was waiting eagerly for this to take place. The crew knew Bette would play the scene with more commitment than she had played anything else in her career. On the big day, not only did the rest of the cast and crew arrive for work, but also everybody possible from every office in the studio and every other picture in production jammed the soundstage to see the event of the season.

Bette had to advance across the living-room, take Miriam by each shoulder, and force her down into a sitting position. Bette strode vigorously to the attack. She took Miriam's shoulders in a powerful grip. Suddenly, Miriam went completely loose, like a rag doll, so that when Bette shook her she seemed to have no bones in her body. Bette stepped back, 'This is impossible,' she said, 'she isn't fighting me.'

Sherman said, 'Miriam, for God's sake struggle with her.' 'But, I *am* struggling!' Miriam said.

The scene began again. Bette walked, took Miriam's shoulders, and Miriam again went slack. Bette gave up. She said, 'It's impossible. I can't do anything with her.' Vincent told her to try again. The scene dragged on all afternoon Finally, by clever camera faking, something approaching an adequate sequence was shot. Bette, knowing everyone was watching, infuriated Miriam by not screaming at her directly. But when she returned home, she screamed at anyone who would listen for over an hour.

Through the entire production, there was trouble over Bette's and Sherman's rewrites of the script. In one memorandum from Chuck Hansen, unit manager, to the studio manager T.C. Wright, Hansen wrote: 'Considerable time is spent in rehearsing, but in my opinion there

228

is still a lot of rewriting being done. Of course, a lot of this is Miss Davis's idea, as she is not satisfied with the dialogue. Nothing can be done about it, as they are trying to make a good picture – only it is being done the hard way.'

Jack Warner cabled Sherman from New York: SEE YOU ARE UP TO YOUR OLD TRICKS AGAIN. RECEIVED THIS MORNING FOURTEEN PAGES REWRITE ON OLD ACQUAINTANCE. WHY DON'T YOU STOP REWRITING THE SCRIPT. IT WAS DAMN GOOD WHEN YOU STARTED. YOU'RE SIXTEEN DAYS BEHIND SCHEDULE. NOW MAKE SOME OF THIS TIME UP AND GET THROUGH WITH THIS PRODUCTION.

There was further trouble when in October, 1943, Bette walked past a record store and saw a copy of the song entitled 'Old Acquaintance' showing her and Miriam toasting each other on the cover. She had never given permission for this and became hysterical, saying that the lyrics printed under the image suggested lesbianism.

Bette didn't stop shouting about this crazy implication of a love relationship between her and Miriam for weeks. She was almost as annoyed when a columnist ran the following comment on the picture being thirty-six days behind due to absenteeism:

Now listen folks, This was the schedule in January:
                    1/5/43.   Miriam ill.
                    1/6/43.   Miriam ill.
                    1/7/43.   Miriam ill.
                    1/20/43.   Bette ill.
                    1/21/43.   Bette ill.
                    1/22/43.   Bette ill.
                    1/23/43.   Miriam ill.
                    1/24/43.   Bette ill.

1/25/43. Miriam ill.
1/26/43. Bette ill.

Is it any wonder, folks, that the picture didn't finish
until St Valentine's Day?

Old Acquaintance turned out to be a great popular
success. Bette was ideally matched in the conflict of
personalities that gave the picture the appeal of a
championship boxing match. Everyone in the industry
made sure they saw it. They knew so much about its
making that it became one of the talked-about movies of
the year.

Stimulated by the experience of shooting the picture –
perhaps more than she would admit – Bette made her
ultimate contribution to the war effort in a horrible
jamboree called *Thank Your Lucky Stars* in which she
flung herself into a wild jitterbug routine with a GI. She
sang a song with arguably the worst lyrics ever written
for public performance, 'They're either too young or too
old'.

The fact that she managed to groan this song without
actually wincing on camera says a great deal for her
commitment to Roosevelt.

Amazingly, Bette managed to make the number and
her subsequent dance one of her most entertaining
moments in pictures, and a perennial favourite of her
fans.

Bette spent the early summer of 1943 in Mexico alone.
From there, she travelled to Butternut in New Hampshire and spent the rest of the season with Farney, who
was on vacation from Honeywell. One afternoon, he was
at the head of the stairs when the telephone rang. Some
weeks before, Farney had had a fall from a horse and it
had slightly affected his balance. He spun around on his
heel at the sound of the phone, tripped, and fell the full
length of the stairs. He cracked his head on the hard

parquet floor of the entrance hall.

He seemed to pull himself together, but this second injury to his head caused – and here is a horrifying parallel to the plot of *Dark Victory* – a growth in the brain. This growth caused symptoms similar to those found in hypoglycaemia or epilepsy. He began to suffer from blackouts, drowsy or dizzy spells; and at times he limped quite painfully. His back had been injured by the fall.

Farnsworth was a silent uncomplaining man's man who thought discussion of physical problems was a sign of weakness. Relations between Bette and Mrs Farnsworth, never comfortable, were strained to the limit. They decided to bring him back to Riverbottom in Glendale where he could rest. But no sooner had he returned with her by train than he began working very hard once more.

He continued his secret war work as liaison between local aeroplane production plants and Honeywell and he also supervised the drawings of aeroplanes executed by Walt Disney's team of animators for the full-length cartoon *Victory Through Air Power*. He also became involved in an affair with a married woman, conducted in great secrecy because her husband was intensely jealous and suspicious.

Bette did not find out about the affair until much later. She co-existed with Farney in a relationship that was more like that of brother and sister than husband and wife.

It is an irony of Bette's life that, scarcely able to achieve more than passing contentment in her private life, she suddenly assumed the role of Miss Lonelyhearts by running an advice to the lovelorn column in *Photoplay*, the reigning fan magazine at the time. Letters poured in from young girls having trouble with their boyfriends, suffering from separations caused by the draft, struggling with hostility from parents, or trying to be actresses. One typical letter from 'a desperate mother' asked her to help a little girl of four named after Deanna Durbin: 'She is a very unusual little girl who can learn poems and remember them indefinitely. She has a natural talent for singing and dancing and I just know there is a place in motion pictures for her. Now, here is my problem. My husband died two years ago and since that time I have been working in a department store, barely getting by. I don't have any extra cash with which to give Deanna the training she needs. That's where you come in. Could you loan me the money to come to Hollywood, or to go to New York, and pay a good teacher to give my baby the start in life she deserves. When she becomes famous you will have the satisfaction of claiming her as a protégé, and at that time she will pay you back every penny.'

Bette replied characteristically: 'Dear Mrs M.L.: I am not answering your letter because you threaten to hate me forever if I don't reply. After all, hatred takes up a lot of time and energy and you really haven't any to spare since you're working so hard and taking care of your small girl. I'm answering your letter because those people who are in the motion picture industry receive thousands of similar letters every day . . . Think of Santa Claus – even he is expected to operate only one night in an entire year . . . You sign yourself "Desperate Mother". I don't wish to be unkind, but no woman should use the future of her child to overcome desperation; that is a job she must do for herself.'

In 1939, the English novelist Mary Annette Beauchamp Russell, known professionally as 'Elizabeth', published in the British *Good Housekeeping* and later with Heinemann and Doubleday a book entitled *Mr Skeffington* suggested by the character of the American actress Fanny Ward, a selfish beauty who had settled in London just before the war. The central figure of the novel was Fanny Skeffington, a dizzy and self-centred society beauty, and the setting was the world of high society in Mayfair and Kensington and of country weekends in mansions in the south of England. Paramount had bought the property but was unable to make use of it; the fashion for British high-flown romances and melodramas had decreased. Warners obtained the rights and assigned the picture to David Lewis. Lenore Coffee wrote a first draft and it was forwarded to Jack Warner's assistant Richard Gully, a cousin of Anthony Eden and an authority on British manners. Gully pointed out that London postmen never use a whistle but knock on doors; no barrel organ player could afford a cigar; a maid would address Mrs Skeffington as 'm'lady' not 'Your Ladyship'; a particular kind of knight of the realm would not wear a flower in his buttonhole; and 'Who else would you like to have to dinner?' should be 'Whom else would you like to have to dinner?' Jack Warner became impatient with these trivialities; he didn't trust anyone on his staff to deal with this pretentious material. He also felt American audiences would become impatient with all the affected social situations, and that, if it had to be done, this kind of property was best left to MGM.

As a result, in July, 1941, Minna Wallis and Andy Lawlor of the Sam Jaffe Agency were authorised by Warners to find a buyer for the property. Not a single person in Hollywood was interested and in desperation Jack Warner and Hal Wallis hired the witty twins Julius J. and Philip G. Epstein to produce and write it. They settled at once on transferring the story to New York in the first part of the century leading up to the present day. Bette had rejected the part when it had originally been offered to her, feeling that whereas she had managed a special accent for *Elizabeth and Essex*, she was not able to speak in an upper-class British accent for this production. When the director Vincent Sherman told Bette he had a new draft script for *Mr Skeffington* she said, 'Oh, brother! I read that turkey years ago. It was a dreary story! I hated that silly affected woman so much!' Sherman explained that the Epsteins had given the trifling material depth and had succeeded in bringing the characters to life. Bette took the material home to Glendale, read it in an evening and called Sherman the following morning. She said: 'It's magnificent. I'm dying to do it. I'll call Jack and tell him.' She telephoned Jack Warner, who was delighted she would go ahead. Production was due to begin in September, 1943. Bette, for once offered a part before anyone else, flung herself into hairdress and make-up tests with enthusiasm. Her excitement was shared by Farney, Ruthie, Bobby, Margaret Donovan and her faithful secretary, Bridget Price.

On 23 August 1943, a hot and sultry Los Angeles day, Farney was in Hollywood discussing the purchase of some real estate with Bette's attorney Dudley Furse. He was walking along Hollywood Boulevard past a cigar store only a few blocks from a home Bette had shared with Ham. Dave Freedman, proprietor of the store, his assistant, Rosalie Day, and a customer, Gilbert Wright, were standing just inside the entrance discussing the war news when they heard a terrifying scream. They ran out and saw Farney. He was carrying a briefcase. He fell straight backwards in an odd, awkward movement, screaming again as he did so. His head struck the concrete pavement and he began to haemorrhage from his nose and ears. His convulsions were so violent that people came running to the scene. Somehow, in the confusion, the briefcase disappeared; somebody must have picked it up. Farney was also carrying a dispatch case which was not taken. Freedman, the cigar store proprietor, called the Hollywood Receiving Hospital, which sent an ambulance. From papers in Farney's wallet, attendants found the address and phone number of his physician, Dr Paul Moore. Moore raced to the spot. He called Bette, who was shocked to tears. But he insisted that she remained at home, while Farney was transferred to Hollywood Presbyterian. It was the beginning of an ordeal even more severe than Farney's bout with pneumonia in Minneapolis. Farney's injury was diagnosed as a skull fracture. When Bette finally came to visit him at the hospital, he barely recognised her.

Reporters constantly besieged her for comment, and police from the Hollywood Homicide Bureau questioned her. Because Farney was on secret war work, there were implicatons that he might have been murdered for whatever was in the briefcase. But the reports remained maddeningly inexact in the press, every day the newspapers contradicting what they said the day before.

Once again, Bette's conversations with Mrs Farnsworth were awkward and strained. Farney continued to hover between life and death. Soon he gave up the unequal struggle. He passed away in his sleep.

The authorities were far from satisfied that the death was accidental. The autopsy report, which has since mysteriously vanished from the files, was disturbing. Assistant County Surgeon Homer R. Keyes told the court: 'A basal skull injury probably caused this man's death. It did not result from the fall, but instigated it. Consider the blood in the fracture. It is black and coagulated, not merely purple and partially congealed as it would have been if the injury had been received as a result of the fall. The fracture must have been inflicted about fourteen days ago. Farnsworth must have been walking around with the condition fructifying until it eventually caused his death.' Dr Keyes went on to say (and his statement was confirmed by others) that the blow must have been caused by the butt of a gun or some other blunt instrument. They dismissed any suggestion that a black and coagulated mass of blood would have remained as a result of the fall at Butternut, which had long since healed; nor could Farnsworth have simply fallen some two weeks earlier in another place.

For some mysterious reason, these testimonies were totally ignored by the verdict, which was death by accident. Nevertheless, the inquest was called before a six-man coroner's jury.

Pale and without make-up after nights without sleep, Bette remained in an ante-room while the other witnesses gave their testimony. She took the witness stand in an acute state of distress. She told of the accident at Butternut but was unable to cast any light on the blow which caused the death.

In complete defiance of the autopsy report, the inquest verdict was that the fall had caused the subsequent death of the subject.

Nobody either then or since has cared to examine the contradiction. The funeral was as quiet as the Farnsworth family and Bette could manage. They had begged the public not to swamp them, and their request was surprisingly heeded. Only a handful of people showed up, in services at the Church of the Recessional in Forest Lawn. Among those present were Jack Warner, John Garfield, Perc Westmore, Ruthie, Mrs Farnsworth, Farney's brother Dan, and Farney's close friend, the famous stuntman and air ace Paul Mantz.

Bette's uncle, Paul Favor, now living at Laguna Beach, performed the service; Bette chose the 121st and 123rd Psalms (Farney's favourites). The casket was banked with floral pieces of gladioli, dahlias and other flowers as it lay beneath the three stained-glass windows of the church.

Shortly afterwards, Bette left for New Hampshire with the Farnsworths and Farney's body.

Bette was back for tests on *Mr Skeffington* on 21 September. John Loder and Paul Lukas were both tested for the part of the hard-pressed husband whose career as a businessman is flawed by his wife's extravagantly silly behaviour. Fortunately, Claude Rains was chosen for the part. Haggard and worn by her long ordeal, Bette looked far from the beauty she should have been for the story when she reported for twenty-six changes of wardrobe tests. Her worst problem was the rubber mask which Perc Westmore made for her to show her drastic ageing following an attack of diphtheria. The mask fitted tightly to the skin which sweated under it and could not breathe properly. Vincent Sherman said:

There was the terrible problem of make-up for Bette. She had to get up at five o'clock in the morning in order to be on the set at nine. Perc Westmore, who was quite an artist in his field, had to put on the wrinkles layer by layer with rubber. By eight-thirty Bette was already fit to be tied. As she perspired under this rubber her face itched. So, late in the afternoon at five or six o'clock, by the time she got the rubber mask off, she wanted to dig her nails into her face. She was nervous and jumpy and uptight. I am sure that contributed a lot to some of the difficulties later. There were times when she just had to stop at five and said that she couldn't shoot any more. She said she was just going crazy with that thing on her face.

There was one scene where she was lying in bed and her hair had fallen out. There was a furry wig she had on. It was a little on the reddish side and she was half bald. When I came in and saw her that morning and looked at it – we didn't have time to test it – I was shocked. I said, 'My God, if I photograph her like that she'll look like a witch.' I told her, 'Gee, don't you think we're going a little too far with this?' She said, 'Don't you worry. My audience will take me in this kind of thing. They don't mind if I do this to myself.' I said, 'I don't know about your audience, but *I* mind it a little bit.' But she felt it was honest and real. I suppose to some extent she was right about that. Perhaps she was more right than I was, although I think I was more right in other places.

Bette would run into her dressing-room and beg Westmore and Margaret Donovan to get the horrible rubber mask off her before she went completely mad.
Vincent Sherman says:

I used mirrors in the picture. I felt a woman as vain and self-centred would always be looking in mirrors. I even had the art director put them downstairs. Eventually, instead of being reassured by her beauty she becomes tortured by her looks. John Barrymore once told me he didn't count the number of speeches he had in a script. What he wanted to know was, 'Who does the suffering?' For an actor that's sometimes more important than the size of the part. What the Epsteins were saying in this script, and what is said in the film is that, 'A woman is only beautiful when she is loved.' *Mr Skeffington* was a study of a charming, feminine woman who was self-centred, slightly superficial but not a completely unworthy human being. One of the things that made Bette hesitate about doing the picture was that she didn't think she was a great beauty. In the normal acceptance of the word perhaps she wasn't, although I felt she looked lovely in the picture. We didn't concentrate too heavily on that so that it wouldn't cause any invalidity to the film itself.

One afternoon on the set, about three days into shooting, a very curious thing happened. A small boy asked to see Bette. It was assumed he was a fan and he was told to come back some other time but he insisted it was a matter of life and death. Bette came out to have a look. She was astounded to see him carrying Farney's brief-case. It had not been seen since the time of his death. Without explaining her interest, she invited the child into her dressing-room. He told her he had picked the briefcase up from the pavement and confessed he had run off with it.

He opened it and showed her the contents without a word. There were numerous bottles of liquor. She was horrified. She had known Farney had been drinking heavily but she had not realised he was an alcoholic. The discovery of the bottles was never shared with anyone. She kept it a secret for many years.

There was a commotion on the set on 15 October. Bette insisted upon having everybody in a dinner party scene be introduced to each other by her as the hostess. The Epsteins as producers pointed out that these intro-ductions were not in the script and would be assumed by the audience to have taken place before the action began. In the peculiarly high-pitched affected voice Bette selected to play the part, she said, 'But a lady would never allow her guests to sit down at a table unless she had introduced them to each other.' 'This is a picture, not a society clambake,' Julius Epstein said. Bette refused to eliminate the dialogue. The rows went on the rest of the afternoon.

The next day, Bette played a sequence in which she arrived in Skeffington's office. In the script, she would simply appear before Claude Rains's desk and make a scene. Bette added lines of dialogue in which she entered the secretary's ante-room, told the secretary to announce her, stood impatiently while being announced and then on being admitted made a lengthy walk across the set to the desk.

This unauthorised piece of business slowed the scene up unconscionably and the Epsteins flew into a rage.

239

They told Bette she should play the scene as written. She refused. She pointed out that when a lady came to her husband's office she wouldn't enter it unannounced. The Epsteins pointed out that the secretary would know her and would simply glance up as she went in; that to show this transition was a complete waste of screen footage. 'But she's a *new* secretary,' Bette explained. 'How do you know?' the Epsteins asked. The absurd and futile conversation went on without resolution.

There was a scene in which Bette sat in a café with Claude Rains and a child. Bette wanted to have Rains bring the child through the door discussing her in the process. The production manager Frank Mattison sent a memorandum to the studio chief Steve Trilling who had taken over from Hal Wallis. It read: 'She wants her name to be mentioned even when she isn't in the scene so no one can ever forget for a second she's in the story.'

The Epsteins sent a memorandum to Trilling: 'There isn't a damn thing that can be done as long as BD is the director.'

By early November the production had slowed almost to a halt because of Bette's changes and additions. Mattison wrote to Trilling: 'It sure is tough on a unit manager to sit by with a show where she is the whole band. The music and all the instruments including the bazooka.'

By 12 November, everyone agreed that Bette was not only the director but the producer too. The Epsteins did something unthinkable, even unique in the history of Hollywood: they walked off their own picture, abandoning it to the star, starting legal proceedings against the studio for denying their privileges as producers. They disappeared for an indefinite stay in New York.

Four days later, on 3 December, Bette was suffering from an irritation of her right eye caused by make-up poisoning. She took a special solution in an eyebath, threw back her head and emptied the solution into her eye. She screamed with agony. A pain lanced her head. She collapsed. Perc Westmore, who was standing nearby, rushed to her aid. Seizing a solution of castor oil he washed her eye out. She was still unable to see in the affected eye. Paul MacWilliams of First Aid took her into the dispensary. He analysed the eyewash. It contained a deadly fluid with a strong acid base, which could have blinded her for life. It could not have been an accident.

Like Farney's death, the mystery remains unsolved. She was in the hands of eye specialists for over a week. By Christmas, the picture was three weeks behind schedule. Bette was doubly tense and distressed following the attempt on her sight. She quarrelled with Sherman constantly. He hated the high-pitched voice she used and the exaggerated rubber mask. He hated her constant interference with the writing and her ceaseless attempts to overbear him in the matter of the direction. Following Farney's death, Bette seemed to have become full of hate, violently intolerant of the slightest sloppiness, weakness or incompetence. And yet, paradoxically, on 21 January 1944, without explanation she turned up for work not wearing her rubber face. It had been called for, and scenes had to be switched around to accommodate her.

Incredibly, the picture was still going on in late February. Jack Warner and Steve Trilling decided it would never end. Warner said to Trilling one day. 'Do you think she'll break shooting to come to my funeral?' Steve Trilling replied, 'Only to make sure they're not lying.'

No sooner had Bette collapsed with relief after five months of shooting and sixty days over schedule than she discovered she would have to do the montage sequences wearing the mask again. She disappeared for a week before she could force herself to undergo the ordeal once more. Frank Mattison wrote a final note to Trilling:

'Thank God *Mr Skeffington* is finally being put in mothballs.'

Bette's behaviour during *Mr Skeffington* was the cause of the first serious breach with Jack Warner. Without Hal Wallis to act as a buffer and control the shooting, with the weaker Steve Trilling in charge, Warner knew nothing but total aggravation. As for the Epsteins, words could not do justice to their fury. They threatened to remove their name from the picture; and when it was released with numerous horrible cuts to compensate for the additions made against their wishes they beseeched theatres and exhibitors, demanding it be taken off. Sherman was almost equally furious over the results. He had begged Bette to tone down her playing and, in the scene in which she finds her husband is blind, by contrast, act with more feeling. She satisfied him in neither case and when he saw the finished cut and realised just how extreme Bette's make-up was in the later scenes, he was reminded of nothing so much as a visit to the mummy room in a museum.

Jack Warner never forgave Bette for her misbehaviour during the shooting, which was enormously over-budget and over-schedule. He hoarded for years some of the memoranda from the production manager Frank Mattison such as: 'I surely would not want to have my own money in any picture being made the way this picture is being made for Warner Brothers. There isn't a damn thing that can be done about it as long as Bette Davis is the director,' or 'I am wondering if it would be possible to speed up the next Bette Davis picture by making it a Bette Davis production, where she would understand all these delays would cost *her* a little bit of money.'

Sherman sums up these views:

There are a couple of scenes I don't like. I don't like the ending after Claude Rains comes back and she discovers he is blind. Something went wrong that day. I never got that scene the way I wanted it. While Bette did a marvellous acting job all through the film, that scene was not as good as I wanted it. But she was very tired. It had been a long time. We had been over sixty days on the film. I think we were seventy-two days on the film. It was an inordinate amount of time. She was exhausted, so I didn't get what I wanted. But you do the best you can. We had all been under strain during the final few weeks of the film, especially due to the rubber mask she was wearing.

Insult was added to injury when Bosley Crowther, all-powerful critic of the *New York Times,* launched an attack on the picture, condemning it and Davis's performance outright. He found the character of Fanny Skeffington insufferable and Bette's performance excessively mannered.

A few days after completion of production in the spring of 1944, Bette, maddened by Warner's arguments over the picture, asked for a release from her contract. Her request was bluntly refused. The Epsteins, upset over the ruin of their picture, didn't speak to Bette for a very long time. She was depressed by the criticisms of her efforts, and scarcely recovered from these when she had a shattering shock.

She learned at last the true cause of Farney's death. Somebody slipped her the news that a few days before he died, Farney had been sleeping with the wife of a colleague. The man, huge and imposing, caught Farney and the girl in bed in a motel near Sunset Boulevard. There was a terrible fight and the man struck Farney on the head with a lamp. Farney only had superficial treatment for the injury and the congealed blood was still on the wound when a combination of this new mishap and the earlier blow from the fall at Butternut combined with the tumour, caused him to have an epileptic convulsion which destroyed him.

As she opened the paper soon after receiving this horrible news, Bette was riveted to a news story. It revealed that the man who had killed Farney had been burned to death in an airplane crash near Los Angeles.

Eleven

BETTE'S ONLY other work of the period was in *Hollywood Canteen* in which she appeared as herself, briskly running the entertainment for the troops and the mass serving of meals. She drove over from Riverbottom in Glendale for ten days of work in an exact replica of the Canteen at Warners. Reviews of the picture were devastating: A group of enlisted servicemen wrote a joint letter to Jack Warner calling the movie, 'A slur on the intelligence and acumen of every member of the armed services.' The charge was well deserved: *Hollywood Canteen* was a horrible example of mass self-congratulation as fifty Warner Brothers stars publicly patted each other on the back as well as themselves while bemused servicemen stood about gaping mindlessly at their glorious hosts and hostesses.

It was a difficult period. Bette had trouble trying to block Farney from her mind. Her two homes, Butternut and Riverbottom, reminded her constantly of her happy times with Farney. Every stick of furniture, the carpets, the curtains, colourings in their bedroom brought back painful realisations that she was profoundly alone. Ruthie remained a consolation and a driving force: she still, even at this stage of Bette's career, insisted on walking in front of her at premieres or first-nights and would never allow anyone to escort Bette but herself. Now that Bette was rich, Ruthie's demands for expensive clothes, furs and jewellery became more and more extreme. She fed off Bette with more determination than ever, and Bette, never forgetting for an instant that she owed much of her career to Ruthie's drive and convictions, never begrudged her mother anything. Sometimes, the sheer pressure on Bette's purse irritated her in spite of herself. The bills poured in, in a stream which threatened even her huge income of over $4,000 a week.

And then, though again Bette never begrudged it, there was the emotional and financial drain represented by Bobby. Bobby was, despite attempts in two marriages, unable to achieve a balanced and comfortable existence. Though she was the last to admit it, she was still eaten by her jealousy of Bette's great career and by her own aesthetic nature. She suffered from increasing dementia in which she became violent and had to be placed in a strait-jacket. She was confined in a mental institution, a private home the costs of which were crippling. Bette was determined she would have the best of psychiatric care and she drained her bank account to this effect. Bette's visits to Bobby in the home were agonising. Patients would gape at Bette and imitate her grotesquely.

It was during this unhappy time that a very curious episode took place. Joan Crawford, the neurotic 1940s star of MGM, had just been signed by Warners to a contract that was to begin with a version of James M. Cain's *Mildred Pierce*. Crawford, many people thought, had been brought in by Jack Warner to threaten Bette's position as Catherine the Great of Burbank. The court began to divide into Crawford factions and Davis factions. For this reason, Bette was careful to avoid actually meeting Crawford.

She knew that the gossip would pretend they had quarrelled, thereby aggravating an already charged situation. So she kept a cool distance, declining to comment in anything except admiring terms when directly challenged on the subject.

But Joan Crawford's attitude was different. For years, she had been a kind of closet king, who had repressed her lesbianism while tormenting her immediate family with a kind of twisted heterosexual rage. She had fought against her nature because she knew that even an inkling that this sainted witch of the West had feet of clay might have caused her downfall. She was admired, fawned on, but never really liked: she was too impeccable to be bearable. Her faults were smoothed down as neatly as the pleats in her immaculate skirts. Her heavy, slightly threatening animal furs and huge imposing face had a daunting quality that defied friendship as strongly as enmity.

The safest procedure was clearly to grovel. Anything less abject might not win her imperial approval. To Bette, all this was nonsense. And yet, she was deceiving herself: she, too, found irresistible the idea of being in command.

Crawford had for years nourished a secret desire for Bette. This greatest of suffering female stars admired this greatest of actresses sexually as well as professionally. As soon as she arrived at Warners, Crawford began sending Bette perfume, flowers and letters begging her to meet for dinner. No lovesick male in those happy, half-forgotten days when women were still wooed by men tried harder to seduce a beautiful woman than Crawford did in her pursuit of Davis. There is something odd, unsettling and grotesque about this: over the years Bette has confided it to friends. Bette returned all the gifts with quick impatience and ill humour, thanking Crawford for her consideration and preferring to explain to the immediate circle that it was merely an effort of Ms Crawford to bring about a truce in the studio conflict.

One night, according to a publicity man, Bette was asked to give a sudden broadcast for a particular charity. She refused, on the grounds she had insufficient preparation. The publicity man went to Crawford and asked her to make a broadcast instead. Hurt by Bette's refusal of her, Crawford instantly agreed but insisted the broadcast be channelled into Bette's dressing-room. Bette was asked to go to her room for an urgent meeting and drove over from Glendale only to find the deafening sounds of the Crawford broadcast played many times too loudly and surging through her room.

Fortunately, the rebuff finally worked and Crawford gave up. There is no telling with what intensity her frustration was vented on her adopted children.

It may be because of this perverse oddity in Bette's life that she asked herself the question whether she could defy the rule of the great sacred monsters of the screen and actually give birth to a child. She had had abortions over the years; she was pushing forty; and at that age there was a risk of the child being deformed or even mongoloid. Clearly, she had no time to waste.

She spent much time at Laguna Beach, where Ruthie had a house and her uncle Paul Favor was living with his family. There she met a twenty-nine-year-old Sunday painter called William Grant Sherry. He was a fairly good looking, lean, hairy, wolfish, dark man with a deceptively mild, quite subdued manner that disguised a moody, forceful personality. He was disappointed in everything. He had not been a successful boxer, because he was too light and wiry and indecisive; and his painting was scarcely more than third rate. He was poor, struggling, and threatened to be as dependent as Ham or Farney.

Jane Bryan Dart says, 'Marrying Sherry was the worst mistake Bette ever made.' The writer Catherine Turney, a friend of Bette's, says: 'I don't think he was at all right for Bette. I remember during their engagement he was a male nurse in Laguna.' The director Curtis Bernhardt says, 'I think Bette quickly tired of Sherry, even though she married him. I remember a party once. He had been placed at her table. The stars' table. It was some studio shindig. He had, she felt, no right to be seated next to her and she ordered him and his place card to another table. He was furious. When she danced with a man who *was* seated next to her, Sherry broke in and she refused to dance with him. When he became angry, she sat down.'

The relationship was a catastrophe from the beginning. It was fortunate that in the endless quarrels and violence of their relationship Bette had the relief of making a film she wanted to do: *The Corn Is Green*, which she had so much admired with Ethel Barrymore on the stage.

She insisted that the performers Rhys Williams, Mildred Dunnock, Rosalind Ivan and Gene Ross repeated their perfect performances from the New York production. She also demanded Orry-Kelly, who had left the studio, as the designer of her costumes.

Perhaps in part because of her unhappiness with Sherry, Bette flung herself with even more than the usual intensity into studying for the characterisation of Miss Moffat, Emlyn Williams's noble schoolteacher in the Welsh village who encourages a young miner to go to Oxford and have a career as a writer. She was very much against wearing a wig which would age her and which the studio called for: she preferred to have her hair dyed grey and straight back, cut very short, like a skull cap over her head. She was excessively nervous about her appearance as an elderly woman, despite the fact that Perc Westmore's make-up was spectacularly effective. After two days using her own hair, she suddenly decided she wanted to test with the wig; then she changed her mind and decided to include a shot of herself with the wig in the work of the day. Eric Stacey, production assistant, wrote to studio manager Tenny Wright:

For your information, if this scene is made with a wig that is approved, it will involve a good two days

249

of retakes at a later date. Mr Chertok is trying to pacify her, and, as the director [Irving Rapper] said to me this morning, what she needs is a psychiatrist, not a director.

On 3 July, Bette insisted on using the wig from that day on and re-shooting the first eleven days of work, which was unthinkable in Hollywood. Jack Warner was furious. 'She flipped her wig!' he said to Rapper. At a charged meeting, in Projection Room Five, Jack Warner, studio head Steve Trilling, Bette and Eric Stacey ran the tests with and without the wig. Bette went over to Jack and said, 'You see, I was right, wasn't I? The wig makes all the difference, doesn't it?' Warner nodded. He told her: 'Yes. The wig's a great improvement. We'll just have to retake the first eleven days.' She kissed him in gratitude.

Shooting proceeded uneventfully for just over a month. Then an event took place which suggested that perhaps, along with her other gifts, Bette was visited by second sight. About three in the afternoon of 7 August, she was very nearly killed.

Bette was shooting the difficult examination scene with the young John Dall who played the miner-writer, when she heard a strange noise above her head. A metal cover for an arc light, high up in the flies above the soundstage, either fell or was pushed and came plunging down on to her head. If she hadn't been wearing the large wig that Jack Warner approved, and she had so strongly fought for, she would immediately have been struck to death. As it was, the wig cushioned the blow. She fell into Irving Rapper's arms and he said, 'Oh, Bette, I never thought you felt that way about me!'

The next night, there was a big studio party, and Bette, despite a headache, attended it in good spirits. She went home to Riverbottom, feeling a little dizzy and

Her second marriage to Farney, New Year's Eve 1940. With them is Bette's sister, Bobby.

Bette with her mother, Ruthie.

With her co-star, Paul Henreid,
in *Now, Voyager*.

Miss Moffat, the schoolteacher, takes in the locals in
The Corn Is Green.

Bette married William Grant Sherry on 8 December 1945.

Confrontation in *All About Eve*.

'By the time the picture was finished shooting Bette was deeply involved with Gary Merrill.' Seen here discussing a scene on the set of *All About Eve*.

Bette arrives back in Hollywood.

What Ever Happened To Baby Jane?

Discussing the next scene with her co-star, Joan Crawford, in
What Ever Happened To Baby Jane?

14

With Joan Crawford in *What Ever Happened to Baby Jane?* 'touching and convincing characters instead of mere grotesques'.

As 'the terrifying mother' in *The Anniversary*.

'She is alive and well and emphatically Bette Davis.'

sick; she woke on Monday morning feeling terrible. The studio files show that no one was especially sympathetic about her plight. The executives were only annoyed that she had chosen a Monday to get sick when the actor Nigel Bruce broadcast a Sherlock Holmes radio show, making it impossible for him also to be shot; theirs were the only scenes called for by the script.

By Tuesday, Bette was suffering from the results of concussion and her headache worsened. She became nervous and sick to her stomach, anxious that she might be stricken with the same brain disease that had killed her character in *Dark Victory*, and had helped to kill Farney. But even on her bed of pain she was adamant about one thing: she had insisted from the beginning that, despite the nerve-racking expense and difficulty, the entire picture must be shot in correct time sequence because it was based on a play. So it proved impossible to shoot scenes for which she was not required, and, absurd though this was, the entire picture had to be closed down until its star came around. A typically irritated note from Stacey to Wright reads:

> We could get rid of two or three $75-a-week singing miners by shooting the end of the picture immediately . . . But I promise you that Miss Davis would raise an awful lot of hell and I don't think it's worthwhile upsetting her for such a small item since she is so much better on this picture than she's been on former pictures.

On 11 August, still feeling a little groggy, and barely able to sleep for fear of the effects from her injury, Bette struggled into work to finish the scene with Dall: the scene in which she presided over his examination. It is clear that Stacey believed the metal light cover, known as a 'barndoor', may have been deliberately dropped on her head by a disgruntled member of the crew.

251

Back on the set, Bette turned out to be unpredictable. She had asked for the cancellation of a scene in which she was riding a bicycle because she had long remembered her accident in Britain in which she fell off a similar velocipede. Now, without warning, she decided to bring it back, which meant breaking her own rule and shooting out of sequence. At first, it proved to be impossible because of the schedule; but over everyone's dead body, she forced the scene in – and then fell off the bicycle.

Her quarrels with Irving Rapper were one-sided: she argued with him. In turn, he left fly at his assistant Bob Vreeland, screaming and yelling until Jack Warner asked him to stop. Later, he apologised to Vreeland, saying, 'I'm sorry, Bob. Miss Davis is making me so nervous and upset, I'm almost ill.'

No scene was achieved without bitter arguing by Davis. A problem was John Dall. He was a homosexual who lived with his mother: they were known popularly as 'the Dalls'. Their devotion was the joke of Hollywood.

All this would have been irrelevant had it not been that Dall had an alarming tendency to swish in scenes in which extreme virility and masculinity were called for. Rapper says:

She and Dall were playing the very important scene when she tells him he must go to Oxford. He was sitting down, and I told him to twist his cloth cap in his hands to suggest indecision and tension. He was supposed to stand up and stride manfully out of the room. Suddenly, he rose and began swinging his hips and wiggling his fanny at Bette. She threw up her hands and said to me, 'This is impossible. We'll have to get another actor.' I said, 'Wait a minute.' I went over to John, who was red with embarrassment, and said, 'Next time you get up, think of the King of England and imagine the national anthem

252

playing and *march* like a soldier.' Rosalind Ivan, who was very good at playing bitches, said, 'He might be happier thinking of the *Queen* of England!' But John was a good sport. I ordered action and watched his fanny nervously. It didn't swish, and the scene was fine.

The Corn Is Green, deliberate and heavily theatrical, nevertheless was an admirable showcase for Davis's talent. Her face, remarkably aged for the occasion, had never been more expressive, nor had her mastery of movement and gesture ever been more vividly displayed. Supported by an admirable cast, she attacked the role with tremendous style and relish, at her strongest in the examination scene – despite the fact that it was done in two halves, divided by her near-fatal accident, if accident it was.

Certainly, there were some people in the studio who hated her. She was so relentlessly demanding, imposing, seeking restlessly for what was best, that many people couldn't tolerate it. Her outbursts of rage and additions of pages to the script was upsetting even in perfectionist Hollywood. She was the opposite of Hepburn, who treated picture-making like a party and gave picnics and sudden, British-style tea breaks during shooting. With Bette, everything was work, work, work: a grim concentration on achievement, on professional brilliance.

In the last months of 1944, Bette's affair with Sherry failed to improve. But they still planned to marry in 1945. She had long wanted to make her own pictures, both to control the material and the director and achieve a tax deduction. In 1945, as the Second World War neared its end, several stars began to set up their own corporations to avoid the vastly increased taxes that the war had brought about. She, characteristically, decided to begin a career as a producer by offering not one, but two Bette Davises in the same picture: *A Stolen Life*, adapted from a picture with Elisabeth Bergner about twins, one good, one evil who were in love with the same man. It was a season for movies about twins: Olivia de Havilland, Bette's old friend, the following year appeared in the melodrama *Dark Mirror*, in which she also played an evil and a good sister.

This was typical of the extreme egotism of stars – that, not content with one of themselves in the movies, they wanted two. Bette often complained that she lacked strong leading men, just as she lacked strong husbands or lovers, but she certainly did not go out of her way to select a powerful actor for *A Stolen Life*. She tried Robert Alda, a smooth, Latin type, and dropped him summarily; she tried Dennis Morgan and found him wanting; finally, she borrowed Glenn Ford from Columbia. Her company was B.D. Inc. She owned eighty per cent of it; her agent Jules Stein owned ten per cent and Ruthie and her attorney Dudley Furse owned five per cent each. B.D. Inc. was to receive the first $125,000 of the net, then Warners the next $232,000, Warners getting sixty-five per cent and B.D. Inc. thirty-five per cent.

Once again, Bette brought in Orry-Kelly to do her costumes. The production was complicated. 'The studio was surprised and dismayed that Bette wanted to be her own producer,' its writer, Catherine Turney, says. 'They felt she couldn't handle all the major problems.'

These problems included the astonishing total of thirty-six sets, a lighthouse constructed at Laguna Beach, three combined scripts and an appallingly difficult scene in a storm in which the bad sister drowns.

Worse still, there was the hair-raising problem of matching the shots in which one twin would light the other's cigarette or touch the other's hair. Herb Lightman explains how cameraman Polito achieved what he wanted:

Bette lighting a cigarette for her twin was executed by having Miss Davis play the scene opposite a double who lit her cigarette and performed other actions at close range. Later, the double's face was 'matted' out and Miss Davis's head literally placed on her shoulders.

In one scene, Bette had to make a complicated matching movement and she had to watch in the projection room her double in action with her. Due to a mistake, her head had not been placed on her double's shoulders. She found herself talking to a headless woman on the screen. She put her face in her hands.

Shooting began in the spring of 1945. Annoyingly, since this was her own picture, Bette fell ill with a mysterious virus and work was delayed for over a week. She then broke out in massive boils all over her face. It is clear this was due to the extreme stress of the responsibility of handling production details; in competition, Glenn Ford announced that *he* had boils on his face – and disappeared for five days to recover.

Bette had several run-ins with the gifted German director Curtis Bernhardt. At one stage, she sent a memorandum calling for his dismissal and then reinstated him with equal abruptness. On the other hand, she admired his strength of will. Bernhardt says:

We began with a tremendous clash on the first running of her wardrobe tests. I thought they were dreadful. She would say, 'Isn't Orry's work wonderful?' And her entourage would murmur, 'Yes, it's gorgeous, darling.' I hated that kind of movie star nonsense. After three costumes, I turned to her and said, 'Miss Davis, don't you think these costumes are too theatrical?' She replied, angrily, 'How can you *say* that? I am *never* theatrical!' I was appalled at her dishonesty. I got up and started to walk out of the projection room. She stood up and followed me, right in the middle of the screening. 'Where are you going?' she shouted. 'Home,' I snapped back. 'What do you *mean* you're going home? These are the costume tests for *your* picture!' She was bursting with rage. I said, '*You* don't need a director. *You need a yes man*!' I told her to her face. We met eyeball to eyeball, and suddenly (she's a wonderful sport) she backed down. She said, 'You know, I think you're right!' And from that moment on she didn't argue with me about the costumes.

Bette had extreme rapport with the charming and talented writer Catherine Turney whose script, with numerous touches by Bette herself, was breezy and vigorously entertaining. In many conversations with Bette, Turney built up the role of the good sister: the problem with the previous version had been that once the bad sister was drowned, the picture fell flat because the character of the good sister was excessively dull.

Turney and Bette together got involved in a cloak-and-dagger operation to sneak Glenn Ford into the picture. Turney remembers:

Glenn was just out of the Marine Corps and inexperienced. Bette and I enlisted the aid of a publicist, a very funny man named Harry Mines. He literally smuggled Glenn on to the Warners lot against Jack's orders and when they found out we had tested him and sent him in to be signed up, all hell broke loose. Steve Trilling, the studio boss, insisted that we have Robert Alda, but Bette was adamant it must be Glenn.

Bette and Catherine together instilled in the picture a strong and salty sense of the Yankee seafaring atmosphere of a seaport in Maine, recreating an authentic mood in a total alien setting with the aid of the director. The picture is perhaps closer to Bette's own world than any other she made. It has a wonderfully brisk and attractive sense of people living lives out in beautifully accurate settings thought out to the last touch of detail in the ornaments: a ship in a bottle, framed in a window overlooking a white and sparkling harbour; a cosy fire on a winter's night with a kindly old man and a pipe to greet the wayward wanderer; light flickering on the ceiling of a lighthouse room when the heroine recovers from near drowning.

Throughout the shooting, Turney says, 'We had endless discussions in Bette's dressing-room about every scene. It would sometimes make the crew very angry, because they didn't realise that good would come from these discussions. Curt agreed with us that we should show deep motivation in the characters. We kept nothing from the original picture except the scene in which the dog doesn't recognise the good sister, who is posing as the bad sister after the latter's drowning.'

Much of the work came from the problem of differentiating between the twins. It was decided early on that Bette should have the same voice in each performance, or the impersonation of the second half would fail to make sense. There were subtle differences, worked out by Bette, Turney and Orry-Kelly in the clothes the sisters wore: Kate, the good twin, wore drab clothes, unpretentious but pleasant; her sister wore fussy pretentious clothes. The biggest problem in the picture was the big storm scene. Bette and her double, Sally Sage, had to get into a boat that was wrought with wires attached to the bottom of a deep studio tank. It was filled with water whipped by tremendous wind machines that churned up fifteen-foot waves. The tank was the size of an Olympic Games swimming pool. Not only did Bette and Sally have to cling to the yacht but Sally had to keep the back of her head to the camera for matching shots. In seconds, both were completely drenched. The sail kept flapping and the jib struck Bette on the head and threw her into the water. Although both she and Sally were good sailors, Bette, probably largely through nerves, became seasick. She sprained her ankle and struck her elbow violently. The shooting, with both actresses soaked to the skin and violently thrown about, continued through three harrowing days. In the last shot, Bette had to slide off the deck while her sister grabbed at her hand and the wedding ring slipped off her finger. The yacht accidentally capsized and Bette went down in the water. Her feet caught in the wires and she was unable to come up. She struggled desperately, convinced that she would drown in seventeen feet of water. At last, she managed to get loose and, striking out powerfully, came to the surface. 'I thought we had lost you,' Bernhardt said. 'Why didn't you dive in and see?' Bette replied.

The effect of this mishap was to give Bette a bad case of influenza and laryngitis and put her in bed for a week. More hazards lay ahead. There was a sequence that called for her to be marooned in fog. She acquired more severe throat problems from the smoke pots used to create a murky atmosphere. Her delicate skin broke out as a result of somebody putting some acid substance in her make-up.

In a slightly less lethal action, a member of the crew almost caused her injury. She was supposed to open the door for a hasty exit and she collided into it violently when it failed to open. She was knocked out cold.

Fast moving and energetic, *A Stolen Life* contained two of Bette's best performances. Some of the interviews given out by the director at the end of the production were notably weird. He told the *Detroit News*: 'With Miss Davis's characterisation, we were handicapped because we could never make Bette cross the room in front of herself. Always we had to have her walk behind her other image.'

There is a curious parallel in the movie between the character of Karnak, the sullen painter who is violently rude to the heroine, ill-treating her while supplying dreadful daubs which she does her best to encourage, and William Grant Sherry. It is almost as though she created a mirror for a living person in a part played with scenery-chewing emphasis by a bad-tempered Dane Clark.

At the end-of-shooting party, Sherry got into a violent quarrel with Glenn Ford, apparently (and quite mistakenly) jealous of him. Bette had absolutely no sexual interest in Ford, nor he in her; and in later years, they became powerful enemies.

Bette married Sherry late in 1945. One would have thought that given the miserable relationship, she wouldn't have made this mistake. More than once, they were seen arguing violently in public. Their behaviour became the gossip of Hollywood. Bette, who had always managed to control the press completely, was unable to stop the ocean of criticism that greeted her marrying someone considered unfit to wed a star. She admitted in her memoirs that the furious opposition of Ruthie and Bobby to the man drove her conclusively into it. It is disagreeable to note that Sherry signed an agreement before the ceremony stating that if and when the marriage ended, he would make no claims on her property. *Photoplay* commented acidly: 'In other words, Bette Davis could try it out, and if it didn't work, it wouldn't cost her anything.'

Bette and Sherry left for a honeymoon in Mexico in November. On the way, Sherry threw her out of the car. In the hotel when they arrived, he flung an ashtray at her head. The honeymoon resembled life in a cave in 10 million B.C. It was a dire warning of what lay ahead, but there was one consolation. Soon afterwards, Bette became pregnant.

Twelve

AT THE beginning of 1946, Bette took the bold step of cutting links to her happier past. She sold both Riverbottom and Butternut within a few weeks of each other, and moved herself and Sherry, bag and baggage, to a new home in Laguna. It was a handsome house, smallish as Bette liked houses, perched on a cliff on Sleepy Hollow Lane overlooking Woods Cove with a striking view of the ocean from every window. The entrance hall was oak panelled and Bette hung British sporting prints on the walls. The library, very small and cosy, she packed tight with crowded shelves of her favourite books. She brought in a desk, typewriter and leather chair to make into an office. The living-room faced north: ideal for Sherry, who was addicted to Rembrandt's north light. He stood his easel by the windows overlooking the ocean, and filled the four walls with his sea and landscapes and still lifes, and a winter scene of Butternut with a large red barn and trees hung with icicles. Bette's favourite rocking chair, coffee table, lazy susan, antiques, all came from Riverbottom. The dining-room was up a flight of stairs; it was furnished in walnut. At the front of the house there was a porch of the kind Bette loved, which embraced the entire façade over a terrace turned into a flowery rock garden. There were pools to swim in between large rocks and a barbecue patio. A huge four-poster bed filled the bedroom, just leaving room for a couple of sticks of furniture.

Bette was busy preparing the nursery and baby clothes that winter. She spent hours dreaming of future projects: a version of Edith Wharton's novel *Ethan Frome*; and *The African Queen*, with James Mason, a picture lost years later to Katharine Hepburn. But all too many evenings were spent in violent quarrels, so that finally, miserable and contrite, Sherry went to a psychoanalyst. His cure consisted of a sudden burst of wifeliness: when Bette came home he, in the words of Louella Parsons, 'Would have her dinner ready for her, bring her slippers, press her dresses, draw her bath, give her massages.' She found this unbearable and, after pretending politely to accept it, exploded. She regarded these duties as her prerogative; Sherry was usurping her by taking them on.

She wanted Sherry to be her equal, financially, professionally, and in temperament and personality. But this dream of a liberated woman had no chance of realisation – and, once again, one wonders if, had she attained it, she would for a moment really have wanted it. Given her consuming ego, she probably could not have endured a matching competition. Yet on the other hand she regretted the fact that Sherry had very little success as an artist; that it was impossible for him to keep up with her financially, and this tortured him. Her friends' and family's dislike of Sherry began to seem to her not so unreasonable. But at least her pregnancy bound them together up to a point – until once more Sherry's temper broke out in a storm and, that winter, Bette even called for Sherry to be put under a restraint because she feared he would do her bodily harm while she carried his child. It was a season of partings and rejoinings, passionate lovemaking and sudden departures of either partner, and above all the constant gnawing hate that destroys as it consumes. It was the most disastrous period of Bette's life to date, more tormenting even than the worst times with Ham. She should have been a joyful expectant mother, bathed in a sense of well-being despite the

261

inevitable medical problems that accompany pregnancy. But she was not. Once more, she was heading for a breakdown; in her late thirties, she felt and looked ten years older.

In this dark period, Bette tried to buoy herself up with a new picture which she entered with decidedly mixed feelings. Given the impossible title *Her Conscience,* which troubled Bette, it was fortunately changed to *Deception.* Because of Bette's condition, it quickly became popularly known in the studio as *Conception.*

Based on a play that had originally been filmed with Bette's idol, Jeanne Eagels, *Deception* reunited the principals of *Now, Voyager* – Bette, Claude Rains, Paul Henreid – with the director, Irving Rapper. Bette had to study the piano for a scene at a reception following a wedding: she trained carefully under the tutelage of Shura Cherkassky, her hand movements matched for some of the more difficult passages by Norma (Mrs Richard) Boleslavsky. A problem in the action was that Bette, despite her streak of physical cowardice, had to fire a gun; she had had to do so, of course, in *The Letter,* but on this occasion she was more troubled emotionally and tried desperately to have the shooting scene changed. The dialogue seemed to her exceedingly pretentious and heavy, and her part was a nuisance: she had to play a congenital liar, a tearful, neurotic woman.

The story was absurd: the mistress of a famous composer is visited by her former lover, a cellist who has been confined in a concentration camp. She has to tell lie piled upon lie to deceive the amorous revenant that she is not involved with the composer. The composer gives the concentration camp victim a cello concerto to perform, intending to destroy his belief in the woman the night following the performance. This rigmarole was very aggravating to the industry censor Joseph Breen, who wrote to Jack Warner: 'From the standpoint of the Code the major difficulty seems to be that this past

262

relationship is not treated as sin; there is no voice for morality; there is no punishment for either of the sinners; and the general flavour is almost one of condemnation for the whole situation.' The script had to be extensively rewritten so that Bette's character ended the picture threatened with the electric chair after killing the composer at point-blank range. Presumably the cellist's subsequent agony at the revelations of the trial was considered punishment enough by the Breen office.

From beginning to end, the making of *Deception* was a nightmare. Bette, more overwrought and hysterical because of Sherry's treatment than she had ever been, painfully conscious of the possible effect on her child, and miserably self-conscious that her pregnant condition showed, spent hours a day in her dressing-room in tears while the production ground to a halt. Since there were only three significant characters, and she was on camera almost every day, the picture was forty-six days over schedule, almost twice its planned period of production.

Shooting began, despite the continuing objections of Breen, in May. Bette was distracted from the first. She was thinking not only of her personal problems but also of her bitter disappointment that Jack Warner refused to allow her to make the story of Mary Todd Lincoln as her next production. In breaks between outbursts of crying and fights at home, shooting the picture and making the long, difficult drive along the coast highway to and from Laguna each morning and evening, she somehow found time to rush off long letters without punctuation, written with telegram dashes instead of full stops, to Jack Warner who was on vacation in Hot Springs, Arkansas, chock-full of demands and requests, ideas and themes, for the Lincoln story. She wrote in one letter during a troubled weekend in Palm Springs that she understood Jack's fear of biographies, 'But to me this is a story of so many women – not just a figure out of history – it is a story of any woman who believes in her husband and pushes him ahead.' She went on that this was a story of a woman who was the power behind the throne, a theme 'apt to be box-office', that the character had a wonderful combination of Scarlett O'Hara and a *Back Street* woman; she cited the success of Katharine Hepburn (that name again!) in *State of the Union*, about the wife of a Presidential candidate, 'and anyway stubborn Davis is asking you to think more about it – I am so truly sure someone in the theatre will do it soon – the Theatre Guild has always been interested – or could I do it as a play? . . . Bye for now – Bette.'

In April, in mid-production of *Deception,* Bette was driving home at night when a car swung out of a bend in the road without warning. In extreme distress after a harrowing day of shooting, and sleepless nights with her unhappy husband, Bette panicked and swerved off the road, crashing her car in the process. The automobile was smashed to pieces and she was knocked unconscious. Somebody picked her up and drove her to her home where she collapsed completely. She awoke next morning with a blinding headache; once more, her fears of sharing the fate of the heroine of *Dark Victory* returned. She managed to pull herself together sufficiently to call unit manager Al Alleborn in person to say she wouldn't be able to work on Saturday. She had a dizzy spell the following morning, and studio representatives called, not to ask her how she was feeling, but to enquire when she would return to work. This upset her fiercely and she called her physician, Dr Wilson, telling him she felt seriously ill.

Wilson came over several times. He took X-rays in the house with his nursing team so Bette would not have to undergo the ordeal of encountering a crowd of fans at the local clinic. He told her, in a scene reminiscent of the diagnosis scene in *Dark Victory,* that he was gravely worried about her condition. There was some evidence of a haemorrhage and possibly a fracture in the skull casing. He told her she must remain flat on her back without moving for several days. Wilson was alarmed to see blood trickling from her mouth down her chin; evidently, she had suffered damage to her jaw, which was to show up in an illness six years later.

The producer, Henry Blanke, and Irving Rapper drove down to Laguna that weekend. Sherry, afraid Bette might die, was in a state of nerves and exhaustion, deeply sorry about his behaviour: like a spoiled child who had suddenly regretted an impulsive action. Bette was too dizzy and hazy to do more than nod at her visitors; she felt sick to her stomach and terrified of the possible results of a further set of X-rays.

Yet, astonishingly, and with iron professionalism, she managed to pull herself together to go to work in two weeks. Precisely how this miracle occurred is a mystery, but presumably her condition was not as serious as everyone thought. However, the dizzy spells came back and she was off work again for several days. She was so run down that she contracted a series of colds and some of her lines had to be dubbed. By 25 May, she was in bed again, with a severe case of intestinal flu, a strep throat and a fever of 101°. Dr Wilson gave her 10,000 units of penicillin; he said on no condition would she be able to work for several days. Wilson told her that the accident in the car and her insomnia because of Sherry had worn her system down to a danger point and that the damp air of Laguna was bad for her with her chronic throat weakness. But she shook her head speechlessly, a thermometer in her mouth, when he advised her to move. Bobby and Ruthie were nearby, and her uncle and cousins, the Favors, and without them there was nothing in life.

Due to the loving care of her mother and sister, and the remarkable Dr Wilson, Bette managed to struggle back to work again in June. But the studio head, Steve Trilling, who had once been the costume director, was unsympathetic, reflecting as he did the tough Jack Warner's slave-driving attitude to the stars. Under doctor's orders, Bette had asked if she could come in at ten A.M. each day to allow for the long drive from Laguna and sufficient time in make-up to cover the marks of grief and sickness in her face – a task which, on this occasion, her devoted Perc Westmore notably failed to accomplish. On 22 June, Trilling suddenly arrived on the set during a break in a difficult scene and called Bette aside. In earshot of other members of the cast, an unforgivable sin in Bette's eyes, Trilling asked Bette loudly if she would please come in at nine A.M. and work till six each day because the picture was far over budget and schedule. Bette said to Trilling, according to a studio memorandum, 'I had an understanding with Colonel Warner that I would start at ten A.M. and leave at five. Some days, I've worked longer hours just to please him. But if I work from nine to six each day' (she started to cry) 'I won't be able to take it. I'll get sick and cause a shut-down again.' Suddenly, she dried her tears and said, sharply, angrily, 'If Colonel Warner wants me to change the arrangement agreed to, why doesn't he have the courage to tell me so himself? Why does he send *you* to tell me? A picture like this needs a lot of rehearsing! Jack knew what he was in for before we started! And they keep adding dialogue! I have to stay up at night learning lines for the next day! And they're long, difficult lines!' Now she started warming up in earnest. In full hearing of the entire company, she shouted, 'You, Steve Trilling, have a lot of nerve, coming down to the set during a shooting day! Discussing me shooting at nine instead of ten each day! And when you *know* we are working and I'm trying to concentrate and I'm about to go into a scene five pages long with difficult, complicated lines!' Bette pulled off her gloves and threw her hands to her face, sobbing so violently that tears started through her fingers. Everyone looked at her astonished; but typically of hard-bitten Hollywood, no one ran forward to comfort her. Steve Trilling went pale, turned on his heel, and strode off the set shaking his head. Bette called her maid. 'Bring me some soda!' she exclaimed. Several of the crew were heard to laugh: they were tired of her tantrums and just wanted to get on with the day's work so they could get home to their wives or girlfriends before sundown.

Bette played her emotional scenes with an excessive emphasis, repeating lines unnecessarily and smoking far beyond the demands of the script. Her genuine emotional condition gave an extraordinary raw power to her playing when it was not downright hammy. She said nothing to anybody and went home in silence. She went straight to bed and called her agent, Lew Wasserman. She refused to speak to anybody from the studio and remained in bed for three days in a state of complete exhaustion.

Warner was angry that Bette had made the scene with Trilling. Devoid of the guts which would have brought about a direct confrontation he sent her a telegram instead which read as follows:

Dear Bette: I am at a loss for words to express myself after having learned of the turmoil that existed last Saturday afternoon and today with respect to the production of your picture. You must not lose sight of the fact that you are in a profession that calls for certain fulfilment of moral obligations to say nothing of legal ones. You are taking the wrong attitude towards our company and me personally on this whole matter in that you would create conditions that are not fair to our studios. We are not responsible for the working hours under which the industry is making its pictures. We have done everything in our power for you, but now you ask us to change the working

267

hours which I find we cannot do after having honestly tried, which was our distinct understanding when I discussed this with you in my office several weeks ago. Am sure you realise our rapport was radical departure from our normal studio operations and if we continue it will create a complete change in our production methods and prove very costly to us. I implore you as a friend and business associate to use your good reasoning. Am sure in the long run you will realise what you are doing now is not the proper thing and am asking nothing unreasonable from you. Sincerely

JACK WARNER

This cable, to which Bette did not respond, marked the beginning of a gradual but increasingly steep decline in Bette's relations with her old boss. The brutal fact was that her pictures were not making the enormous profits of previous years; that a new and tougher industry was less indulgent of the behaviour of the old-time stars.

On 24 June 1946, the unthinkable happened: a member of the legal division sent a telegram to the production chief which was to be rephrased and delivered to Bette in Laguna, placing her on suspension for absenteeism. At the last minute, Warner panicked, and the cable was never sent.

Back to work at the end of June, Bette slammed into her dressing-room in a fit of rage over rewritten dialogue and severely injured her finger. The pain was excruciating, the nail smashed and black. It didn't help her when Al Alleborn chose that moment to tell her she was threatened with suspension at any minute.

With her finger in a bandage supplied by Perc Westmore, Bette stopped the shooting for the first time in her life and demanded that the entire crew including the producer and director and other players gather around

her. Extremely distraught, she said, 'Many of you have
been on pictures I have made previously. There are
certain things you should know. You see my finger is
badly hurt. The studio seems indifferent. I am appalled
that the crew has been called in to work every day I've
been off sick when Trilling *knew* you would be wasted
because I couldn't come in. It shows terrible lack of
consideration for you. I hate being put in a position like
this. When Trilling and Warner make it seem my fault
the crew is called in every day, when they know it's
impossible for me to come to work.'

Jack Warner was furious at this sudden labour meeting: the first of its kind in the history of Hollywood: the
first time a star had presumed to complain about her
employers to a crew. So what if she was the queen of the
lot and earning $8,000 a week? She still had no business
to criticise her betters!

The rift between Bette and Warners was never to heal.
It was probably just as well that she gave birth to her
child soon after the picture's disastrous previews and
shattering reviews.

The birth was difficult: a Caesarian section.

The child was a very pretty girl of ten pounds, ten
ounces. Bette, lovingly, named her Barbara after Bobby
and called her, from that moment on, 'B.D.' Always
extreme in her emotion, Bette became ecstatic over the
child and for a time her relationship with Sherry was
cemented. There can be no doubt that, intensely family
conscious like all New Englanders, Bette had never
really cared overwhelmingly for any human being outside of her mother and sister – until B.D. came along.

Bette immediately took a year off work, over a
grudging Jack Warner's complaints. Motherhood
absorbed her torment and nervous strain and for a
period at least she was reasonably serene. Her health

suddenly improved; she had great fun entertaining columnists she normally despised – Louella came to coo relentlessly over the child who somehow survived the presence of this witch at her cradle, Hedda descended like a bird of prey in a feathered hat to bless the newborn. Bette acted up magnificently, sitting up in a bedjacket against large New England pillows, displaying her gurgling offspring to these alarming visitors.

Becoming a mother at almost forty had its risks, but Bette had triumphed over them. She began to live the life the fan magazines had been busily inventing for her. She took B.D. for dips in salty rock pools; waved Sherry goodbye when he went to flying school; joined him, family and friends at weekend barbecues; took in movies and summer theatre; filmed B.D. in home movies with Irving Rapper-like expertise; and, in her own words, undertook a regime of darning socks, sewing on buttons, and, 'doing what any family does – a family that is sufficient unto itself – the only really important thing for everyone in the world – the one thing really worth striving for . . . I cannot ask for more than to have life continue as it is. I have my family – my work – I can look the world in the eye. I am happy.'

Back under psychiatry again, Sherry became intrigued by a novel about a sensitive young Navy man planning to be a priest and a nervous spinster poetess in New York. Sherry, perhaps trying to compensate for the misery he had caused Bette, urged her to take on the story. Trying to please him, she agreed, though she was worried about the property. To try to protect herself, she asked her friend Catherine Turney, whose writing she much admired, to make the adaptation.

A New York stage director, Bretaigne Windust, was brought in to make the picture, because of his intimate knowledge of the New York social milieu in which the story was set. Bette kept writing notes through the spring of 1947 to Turney in Manhattan saying such things as, 'I

270

am very rested and very ambitious to do something really outstanding – and I don't feel this, the way it is, answers the requirements.' Turney wrote and rewrote but the script, finally called *Winter Meeting*, was never completely satisfactory. One of the problems was that Richard Widmark, who would have been ideal in the part of the priest, and who gave a brilliant test, was felt by the studio to be too closely identified with his part of a giggling villain in the picture *Kiss of Death*. Instead, Trilling cast the wooden and awkward Jim Davis, who was hopelessly outclassed by his namesake. The script was filled with yards of dull talk which irritated Bette; Sherry, who influenced the choice of Jim Davis and the acceptance of the final draft, proved to be quite mistaken in his influences.

The picture was a dull and uninspiring experience to make, received bad reviews, and lost a fortune. Nevertheless, it is in many ways one of Bette's more interesting pictures. Cleverly made, photographed with great artistry, it is at times a sensitive and moving study of loneliness and lack of fulfilment: rare themes in motion pictures. And Bette's performance was finely and delicately drawn, conveying a subtle sense of pain behind the confident surface. In counterpoint to the anguished story of sexual deprivation there is the sharply witty characterisation of snobbish New York social life, enlivened by the acid portrait of an effete Manhattanite by the admirable John Hoyt.

Although *Winter Meeting* was preferable to the overheated *Deception*, the picture proved to be the catastrophe of Bette's career. Jack Warner's impatience with her over her behaviour on *Deception* would have been replaced by forgiveness if *Winter Meeting* (for which she can be held responsible) had been a commercial hit. But the delays in *Deception*, the long absence following the birth of her child, and now this fatal mistake in production destroyed his confidence in her and as an asset. By

1948, her career at the studio was already doomed.

Her next picture, a comedy called *June Bride*, barely broke even, and Bette, looking like her daughter in *Deception*, was, despite a brisk appearance, far from pleased with the shooting. Although she appeared in fan magazines praising the brilliance of her co-star Robert Montgomery, she disliked him intensely. Possibly her hatred of Montgomery is the reason for her exceptionally mannered comedy playing, notably lacking in sympathy and warmth in the love scenes.

One pleasure of the shooting – perhaps the only one – was that Bette formed a new friendship. She very much liked the young actress, Betty Lynn, who played the bride of the story. They have remained close to this day.

1948 was a watershed year before a disaster. Barely able to tolerate her marriage, still finding satisfaction in her daughter, Bette spent much of the time trying futilely to get the Mary Todd Lincoln story and *Ethan Frome* off the ground. Unable to do so, she had to settle, early in 1949, for an absurdity called *Beyond the Forest*, a novel written by Stuart Engstrand, who, perhaps after reading the reviews, walked into a lake and drowned some days after the book appeared.

In *Beyond the Forest*, Bette played a small-town housewife who yearns for the big city: Chicago. Against a background of smoke-belching mill chimneys not unlike those which defaced the sky in Bette's birthplace of Lowell, Mass., Rosa Moline is tormented and repressed. Bored with her sensible, down-to-earth husband, she becomes embroiled in a steaming affair with a *macho* businessman who later turns her down when she throws herself at his head. The plot involves a forced miscarriage, seductions, violent arguments and arrivals and departures in heavy rain, all accompanied by the hot-house rhythms of Max Steiner's score. In the last scene,

Rosa, half-dead, wanders distractedly towards a train, winding up, in a dramatic demise, firmly on the wrong side of the tracks.

The director was King Vidor, the most gifted craftsman Bette had worked with apart from Wyler. Yet Bette was unable to relate to the sober, subdued and warmly human man. He was neither subservient nor overpowering: he was in a class by himself. She couldn't cope with his serious, controlled intelligence. And she overcompensated for the weaknesses in the writing by assuming a fantastic guise. She wore a long black wig, garish make-up, and ugly print dresses, and used all of her most extreme vocal and physical mannerisms in a rather desperate parody of herself. It was the beginning of a definite change in her approach to acting: a kind of exaggeration of all the elements that distinguished her as a performer.

As so often before, Bette was infuriated by the hypocrisy of the Breen office. When she visited an abortion clinic in the picture to get rid of an unwanted child, Jack Warner on Breen's instructions removed the clinic sign and put up another with the word 'psychiatrist' painted on it. King Vidor says, 'I don't think that fooled anybody. It was still obvious that she was trying to get rid of her baby.'

Vidor recalls countless problems with Bette. He says:

One day we were doing a scene in which Joe Cotten who plays her husband, a doctor, had given her a prescription in a small bottle. She picked the bottle up in disgust and threw it at him. I felt she threw it too weakly: I could see she liked Joe. Her gesture was far too lacking in the necessary anger. I said to her, 'Bette, try it again!' She refused.

Bette was infuriated that Vidor overrode her in the gesture. She was not accustomed to being told what to do in so severe a manner. Tragically, she didn't realise that already her position was in danger. That she should not have dared to cross a famous director in this difficult period of her career. No longer box-office, she was no longer indispensable. It was her fatal mistake that her usual sense of realism failed her then.

She clashed with King Vidor again a day later. He says:

> The only other point during the shooting which might have bothered her was a scene where she was dancing with [the actor] David Brian. And there's this technique that's been used since the advent of sound – and it's still used – when you shoot a couple dancing they speak their lines when their faces can be seen. After one take that we did I said to Bette, 'I want to do it again, because when you swung around to speak your line you weren't facing the camera.' In fact, he was such a big fellow, David Brian, that she was completely covered. Today I wouldn't think anything of it, but this was the way things were done then. People were used to seeing the actors' faces when they spoke. So I said to Bette, 'Let's time it better so that they can see your face when you talk.' And Bette said, 'Oh, my God! Haven't they seen my face enough?' She went on in a loud voice, much louder than mine. So I said, 'That gives me a good idea. Let's do it again and fix it so they can't see your face at all.' She said, 'That's an excellent idea.' I told her, 'Keep your face hidden down there.' That must have burned her up something awful. And that's how we did it, so we couldn't see her face at all.

Bette called her agent, Lew Wasserman, and a meeting was held next morning at the studio, rather oddly on the set itself, between Wasserman, Bette's lawyer and the studio's legal people headed by Roy Obringer. She told the assembled group she refused to work that day. Word of this was brought to Jack Warner who insisted upon seeing Bette immediately. As it turned out, she was already on her way to his office. She stormed in and said, very loudly, 'Jack, if you don't get another director, I want to be released from my contract. It's him or me.' Warner looked her straight in the eye. 'Okay, Bette, it's you!' he said.

She froze for a moment, unable to believe what she was hearing. Then she stormed out. Warner was delighted at the opportunity to cancel Bette's contract. King Vidor says:

It took him fifteen minutes to draw up the papers and have her sign them on the set. But it says a great deal for her that she took the news after almost twenty years at the studio that had made her great without carrying on about it. She cooled off suddenly and did the rest of the picture like the pro she was. Suddenly, I saw the stuff she was made of. I lost all dislike of her.

The realities were there. Bette's pictures were more costly to make than those of other stars. They were not doing well at the box-office. That was all that mattered in Hollywood. She was let go without a tremor.

Thirteen

WITHIN TEN days of the disastrous press screening of *Beyond the Forest,* Bette filed a suit for divorce against Sherry. It was agreed that Bette should have custody of B.D. with visiting rights by Sherry; that Sherry would not take B.D. out of the county of Los Angeles without Bette's written consent or outside the state; that Sherry would pay monthly maintenance.

Sherry took the serving of the papers badly, and became severely depressed. An attempt was made to patch up the marriage without success. By May of 1950, it was all over.

By one of those unappealing ironies that marked Bette's career, Bette made as her next picture *The Story of a Divorce,* a bitter account of a collapsing marriage. It was directed by Curtis Bernhardt at RKO; Bette's first picture away from Warners in almost two decades. Intelligently written, harsh and lacking in major compromises, *The Story of a Divorce** was much superior to Bette's recent vehicles at Warners. Bette ended it in a dark mood.

Bette's character in the picture had to appear as fifteen years old in one scene: a major challenge for an actress of the age of forty. She carried off the deception with amazing expertise. It was one of her finest performances, at its most striking in the scene in which, grim and determined, the wife attends a meeting to discuss alimony. The greed and cruelty of a detective, the stupidity

*released as *Payment on Demand*

276

of lawyers, the sterile atmosphere of the house where the couple quarrel, all are admirably realised. The direction is consistently intelligent; there is no attempt to soften the pitiless ambition of the central female figure.

At the end of shooting, there was a party into which Sherry barged. Bette had specifically excluded him from it, knowing he would cause trouble. He strode on to the set and dragged Bette from a table. She told him to leave at once and not come back. Barry Sullivan came over and said, 'Why start trouble again? Why don't you have a sense of humour? The company's worked very hard and everybody's trying to relax.' Once more, Sherry took a swing at Sullivan; he was dragged off by studio police.

During the last week of production, Darryl F. Zanuck, boss of Twentieth Century-Fox, got into a serious jam. He had cast the comedy-drama *All About Eve* with Claudette Colbert in the part of a temperamental star based on Elisabeth Bergner, who is threatened by the emergence of a younger actress. Zanuck had never liked Davis: he had quarrelled with her violently over the administration of the Academy of Motion Picture Arts and Sciences during the brief period when she had been president. At first, she didn't take his calls. But he finally reached her and explained that the picture was already starting to shoot in San Francisco and there was no time to waste. He rushed the script to her by special messenger; she read it in less than an hour and a half, fell in love with it at once, and called Zanuck back to say she would immediately go ahead.

The part of Margo Channing was perfect for her. Roy Moseley, a friend of Bette Davis's, described the circumstances on which the plot was based:

Bergner was appearing in *The Two Mrs Carrolls*, and a young actress playing a small part came straight to Bergner to say she would be quitting.

And Miss Bergner said, 'Why?' And the young actress said, 'Because I'm not good enough, not good enough to be with you. You're so magnificent!' Bergner persuaded the young actress to stay on. The young actress was Irene Worth. The difference is, of course, that Bergner and Worth have remained friends to this day. There was an emulation, but not in an evil sense.

The little known fact is that the part of Margo Channing was originally written for Gertrude Lawrence. She was actually signed to play it. But in the drunk scene where 'Liebestraum' is played on the piano, Lawrence insisted on singing with it. The director, Joseph L. Mankiewicz, refused to allow this, and suddenly Lawrence stormed out.

Bette travelled to San Francisco in a state of great excitement, eager for work in her best picture in years. Although she didn't like Mankiewicz, finding him brutal, self-opinionated, tedious, wordy, obvious and much too slow at work, she was lost in admiration for his ability as a writer. She was also, with her customary professionalism, not shocked to be surrounded by actors of equal importance, fine players like George Sanders, the brilliant Thelma Ritter, and Anne Baxter; she welcomed and thrived on the vigorous competition for the audience's attention. And of course she was accepted at once with enormous enthusiasm into the acting company.

For years, Bette has denied that she based her performance of Margo on any particular performer. But there's no escaping the fact that her hairstyle, gestures, movement and sometimes the voice completely reflected Tallulah Bankhead. Mankiewicz almost certainly directed Bette as Tallulah without even telling her.

Mankiewicz has said of Margo Channing that he reduced her age from over forty-five to forty in making some adjustments to Bette's character.

Forty years of age. Four O. Give or take a year the single most critical chronological milestone in the life of an actress. *Look,* I knew these women. I'd been in love with some – I'd worked with many of them. In the early 1930s I'd watch them roll into Paramount and Metro at six-thirty in the morning on their way to hairdressing and make-up. Drive in usually with the top down, their hair all blown by the wind, no lipstick, their own eyelashes, wearing anything from a poncho to a polo coat – and I'd think Perc Westmore should be arrested for so much as touching a powder puff to their loveliness. Well, by the late thirties they were driving with the top up. Then, in the forties they started wearing scarfs. And by 1950 large hats. The pancake was getting thicker, the make-up took longer, the cameramen started using specially built little banks of 'inkies' to iron out wee bags and sags.

The day before beginning work, Edmund Goulding, who had directed Bette in *Dark Victory,* called Mankiewicz at the San Francisco hotel and said, 'Have you gone mad, dear boy? How could you hire such a woman? She will destroy you. She will ground you down to fine powder and blow you away. You are a writer, dear boy. She will come to the stage with a thick pad of long yellow paper. And pencils. She will rewrite everything. And then she, not you, will direct. Mark my words.'

But no problems awaited Mankiewicz of this kind. Despite her reservations about his character, she told him straight out, 'I am neither Lady Macbeth nor Portia; I'll play either at a drop of a hat, anywhere. If I make a horse's ass of myself on the screen, it is I – me – Bette Davis – who is the forty feet by thirty feet horse's ass as far as they [the audience] are concerned. Not the writer, not the director, the producer or the studio gateman –

nobody but me. I'm up there as a representative horse's ass for all concerned. I made up my mind a long time ago, if anybody is going to make a horse's ass out of me, it's going to be me.'

Mankiewicz admired Bette enormously. He has consistently praised her. He wrote: 'On the first day of shooting, I was marking Eddie Goulding's words. I had my antennae deployed to pick up possible storm warnings. Miss Davis arrived on the set fully dressed and made up, at least a quarter of an hour before she'd been called. Bette didn't even glance at the set. She lit her cigarette and opened the script – not, as I noticed at once, the scene we were doing that first morning . . . Bette was letter perfect. She was syllable perfect. There was no fumbling for words; they'd become hers – as Margo Channing. The director's dream: the prepared actress.'

Milton Krasner recalls that from the beginning, the picture was a completely happy experience. Delighted with the script and ideally cast in every instance, the company relished the filming, and their relish shows on the screen. The picture perfectly hit off the overheated, witty, dangerous world of theatre people even while it glamorized that world legitimately to appeal to public taste. One's only serious question is whether cynical finely-tuned people of this kind, alert to the presence of ambition and deception in their midst, would for an instant have accepted Eve, the relentless phoney young actress, as one of them. Her line of fake sentiment seems false; too false to be accepted. And for all Anne Baxter's cleverness, it is hard to believe that an untried actress could suddenly emerge to fame and fortune with little more than cunning and a smooth line in pathos.

By contrast, the playing and writing of the other parts is consistently watchable and convincing. Bette got along famously with Celeste Holm, who played the cool, dignified writer's wife in expert contrast with Margo's tantrums and storms. Bette often told friends, 'That scene in the car. When her friends maroon Margo in order to give Eve a chance. I couldn't have played it if I hadn't had Celeste with me. She was so perfect.' By contrast, Celeste Holm had not been as flattering about Bette. She complained particularly that Bette and the romantic lead, Gary Merrill, spent all that time together and ignored everyone else in the company.

This is unlikely. But it is true that Bette found Merrill enormously attractive, that he was powerfully drawn to her. Like Sherry, he was a man with a strong temper, who allegedly overindulged in the bottle; he was extremely virile, hirsute, and in some moods witty and appealing, with an odd combination of a primitive caveman physique, a carved all-American face, and a nimble challenging mind. Drawn always to very physical men, unpretty and rugged, Bette was captivated by Merrill. Of all her husbands, she almost certainly cared for him most deeply. He was her match in temperament if not in talent; her match in his drive and fierce commitment to his profession, his intelligence and understanding. But he was emphatically not her match in being able to fulfil his ferocious drive in achievement of a high order.

By the time the picture was finished shooting, Bette was deeply involved with Merrill. It was an impassioned relationship, as impassioned as any Bette had known. And once again she was blinded by her strong physical drive towards domineering, extremely masculine men; blinded to the fact that the price she would pay would be in an attempt to overwhelm her, to consume her. Bette committed herself to Merrill within only two months of their meeting. The divorce with Sherry was rushed through on Independence Day; Bette's independence only lasted for twenty-four days. One would have thought she would have wanted to draw breath, to enjoy a calmer life as a famous, highly individual woman for at least a little while. But instead she impetuously eloped with Merrill to Mexico, married him in late July, and flew with him to New England for a quick honeymoon marked with quarrels.

At first, she and Merrill managed to make a go of it. They had in common more than she had had with her previous husbands. Although she had striven almost too strenuously to interest herself in Ham's dance music, Farney's aircraft design and Sherry's painting, these occupations were alien to her, creature that she was of show business. She was far more interested in discussing pictures and picture people than in trying to follow a musical score, an aircraft blueprint or a seascape design. Merrill was steeped in show business. He was a charming, typically aggressive, vain, self-conscious driven actor who perhaps even at that stage was painfuly aware that he wouldn't make it to the top flight of stardom. She and Gary knew some of the same people; their lives moved in similar circles. Ruthie and Bobby, and the Laguna Favors, all felt that Merrill at least came within distance of Bette's professional position and that he wasn't open to the suspicion of using her.

Along with her new marriage, which filled her with a surprising optimism, Bette knew a triumph in the international success of *All About Eve*. Her performance of Margo Channing, at once extravagant, absurd, tragic and witty, attracted the most lavish praise she had received in years. Her brilliantly sustained acting was the result of years of technical refinement; above all, the development of a sharp and knowing worldliness honed fine by experience. Nobody who had not been part of the theatre in her early days could have played with such understanding of the theatre. No one who was less than a great actress could have made one believe that Margo Channing herself was great. Margo Channing and *All About Eve* represented the peak of Bette Davis's career. It is appalling that she didn't receive an Academy

Award; but she was consoled by the New York Film Critics' Circle Award, the San Francisco Critics' Award, and an Oscar nomination.

As always in Bette's life, nothing ran smoothly. It would have been the joy of her life if Merrill could have sat with her in the fake Oriental interior of Grauman's Chinese Theatre on 9 November 1950, and seen *All About Eve* with her from beginning to end for the first time. But he had been sent by Zanuck to Germany to make *Decision Before Dawn* – ironically, since that picture was directed by Bette's former lover, Anatole Litvak. And shortly afterwards, Bette had a quarrel with another of her former flames: Howard Hughes. He owned RKO, and wanted to change the ending of *The Story of a Divorce,* along with the title, which became *Payment on Demand.* Bette was furious when Hughes literally destroyed the ending of the picture. It was supposed to show that the wife in the story was as relentless as ever, confronting her future without hope. Instead, the ending was softened and made ridiculous. Bette argued with Hughes in vain, their close feeling permanently fractured, their powerful mutual attraction long since forgotten.

One would have hoped that Bette would have gone from *All About Eve* to another triumph – but a disastrous professional mishap occurred instead.

The English screenwriter and producer Val Guest had written a script, *Another Man's Poison,* from a heavy, melodramatic stageplay. He had designed the movie for Barbara Stanwyck, but a problem arose. Val Guest says:

Stanwyck was all signed and fixed for it, and one of her understandings if she came here to do it was that we would pay for her fare to Rome to see her husband, Robert Taylor, and she could spend Christmas with him, and then come over to do the film. She went to Rome to surprise him, while he was shooting *Quo Vadis* and she *did* surprise him – having an affair. And from Rome she called me to say, in tears, 'I'm sorry. My whole life is in shreds. After all these years we've been married! I've got to go right back home and arrange a divorce. I'll have to bow out of the picture.' So I said, 'Work is the best thing you can do at a moment like this.' But she replied, 'No, no.' She had to go back to California. So there we were with a picture, a unit, a studio booked, and no star. What could we do?

As so often before, Bette was second choice. Douglas Fairbanks, Jr., who partly owned the picture, sent the script to Bette who inexplicably liked it. She evidently saw a chance for her to co-star with Merrill: perhaps this overrode her better judgment. The story cast her as a thriller writer having an affair with a handsome young engineer in a house in Yorkshire. Her husband is a convict who comes back unexpectedly and she poisons him. The rest of the story involves a series of absurd events including attempted murder – and an impersonation of quite extraordinary implausibility. In the last scene, Bette accidentally swallows a brandy glass full of poison, laughing uproariously when she discovers she is the victim of her own lethal dosage.

Just before leaving for England, Bette and Merrill adopted a pretty little girl, Margot Mosher (Merrill), who at that time seemed to be a normal baby. With no inkling of the tragedy that lay ahead, five-day-old Margot appeared to be perfect; she underwent the mandatory medical examination without a problem. Bette, who had been advised not to have any more children herself, adored this sweet child, and adopting Margot bound Bette and Merrill very close together. B.D. was three years old and Margot was presented to her as a 'wonderful surprise'. While B.D. closed her eyes, Bette put

Margot in the child's lap. B.D. opened her eyes and screamed with joy.

Bette, Merrill, Bette's long-time maid Adele, B.D., Margot and two nurses sailed to England aboard the *Queen Elizabeth*. They arrived after a rough crossing in freezing winter weather at the beginning of December, 1951 to be greeted by a hostile press, rationing, harsh post-war austerity and an England that was far removed from the glowing prosperous country Bette remembered perhaps unrealistically from the late 1930s. The press was so vicious, dubbing Merrill 'Mr Bette Davis', that she threatened to go straight back to America when the *Queen Elizabeth* returned.

She arrived at the Savoy Hotel in a flaring temper to face a disagreeable press conference. She wasn't feeling well and looked haggard and worn – which the press photographers exploited cruelly. Perhaps because of the extreme openness and depth of her emotion, and an increased fondness for alcohol, she had aged very suddenly and looked much older than she did in *All About Eve*. Few reporters failed to notice this.

As a result, her insecurity was enormously increased. Val Guest, who went to the Savoy to talk with her, says, 'She was very uneasy. She had struggled and got to the top and viewed anyone she didn't know as the person who was going to undo fifteen years of stardom and slogging. I tried everything, foul means and fair, to win her confidence. At last I did. She showed a toilet sense of humour, she was loud and boisterous, but even then there was a problem: she had no sense of humour about herself.* She took herself seriously to the point of excluding humour. Because herself was her career.'

Irving Rapper, who had directed *Now, Voyager* and *Deception,* was imported as director. Robert Krasker was chosen as cinematographer. Bette was very nervous of working for the first time with a British cameraman. Conscious of her ageing appearance she was afraid of a

*Mr Guest was wrong!

285

cinematographer who wouldn't protect her as her
favourite Haller and Polito had done. She had reached
an age at which the cameraman was as essential to her as
the make-up artist, and considerably more important
than the director since she could be relied upon, at least
in this instance, to do much of the directing herself.

She agreed to Krasker's selection on the interesting
ground that he had won an Academy Award. Val Guest
continues:

> She would *only* have an Academy Award-winning
> man. She insisted on having photographic tests
> done with him before we started production. Bob
> was not a 'glamour' photographer but a very fine,
> realistic cameraman. We all went in to look at the
> tests. Everyone was terrified of Bette. She didn't
> dole out warmth that day! The lights went down
> and the tests came on the screen. I could see Bette
> was very unhappy about her haggard appearance.
> Suddenly, she snapped open a cigarette lighter, lit
> up a cigarette, and said, with an acidity only she
> could manage, 'And for *what* did this man get his
> Academy Award?' Bob had won it for *The Third
> Man,* which was shot in war-torn Vienna. And
> someone at the back of the projection room said, in
> answer to her question, and very loudly, 'For
> shooting ruins!' There was immediate chaos. Bette
> yelled out, 'Put the lights on! Stop everything! Who
> said that?' No one owned up, needless to say. She
> stamped out. But afterwards, more tests were
> done, and she was pleased. She was a sport. She
> kept Krasker on.

Work began at Walton Studios. It was miserable from
the beginning. Bette realised she had been insane to take
the script on in the first place. She argued constantly
with Irving Rapper, and virtually controlled the shoot-

ing, insisting on rehearsing scenes over and over again, dismissing an anxious camera operator who explained the difficulties of a staircase shot with a sharp, 'I don't know about that. It's *your* problem!' She tended to fluff her lines, overplayed some scenes, and underplayed others. She smoked forty cigarettes a day, rising to sixty during particularly strenuous days. At one stage, after completing a staircase scene, she was so exhausted she lay at its foot without being able to get up.

She gave one of the worst performances of her career in the movie. When Rapper complained of her excessive intensity, she threw a bucket of water over him. She called her male romantic lead, rival to Merrill, Anthony Steel, 'a beautiful prop', which infuriated him. When they played a love scene on a bank, they rehearsed over and over again, and finally Bette said, 'Look, just let me do it. Do nothing. Let me do it.' She wound up on top of him, completely blocking him from the camera.

The entire unit took off to the Yorkshire moors and had to sleep on couches in farmhouses. One night, everybody gathered in damp and chilly conditions, feeling thoroughly depressed, before a radio to hear the broadcast of the Academy Awards. Screwed up to an extreme of tension Bette quipped cheerfully, pretending not to care whether she won or not. The rain beat down outside. The announcements droned on and on.

Everyone expected to hear tremendous news. When the words, 'And the winning actress is . . .' came over the air, Bette jumped up. At the words 'Judy Holliday' she sat down abruptly. She gave the performance of her lifetime in front of the others, lying with consummate bravery: 'That's *good!* A *newcomer* got it! I couldn't be more *pleased!*' Not a soul believed her.

Bette stayed at a place called Greatfosters near London. A consolation of the shooting of the picture was that she enjoyed the hotel and Merrill proved to be unusually affectionate. Once more, as she had done in the late 1930s, she liked the English people. The Elizabethan atmosphere of the hotel – the family occupied a wing – fascinated her and sometimes at night she poked about, looking for ghosts and secret passages in a humorous child-like mood.

Bette was enormously relieved when *Another Man's Poison* was completed and the Merrills could set sail for America (Bette still hated flying) on board the *Queen Mary*.

On the way back, in heavy weather, Margot seemed to cry excessively. But still Bette had no inkling of what was to come.

Another Man's Poison was a critical failure and scarcely broke even at the box-office. It was a film so embarrassingly bad as to be virtually unwatchable today. Bette returned to California in a surprisingly good mood, delighted with B.D. and Margot, enjoying her role as a mother, still convinced Merrill was right for her. The couple, who had been living briefly in Malibu, moved into a large ugly house in West Hollywood and began reading scripts. Gary received the first offer: Zanuck sent him the screenplay of an omnibus picture, *Phone Call from a Stranger*, in which he would play the survivor of an air crash. Bette insisted on playing the small part of a crippled woman injured in an underwater swim. Zanuck was amazed she would want to play what was in essence a bit part and this may have been a mistake in her career. Many people felt she was slipping; in fact, this desire to appear in a supporting role had surfaced before: when she had wanted to act the part of Cassie Tower in *King's Row* and when she had acted a bit part as a nurse in Irving Rapper's *Shining Victory*.

She gave an admirable performance in *Phone Call from a Stranger* giving great depth and honesty to lines all too clearly suited to a character called Hoke. She and

Merrill decided B.D. and Margot needed a baby brother, and they adopted a little boy, naming him Michael Merrill.

The signs of a declining career were ominous. After the triumph of *All About Eve,* there had been nothing more than a melodramatic failure and a small part in an episode picture. And now came a depressing example of Hollywood hackdom: *The Star,* a story of an actress down on her luck, reduced to selling lingerie at the May Company, arguing with a ferocious family and driving about drunkenly through the Beverly Hills settings of her former glory. A weakness had begun to show itself: poor judgment of scripts – the downfall of many performers. She had thought the script of *Another Man's Poison* was good, but at least she had become disillusioned when work started on the picture. In the case of *The Star* she continued to admire the script until the end of shooting. And she made the mistake, tactical as well as professional, of acting a failed performer: an open invitation to critics who said she was all too visibly a failure. Several reviewers seized on the publicity flimflam for the production ('The orchids . . . the furs . . . the diamonds that were the star's were all gone now . . . and nothing remained . . . but the woman!').

The picture was directed by Stuart Heisler and co-starred the heavyweight, rather Neanderthal Sterling Hayden, a man of many talents flawed by a streak of intellectual pretension. Shot cheaply in twenty-four days, the picture's chief merit was that it gave a seedy, authentically grim picture of Hollywood in the 1950s.

Bette clashed with Stuart Heisler on the first day they met. Heisler says:

I got into the damnedest wrangle with her about the script. I said, 'These writers, for Chrissakes, they're silly. All they're doing is pussyfooting you.' And she said, 'What do you mean? I like those

289

little touches.' I said, 'They don't mean a damn thing. You've got a subject here that's got guts in it. These little things they want you to do, Christ, they'll ruin the whole picture. Just throw the whole thing out of the window.' And she went into the goddamnedest scene and I thought, 'Oh, shit, this is it.' Anyway, we went through the script and I kept telling her, 'That's no good, that's no good, that's throwing time and effort away.' At the end, she shrugged and gave in. I loved her for that and we never argued again.

Heisler shot almost the entire picture in first takes; Bette enjoyed the challenge. Her keen mind ensured a degree of realism, particularly in the scene when the actress is dismissed from the lingerie counter at the May Company: a bitter moment evoking those days before customers in department stores were reduced to helping themselves from the racks. But not even she could save the poverty row atmosphere of the picture, with its grey, grainy images. *Time* magazine said that Bette was 'down to her last thousand tantrums,' and today the picture looks that way. It is unfortunate that while eagerly accepting the script of *The Star,* Bette turned down the screenplay of *Come Back, Little Sheba,* William Inge's play about a drab housewife that would probably have restored her position as a major star.

During the shooting of *The Star,* Bette formed a new friendship that would last the rest of her life. There was a scene in which a child, the star's daughter, Natalie Wood, was to fall in water from a pier. Stuart Heisler wanted to throw Natalie in; the little girl was terrified, and cried hysterically. Bette heard Natalie's cries, came out of her trailer, picked Natalie up and said to Heisler, 'If you make Natalie do this, I'll walk off the picture. Who do you think she is? Johnny Weissmuller? You mustn't do this kind of thing to a child.' Heisler backed down and Bette took over the direction of the scene.

In the summer of 1952, Bette began to think of returning to the stage. Somebody came up with the idea of her following Judy Garland into the Palace in New York, playing scenes from her pictures and singing various numbers. Fortunately, this ghastly idea was never realised. Instead, she was approached to appear in a scarcely more inspiring format, in an absurd musical revue called *Two's Company*. Vernon Duke came to the house in West Hollywood and played the tinkly score, which contained not a single memorable number. But Bette's disastrous judgment drove her into this catastrophe.

She made a mistake as serious as undertaking a show which called for singing and dancing, neither of which she could manage with more than minimum competence. She also refused an understudy, which meant that severe pressure was put on her not to be absent for a single performance.

Bette had for some time had tooth problems. But, obsessed with work and career, she didn't have the patience (or the time in a busy schedule) to face a dentist. The poison from an infected tooth drained into her system without her knowing it and caused her to feel tired and ill much of the time. Moreover, the awareness that she had rendered herself literally irreplaceable made her weary and strained. She and Merrill moved from West Hollywood to New York and she went into gruelling rehearsals. She wound up exhausted by her commitment and intensity, by forcing her voice when she had no singing ability and stretching her forty-three-year-old body to the limit in order to manage complicated stage movements. Her lack of a basic callisthenic training programme each morning through her life and her fondness for smoking and alcohol told on her severely. She had forgotten that a stage star has to have the physique of an athlete in order to stand and move about for hours at high pressure night after night.

Two's Company opened in Detroit in October. She went on the stage completely wrung out, feeling seriously ill after a night without sleep during which Merrill had in vain begged her to relax. She had to go on stage in the opening scene in a large magician's box. It was airless, cramped and hot and Bette, when she burst out of it, suddenly felt giddy. She sang a horrible song called 'Good Little Girls' and then the lights began to swim in front of her. Just as she entered the third chorus, she blacked out. The audience screamed as she fell forward, jarring her chin. Merrill rushed to her side as the curtain was rung down and said to her sharply, 'Get up, Bette, get up!' It was the right thing to do and she was grateful for the instruction. She struggled to her feet and walked out front to deliver the memorable quip, 'Well, you can't say I didn't fall for you!' Incredibly, she forced herself to complete the performance, which involved several complicated musical numbers and some dance movements. She had never been more painfully aware of the pressure of knowing that she had to go on because people had bought tickets to see her, and that her replacement by an understudy would result in the play closing and the bitter disappointment of her former mentor, the producer John Murray Anderson.

With fairly good reviews, the show proceeded to Pittsburgh and Boston. Bette cut the opening song from the show: superstition got the better of her. When she arrived in New York in the icy December of 1952 the poisoned tooth had severely weakened her system. And added to the physical illness was a psychosomatic one. The sickness of fear that she would let herself and everybody else down; that she would not return in triumph to Broadway; that she would not be the big Broadway star everyone would expect after her performance in *All About Eve*.

292

She was so sick she was unable to attend rehearsals. John Murray Anderson had put in a great deal of work in changing the show at the last minute. She had to go on without being able to prepare for changes.

She struggled through the opening night, imitating Tallulah Bankhead, her beloved Jeanne Eagels, a hillbilly singer complete with briar pipe, a tenement dweller and a torch singer. The reviews were devastating. Brooks Atkinson, who had encouraged her at the outset of her career, wrote, 'No one should be surprised to discover that her severe performing is on the elementary side – colourless and monotonous. She had never had a chance to learn the sharp techniques of musical acting.' The critic of the New York *World Telegram* took a more mixed view: 'Her dancing is likely to consist of hip rolls, marching and none too steady lifts by a whole corps of male partners. Her singing is deep, husky, very articulate and rhythmic, but not very musical. In sketches she can do almost anything better than whip off a laugh line. But . . . Miss Davis is electric, as she always had been on the screen . . . Somewhere along the line you are dazzled and in the end awed.'

Bette was devastated by the reviews; she was convinced that critics were inspired by snobbery about Hollywood stars. However, she was cheered by the packed houses, and the show ran successfully on her name to predominantly gay audiences through the long winter into 1953. But the infection continued to drain into her neck and shoulders, causing pain that was often very severe. In early March, she had to be injected daily at the New York Hospital with penicillin and pain-killing drugs to get her through the performances. She managed to survive a special benefit for actors. But after the Sunday night performance she was rushed to hospital where Dr Stanley Berman extracted the infected tooth. Examining the jawbone, Berman discovered what he had feared most, that she had osteomyelitis, a disease of

293

the bone that was very rare in adults. He told Bette she would have to have a major operation in which the diseased tissue would be scraped from the jaw. The play was closed immediately and the road tour cancelled.

The ferocious Walter Winchell immediately told his public that Bette had cancer. Propped up miserably in her hospital bed, Bette read this ugly lie in Winchell's column and fired off a demand he retract it at once. He did – and published the telegram in his column. But many people still believed she was stricken. It would be three years before she recovered completely. And a worse suffering lay immediately ahead.

Fourteen

DURING THE run of *Two's Company,* Bette's misery had been increased by the strange, unsettling behaviour of little Margot. The child had continued crying all night even at the age of two: sobbing hysterically and sometimes throwing her bedclothes on the floor. Margot took an exceptionally long time to adjust to her new parents and would alternate excessive affection with unexpected bouts of hostility. Ruthie warned Bette that similar indications of mental and emotional imbalance had been found in Bobby when Bobby had been a little girl. Bette and Merrill did their utmost to create a normal home – in the face of the painful realities of show business, with its basic insecurity and enforced shifts of residence: drastic threats to the stability of any household.

It soon emerged that there was a far worse problem than simply a severe emotional disturbance in Margot. In the period following *Two's Company,* the Merrills moved to a large house, rather gloomy in winter months, and situated high up over the ocean at Cape Elizabeth, Maine. They embarked on life in their new residence with a kind of manic enthusiasm peculiar to film and theatre people, remodelling, refurnishing, working on the garden and keeping a succession of servants in a dither of excitement followed by joyous anxiety. Within weeks, the imagined idyll had turned into something approaching a nightmare.

One afternoon, when Bette was paying a visit to her

neighbours, she rashly left three-year-old Margot on her own in the automobile. When Bette emerged, she was disturbed to see that Margot had angrily stripped off all her clothes on that chilly day and flung them into the drive. The neighbour made light of this, but Bette felt a stab of unease. And when, a few days later, Margot again flung off her clothes and threw them through a window, Bette realised something serious was wrong.

Night began to prove unbearable. Margot would not just cry, but suddenly jump to her feet and scream like an animal, almost cracking the bars of the crib. Every effort Bette and Merrill made to have her settle down proved futile. Often, the Merrills would be up all night struggling with Margot – doing everything possible to make her relax.

One morning, Bette came in the playroom. She had, some weeks before, given Margot an adorable kitten, and had been worried because Margot seemed indifferent to the pet. On this occasion, Bette was pleased to see Margot fondling the creature. As Bette opened the door a look of hatred distorted the child's face. Margot squeezed the throat of the terrified animal until it began to choke to death. Bette screamed with horror; she came perilously close to striking Margot across the face. She snatched the kitten from her – and began to cry from desperation and exhaustion after a week virtually without sleep.

Still recovering slowly from the painful operation on her jaw, and the distress caused her by the column suggesting she had cancer, Bette came as close to a nervous breakdown over Margot as she had since Farney's near death from pneumonia and her frantic air flight to him in 1943. Often, her quarrels with Merrill came about because they vented on each other an anger that sprang from frustration; an anger that it was not in them to vent on the child.

A horrifying episode took place in the summer of

1953. Bette and Merrill tried to encourage B.D., Margot and Michael to play together, so that Margot would feel she was a member of a family that loved her and wanted to protect her. But B.D. found it difficult to sleep with Margot and had to be kept in a separate room.

During a hot late afternoon, Michael and Margot were playing together when Margot suddenly pulled Michael's hair out by the roots with a strength astonishing in so small a child. Bette heard the screams and came running. The two children had disappeared. Almost vomiting, her stomach in knots, Bette ran all over the house looking for the children. Then she heard a scream from the bar. There was a sound of shattering glass. Bette opened the door. She felt dizzy for a moment at what she saw.

The floor was strewn with broken cocktail glasses. Michael was covered in blood. Margot stood laughing as she watched him bleed from the many cuts on his shoulders and arms. She had a piece of broken glass in one hand.

Bette broke down completely. Fortunately, Merrill proved to be a tower of strength in this agonising moment. He cleaned Michael's wounds and soothed him. It was obvious, Bette wrote in articles over the years, that Margot needed professional help. Bette and Gary took Margot to New York's Presbyterian Hospital for tests.

Waiting for the results of the tests was an appalling experience. Bette was worn out physically and mentally when she went in with Merrill for a meeting with the doctors at the end of a week. They broke it to her that the child wasn't merely displaying symptoms of dementia. She was also brain-injured and must have been from birth. Her I.Q. was sixty and would probably never improve. The brain damage was incurable and was probably caused by the mother taking a drug to abort the child.

In this desolate moment, the doctors tried to provide

some hope. They told Bette and Merrill that she could at least be given some degree of training to enable her to adjust better to her surroundings. Infinite care and patience would help. It was a question of Margot being sympathetically controlled. Normal people and things would drive a retarded child into desperate anger and frustration. The doctors asked Bette if Margot seemed to have unusual strength for her age. Bette explained that Margot actually threw heavy chairs and tables out of windows without injuring herself.

The doctors advised the Merrills not to continue having Margot at home. It was obvious that centring an entire life around a sick child would ultimately and most seriously affect Bette's health. At forty-four, the suffering that her always excessively nervous temperament endured through Margot had aged her drastically. Her shockingly haggard appearance alarmed Ruthie and Bobby so much when they came to visit that they insisted on Bette returning Margot to the adoption agency on the grounds that the child had been illegally supplied.

Bette violently disagreed. Her motherly instinct made her want to devote herself utterly to giving Margot some degree of light in the hell in which she lived. But her family, Gary and the doctors finally overrode her obstinate and well-intended objections. They induced her to take Margot to an institution known as the Lochland School on Lake Geneva in northern New York State. Florence Stewart was the director: a genius in the field of retarded children.

The Merrills drove to Lake Geneva in agony of mind at parting with Margot and submitting her to an alien environment. But as soon as they saw the Lochland School, which they had feared would be a grim institution with guards and high walls, they were deeply relieved. The school was in a converted nineteenth-century mansion with a new brick schoolhouse in the grounds and many oak and elder trees shading the smooth green lawns that rolled down to the nearby lake.

They were even more pleased when they met Florence Stewart. A warm, lovable, but firmly disciplined woman, she exuded good sense and efficiency. She took the Merrills and Margot to meet many of the retarded pupils, showing how they were taught coordination, peaceable cohabitation and various crafts that could control their extreme nervousness. The children were given special clothes, which, though attractive, were as effective as strait-jackets in preventing them from leaping from their beds and causing themselves injury at night. Miss Stewart explained that the first essential for a retarded pupil was for her to feel she could contribute something to the world; that she was not a useless near-animal whom people barely tolerated; that she must be constantly praised because retardation brought with it a profound, inborn inferiority complex.

Bette and Gary didn't immediately decide to leave Margot at the school. They needed some time to think about it. They drove back to Maine. As they made their way along a leafy country road Bette suddenly burst into tears. The idea of sending her beloved daughter away proved too much for her. But with her usual common sense, the New England pragmatism that overcame the more hysterical strain in her nature, Bette pulled herself together and realised her tears were selfish. Her mind was made up. Merrill was greatly relieved.

A week or so later, Bette, again fighting back tears, her vitality very low, dressed Margot in a little sailor suit and Gary flew the child back to school.

Bette was constantly in tears after Margot left – wondering if she could endure much more. But she rallied, and, with Margot gone, began to enjoy some desperately needed sleep. She learned not to call the school too often; to control her overwrought nature and let the teachers get on with their training of Margot. She would go over to Lochland; and in the summer and at

Christmas Margot came to stay, showing signs of improvement but still unable to control her rampant, terrifying hostility.

Their life should have been completely peaceful during this period of semi-retirement. But even though Bette was inactive, recovering through late 1953 and into 1954 until at last she began to feel strong again, Merrill had to go on working for the sake of his career. And here was another problem. It was a torment to this driving and ambitious actor that all the way from the heights of *All Above Eve* he was suddenly reduced to motion pictures of surpassing mediocrity like *A Blueprint for Murder, Witness to Murder, The Black Dakotas* and *The Human Jungle*. The worst blow of all was that at thirty-eight his contract at Twentieth Century-Fox was summarily cancelled. Sometimes, he would fly with Bette, B.D. and Michael, Bette hating every minute of the air journey, to shack up in a Los Angeles hotel, trudge grumblingly through weeks of futile shooting and at the end have a crushing sense that his career was virtually over. To anyone as driven and violent as Merrill, this was nothing short of a catastrophe. Bette alleged he would slam his fist on walls or tables. She said he took to drinking bouts, trying to douse his disappointment – Bette testified later under oath in court – in the use of alcohol. The result was that his robust constitution and powerful physique were undermined by shaky health and extreme nervous distress. The marriage somehow kept going, perhaps more because of love of the normal children and concern for Margot than anything else. The misery the Merrills endured over Margot was a binding factor; but by the early months of 1954 Bette had begun to drink herself.

For the sake of sanity, Bette needed to work again. Zanuck came to the rescue. He found a script which would, he felt, restore her to the top: *Sir Walter Raleigh*, later retitled *The Virgin Queen*. She liked the script, which dealt with an older and more subdued monarch than the ferocious figure of *The Private Lives of Elizabeth and Essex*. The problem was that Merrill was in a TV series in New York and there would have to be a separation. But the couple agreed that this mightn't be a bad idea. The ordeal with Margot, Gary's alleged drinking and quarrels had made living together increasingly painful in recent months. For every cookout, lobster picnic or beach visit, for every evening of laughter and family games, each could count at least a dozen traumas and turmoils that year.

Once more, in February, 1955, Bette found herself back in Hollywood. CinemaScope had come in, temporarily revitalising the industry but reducing motion pictures to watery versions of the stage. Because of the peculiar demands of the wide screen, performers found themselves compelled to learn full scenes, to make exits and entrances without the protection of clever cutting, and to meet the requirements called for by Broadway or the West End. Needless to say, this was no problem for Bette, but she resented the ugly blueish tints of DeLuxe Color and the clumsy CinemaScope cameras.

She was also suffering from an old problem that was aggravated by middle age: the extreme sensitivity of her pale blue eyes to both indoor and outdoor powerful light; and her delicate skin which, still missing the top layer after her burning incident as a child, freckled and scorched in scenes calling for direct sunlight. *The Virgin Queen*'s cameraman, Charles G. Clarke, remembers, 'The stronger the sun, the deeper the shadows, and the great problem with lighting exteriors is filling the shadows. Bette didn't like the bright lights too much. She kept saying to me they were too intense for her. And she thought she knew something about cinematography and lighting. A couple of times she'd try and tell me my job, but I don't put up with that kind of business.'

Clarke remembers a particular incident:

One thing I recall was when we were working in a courtyard. It was supposed to be an English courtyard. It was an exterior, naturally. And when I'd finished lighting it, she demanded that the whole thing be diffused. That meant breaking for lunch and having the grips come in and hanging and stretching these diffusers all over the set. I think her main reason for demanding that was just to show that she was the star. If it had been necessary to use diffusers, I would have done it in the first place. That cost us a couple of hours.

Bette's quarrels with Clarke had to be refereed by director Henry Koster, who had made his name with the Deanna Durbin pictures. On one occasion, Bette was seated on a bed, her hair shaved back, in an ugly red wig, feeling terrible. Clarke took what seemed to her an unbearable amount of time setting up the lights and moving the camera on instructions to his operator towards the bed. Suddenly, unexpectedly, she exploded against the infuriated Clarke and production stopped for over an hour while the savage words flew to and fro.

Bette's regal behaviour, appropriate to her role, upset the entire unit. The brutal fact was that she no longer occupied the supreme position in Hollywood that would justify behaviour acceptable at Warner's in her heyday. Marilyn Monroe was the queen of Twentieth Century-Fox: not Bette Davis. This fact was often and painfully brought home to her. But Zanuck, surprisingly in view of his ruthlesssness, was very supportive, and gave Bette extraordinary licence – and a dressing-room almost comparable with Monroe's.

The picture lacked the splendour of *Elizabeth and Essex*. It was a somewhat dowdy production, drab and pedestrian, and the public notably failed to respond at the previews. The result was that the studio virtually

302

threw the picture away, and it lost money: sure sign that Bette's star was rapidly fading.

Back in Maine, at the house they called Witch Way ('because a witch used to live in it,' Bette used to say), the Merrills continued their uneasy, spiky marriage. Their separate schedules (Merrill was still making third-rate thrillers) and their temperaments did not lead to comfort and ease between pictures. Bette tried to occupy herself with new scripts. At last she found one she liked, written by Daniel Taradash and Elick Moll, *The Library*. The picture was written in 1951, when Joe McCarthy and his red-baiting was at its height. It was a story directly antagonistic to McCarthy's point of view: about a librarian accused of left-wing commitment. The story included a ritual burning of books.

Mary Pickford originally was supposed to have left her long retirement of nineteen years to make the picture. But she was annoyed when a headline in the New York *Herald Tribune* announcing her comeback was headed 'Life Begins at Fifty-Eight'. And within days of her committing verbally to the project, the right-wing forces closed in on her. The ferocious Hedda Hopper called her and asked her if she had gone out of her mind wanting to appear in a Red motion picture. Pickford panicked that she would be identified with the left wing and backed out after only one reading. The right-wing Barbara Stanwyck and Irene Dunne were approached, but predictably declined. Once more, Bette was fourth in line for the part and accepted it immediately.

Daniel Taradash and the producer Julian Blaustein flew to Maine to discuss the script with Bette. She was so determined to make it, felt it was so important, that she took a very small sum of money up front against a percentage of the gross. But no sooner had she agreed to go ahead, feeling that the part of an embattled librarian would be a wonderful opportunity for a big performance, than Harry Cohn, boss of Columbia, decided the

McCarthy era was ancient history and no one would want to see the picture. It was only when producer and director agreed to make the movie for no money and a profit share that he agreed to go ahead.

Bette began shooting the movie, retitled *Storm Center,* in the suffocating August of 1955. It was shot in the pleasant small town of Santa Rosa, California, where Hitchcock had made *Shadow of a Doubt.* Bette enjoyed Santa Rosa, the warm and friendly people, the pleasant setting with its tree-lined streets and lack of pressure. But as always there were problems; her nerves began to fray as the shooting went on.

A major casting problem was the child actor Kevin Coughlin, who later became a casting director. Sensational at the reading, crying convincingly on cue, he never cried again. Taradash says, 'His mother was on the set, and it would make me sick because she would take him away and pinch him to make him cry on cue but it failed to work every time.'

In spite of her love of children, Bette became impatient with Coughlin and with Taradash's incapacity to direct the child. A writer, Taradash had little or no feeling for direction. And Bette herself was irritated by this. She was also infuriated because local women's club leaders beseeched her with letters warning her that the film was subversive and that for the good of herself and her children she should walk off the picture. There was one gruesome experience during the shooting, followed by a surprise. Taradash says:

One day, Bette had a day off. We were shooting a scene in which Kevin Coughlin and some of the neighbourhood kids discuss communism. They wandered along a street with small residential houses. As we passed a front door, a hag with wild hair jumped out and screamed, 'I told you motion picture people I didn't want you around. Now you get the hell out of here or I will call the police!' She screamed on and on and on. My God, I was terrified! I said to the assistant director, 'Didn't you get permission from all these residents? Didn't you get releases? You should have given them fifty dollars apiece.' 'Fifty dollars?' the old harridan shrieked. 'You're out of your ever-loving mind! Think that would buy me off? You're crazy, the whole lot of you! I'm calling the police right now!' And then suddenly the hag pulled off her grey wig and stood there holding her sides with laughter. It was Bette!

At times, Bette changed from joking to toughness. Taradash says:

She *can* be tough. She had worked with Willie Wyler, who would often make actors and actresses do ten, fifteen, twenty takes without telling them why. There was one scene that I did with her, where you could see the title of the book, *The Communist Dream*. It was a close shot of her as she's replying to the city councilman. I wanted it framed so that you could see the title of the book as she talks about it. It was a long speech and she did the take perfectly. But the camera operator whispered to me that the aperture was set so that the book could not be seen. So I asked him if he changed the position of the camera a bit, could he get the book in without any trouble, and he said yes. So I said, 'Bette, I'd appreciate it if we could do it once more.' And she said, 'Why?' I didn't really want to tell her the truth, so I said, 'I don't know why.' And then she said, 'Well in that case I'm not going to do it.' She said, 'If you can't tell me what change you want, there's no point in doing a scene over for no reason.' I said, 'Bette, I really know, I just have some kind of a feeling we ought to do it again.' I didn't want to tell her the reason, because I was afraid she would blow up and say, 'If I can be a pro you can be pros too, and if you want something in the shot, then get it in the shot.' So I said, 'I really don't know, I just feel we can do it better.' I tried to be as vague as possible. 'I just can't articulate it, Bette.' Finally I said, 'All right, Bette, if you don't want to do another take, then we won't do it.' And then she said, 'Oh, all right, go ahead . . .' The irony of this story is that I discovered later that the first take turned out to have a negative scratch on it. So the second take was wonderful for two reasons: we got the book in, and there was no scratch on the negative.

Bette was very lonely during the shooting. She missed Merrill; there were rumours that they had actually separated: rumours which were unfounded but still unsettling. Moreover, many of the crew were having affairs with people in the town or brought their wives in; producer and director were too busy to escort Bette to dinner or cocktails at night. They were preoccupied with preparing the pages for the next day's work. She usually ate dinner alone.

Back in Hollywood, Bette was given the star dressing-room. One day she heard a noise from the wall next to her dressing-table. She was astonished when the wall flew open and Harry Cohn walked in. He began to make an obscene gesture. She snapped in her best frost-and-fire manner, 'How dare you come in here. Get out immediately and don't dare come back!' Suddenly sheepish, the all-powerful studio boss turned on his heel and disappeared. Later that day, Bette told Daniel Taradash of this alarming apparition from the woodwork. He said, 'Oh, Bette, I wouldn't flatter yourself too much. He hadn't been told they moved Kim Novak to an even bigger dressing-room last night!'

Storm Center was as worthy as it was dull and notably failed to set the box-office on fire. Bette felt her hopes dashed; she was slightly revived by being offered the leading role in Paddy Chayevsky's *The Catered Affair*. And along with it the chance to rent Fay Bainter's attractive house at Malibu.

The Catered Affair was made at MGM under the director Richard Brooks. Bette played a Brooklyn mother, overweight, grey-wigged and unattractive, but with great warmth and charm. Bette was strongly attracted to Brooks, an appealing and handsome man's man: sure sign that her marriage to Merrill, with its endless conficts of ego and schedules, was now in even worse trouble. She made a curious indirect reference to Wyler during one conversation with Brooks. Brooks recalls:

One day, after we'd been shooting a day or two, we were sitting around. I was lining up a shot and she was sitting in a chair beside me. She said, 'Do you think it's going to be all right?' And I said, 'I think we're getting into it.' She fell silent and didn't say anything. And I said, 'You know, probably every director you've ever worked with has been in love with you.' And she said, 'Really? Why?' I said, 'I don't know why. But that could happen. You're a very sensual woman.' She didn't say anything. I went on: *'Jezebel, Dangerous, Marked Woman, Little Foxes* – in all those pictures you can see the love that your directors had for you. I don't know if any of those loves were consummated, but I can see it on the screen.' And she said, 'You can?' And I said, 'Yeah – it's up there.' She said, 'You're crazy.' She then said, 'Name the pictures where you think it was consummated.' So I named a

307

couple. I'm not going to tell which ones. She said, 'You really think you can see it up there?' And then she said, 'Well, we could have been great together – but I was a coward.'

Brooks remembers that there was a difficult scene in which the housewife played by Davis had to come apart under pressures of arranging her daughter's wedding. She had to start sobbing as she left the parlour, walk down a hallway, and enter a bedroom where she completely broke down. The husband (Ernest Borgnine) was in the kitchen swilling beer. 'I asked Bette not to lie on the bed sobbing as the script indicated,' Brooks said. 'I asked her to sit on a chair, put her arms on the bed, lay her head on her arms and just sob her heart out.'

Brooks explained the scene to Bette. She asked him, looking him straight in the eye, 'What kind of crying are you talking about?' Brooks got the impression that she had so vast a repertoire of emotion she could turn on tears instantly at any degree of intensity that was called for. He told her, 'From the belly. I don't just want to see tears in your eyes. Your whole life is falling apart.' Bette told him, 'Fine. I'll do it. But I can only do it once. Can you get it in the first take?' He told her, very honestly, that he wasn't sure. For two hours, he laid out the scene in terms of camera movement so that the camera could follow her all the time in one continuous take, that wouldn't have to be shot again. The camera could not be mounted on tracks because Bette might stumble. Finally, the camera was mounted on a three-wheel dolly. Brooks said, when he was ready, 'Are you OK, Miss Davis?' She had spent the whole two hours in deepest concentration. She replied, 'I won't say anything. I'll just nod to you when I'm ready.' Five minutes later, screwing up her emotions, she nodded. Brooks shot the scene perfectly; Bette built the emotion from the first sob to the final storm of hopeless tears. It was one of her finest moments on the screen.

There was another wonderful moment at the end of the picture. The husband and wife are left alone in their depressing apartment. All the poison of their many quarrels has drained out of them and now they are left with nothing except four walls and little or nothing to say. And at last they go to the church for the daughter's wedding. A lovely touch had the father start to get into the taxi ahead of the mother and then remember his manners and open the door for her. Bette's laugh at that moment had to be a combination of sheer amusement, resignation and an understanding of her husband's reality. Brooks says, 'One laugh told it all. She stopped as she got into the taxi and she looked at him and the look was wonderful. She was of course so supreme a professional that she instinctively knew where the camera was even though she couldn't see it. Her laugh was so joyful, it ended the picture perfectly. What an actress she is!'

Much of the performance was modelled by Brooks on his mother. Bette wanted to know what his mother was like. Brooks said, 'She suffered all the time.' Bette asked, 'What kind of suffering?' Brooks told her, 'My mother would just put her hand on her heart and say, constantly, "You want to make me suffer? You want to do this to me?" ' Bette understood instinctively what he meant. Brooks comments, 'She was terrific. So very funny. And just like my mother! I almost came apart. Although she wasn't trained in a Method way, she was a method actress in a sense. Her capacity for invention was amazing. She reached for the essence of a scene. She knew how to transmit feelings. It's instinctive with her.'

The mother in *A Catered Affair* remains one of Davis's towering peaks of achievement. She subdued all of her mannerisms and affectations in order to give a harsh, uncompromisingly realistic performance that no doubt compensated her for not getting a similar part in *Come Back, Little Sheba*. She went to Brooklyn and bought cheap dresses off the hook. She watched neighbourhood women and caught the Irish-American intonation in their voices to perfection. To this day, Brooks remains overpowered by her. Years later, when he was directing Geraldine Page in *Sweet Bird of Youth* he wanted Miss Page to walk down a Hollywood staircase with the style and command of a beautiful motion picture star. Miss Page had been told by a vicious acquaintance that she was a fool to consider herself attractive; that she was all too well cast as a faded beauty who had to buy sex from a gigolo. This so seriously affected Geraldine Page that she was unable to play the staircase scene correctly for the director. In a fury, she asked Brooks, 'What the hell are you talking about? What does a movie star walk like?'

Brooks, knowing she would be offended, told her not to be and advised her he would be rushing the print of a picture to her so that she could see the way to walk downstairs like a star. This was, of course, a blow to any actress's pride but Miss Page bravely confronted the task of seeing an example laid before her. She went into a screening room and suddenly *A Stolen Life* came on the screen with two Bette Davises walking downstairs. Fortunately, Geraldine was a sport. She went straight to Richard Brooks and said, 'It was wonderful. Don't say another word. I know exactly how to play the scene.' And she did.

It is appalling that Bette did not win an Oscar for *The Catered Affair*. And it is unfortunate that *Storm Center* was released so soon afterwards, out of sequence, because it proved to be ineffective and dulled the impact of the finer picture.

In 1957, Bette spent as much time as possible visiting Margot. The child was still at Lochland School, and Bette described her slight progress in an article entitled 'It Could Happen to You.' She wrote:

For example, you can tell an average child for maybe one week – don't forget to brush your teeth. It took almost a year to teach Margot to do it. Lacking coordination, it is difficult for retarded children to learn to dress themselves so that clothes must be provided with oversized buttons at first. They walk slowly, they dress slowly, they start out and forget where they are going. They require infinite patience and no parent can possibly give them this most rigorous of over-and-over training in the world.

Although Margot is a very well-trained little girl by now she can only behave up to a point. Then she becomes exhausted. It's a part of the training for the children to be of use to themselves which gives them a feeling of accomplishment. This is why school is so essential. Every human being, normal or retarded, must have something he can do well. And praise for a child is so important. We are all starved for it.

Margot weaves and makes things. She writes letters, though it takes hours of course, and she truly adores coming home for visits. With her, one must be very quiet, though firm. I must talk to her in short sentences, or it becomes too complicated. Retarded children require lots of rest. They can listen to music by the hour. You can tell they respond to it because they always rock back and forth.

By contrast with Margot, B.D. turned out to be a happy and well-adjusted child. She grew very tall and big-boned, a strapping youngster who could take Bette on any time in an argument and win. Bette loved her more than any human being. She devoted herself to her with driving intensity to make sure she had the best education possible. She had a strong rapport with her;

311

she often had her on the set to watch her work. But she was relieved in a way that B.D. seemed to have no ambition to be an actress herself. Perhaps B.D. had seen too much of the misery of it.

In the late 1950s, Ruthie lived in Laguna, still in the grand style to which she was accustomed, costing Bette a fortune with her bills. Bobby continued to be in and out of sanatoriums, and the cost of B.D.'s schooling, Ruthie's high living and Bobby's expensive nursing home was crippling. The pressures were severe and often made Bette ill; she had to carry so much on her famous shoulders, and all her money was running away. But she was happy to give herself and her income to her dependants.

Bette worked in television in the early months of 1957. She told Cecil Smith of the *Los Angeles Times* on 10 March 1957, 'I had to get into the medium eventually. I had to find out what this new thing was. And now that I'm in it I love it. Simply love it! Such wonderful economy. They're making films the way we used to make them. Back twenty-five years ago when I began. Movies have become so enormously wasteful, so time consuming. The thing that happened in the movies – the technicians took over. Now television's giving back that acting to the actors again. We used to make six, eight pictures a year. So these television schedules – rehearse two days, shoot three – don't terrify me. I like them.' But she was afraid of live television: she panicked over the difficult costume changes in Playhouse 90's *If You Knew Elizabeth* and, for the first time in her life, actually backed out of giving a performance. Claire Trevor ultimately played the part.

Her best opportunity in years came early that summer; she was offered the important part of the mother in *Look Homeward, Angel,* adapted for the stage by Ketti Frings from the novel by Thomas Wolfe. The play was excellent, she deeply admired Wolfe, and she was looking forward to working with such practised performers as Rosemary Murphy, Hugh Griffith, Arthur Hill and Anthony Perkins . . . when yet another, unexpected accident occurred that marred her life.

In June, Bette moved into a new house in Brentwood. A Mrs Clark, a real-estate saleswoman, took her to see the house, owned by Mr and Mrs Ronald Buck. Bette explored the house with extraordinary thoroughness, neglecting only to open a door to the basement. Indeed, she wasn't told there was a basement; seeing a particular door, she assumed that it led to a closet. She moved in on 29 June. She noticed the previously hidden door; she could tell from the jamb that it opened inwards; she pushed the knob, took a tiny step forwards, and suddenly felt the ground give from beneath her feet. She plunged into black space and felt agonising pain as she hit a hard stone floor. She must have dropped at least twenty feet. She lost consciousness and when she came to felt excruciating agony in her back and the right hand she had instinctively thrown out to block the fall. She managed to crawl up the steps and see what had happened. The door opened inwards over the top step of the stairs which was about nine inches wide and seven inches below the level of the hall floor. There was no landing at the top of the stairway and only a tiny sill. The stairway was less than four feet across; it had cement walls at its side and no handrails.

The pain was so acute she was unable to move. When a neighbour finally came to her rescue (Merrill was not present), it was discovered that she could not walk and had to be placed on a stretcher and rushed to hospital. She had broken her back and was very lucky indeed that, unlike David Niven's first wife, who had suffered a similar accident, she had not been killed.

She sued Mr and Mrs Buck; the real-estate woman Mrs Clark who had failed to show her the door; and Lelah Pierson, the real-estate agent employing Mrs

Clark. Five years later, Bette was awarded a verdict of $65,700.

It cost her most of that amount in hospital fees and lost work, as well as the heartbreak of losing *Look Homeward, Angel* to the admirable Jo Van Fleet. The hospital expenses, the huge costs of maintaining Margot and giving her other children the finest schooling, her several moves and the problem of maintaining the life of a star on drastically reduced income severely drained Bette's financial resources. Almost fifty, she was very far from a rich woman and had to work, despite the agony that followed the severe and dangerous surgery on her shattered spine. It says much for her New England constitution that she wasn't permanently crippled; but she was never free of recurrent back pain for years afterwards.

Incredibly, given her condition, only six months after her accident, Bette appeared in a thriller on television called *The Cold Touch* in which she had to make her way along a high building ledge in high heels. And then yet another accident occurred.

Merrill and she had patched up their fractured relationship. Their mutual humour and shared interests helped them overcome their existing hostilities, and they also shared the joy of seeing B.D. and Michael grow up into strong, healthy and handsome children. After several months staying with Bobby, whose mental health had much improved, at Laguna, greatly tended by Gary and Ruthie, Bette moved into the Château Marmont with Gary and began working on a pilot for a series called *Paula*. The night between rehearsals and commencement of shooting, some faulty wiring or perhaps a fallen cigarette caused the drapes to burst into flames in the middle of the night. Smoke enveloped the Merrills in heavy clouds. They were awakened in time by a scream from a woman down the hall and staggered from the room choking.

Fifteen

CAMEO ROLES are often considered death for major actors. But Bette was anxious to earn money in the spring of 1958 and was very glad to receive an offer of $50,000 for two days' work as Catherine the Great in *John Paul Jones,* an adipose epic in which she would speak several lines in Russian. Accompanied by B.D. and Bobby, she travelled to Spain on the *S.S. Independence;* she was perhaps glad of the separation from Merrill. She also had another script in her suitcase. She was to go to England to make *The Scapegoat,* by Daphne du Maurier, in which she would be cast as a monstrous, cigar-puffing morphine addict confined largely to her bed and playing mother to Alec Guinness. She decided in advance she would adopt the 'Japanese' rice white make-up she had used in *The Little Foxes,* and a costume from that picture, let out a little for her increased weight.

Shooting the brief sequence from *John Paul Jones* was not a pleasant experience. The director, John Farrow, Australian husband of Maureen O'Sullivan, father of Mia Farrow, was a boorish drunken lecher with a foul mouth increased by the pain he was suffering from a mortal sickness resulting in part from his addiction to alcohol. At his best a fine director, he was now on his uppers, and directed Bette with a leaden hand. The producer, Samuel Bronston, was in severe financial straits and every conceivable corner had to be cut in the production. Farrow asked Bette to play her part on a single note of voracious sexual intensity, and this irritated her, but, undoubtedly, the movie queen in her vibrated to the challenge of portraying what Farrow insisted on calling 'the Queen of all the Rushes'.

With loud sighs of relief, Bette, her sister and daughter took off for a vacation in Italy. Tourists froze in their tracks as Bette swooped down on the Vatican, toured the Sistine Chapel and trudged around St Peter's; the Italians adored her, and noted in the press her volcanic enjoyment of everything she saw and everybody she met.

The Latin atmosphere, with its deafening noise, antic enthusiasms and violent extremes of emotion suited Bette perfectly. After a trip to Milan, she flew with her relatives, in the finest of humours, to England.

Bette had high hopes for *The Scapegoat*. The director, Robert Hamer, had made the brilliant ironical comedy *Kind Hearts and Coronets* with Alec Guinness, and Bette felt that the combination would work again. But from the beginning it was obvious to her that it would not.

Although she herself enjoyed drinking, very occasionally to excess, she hated people who were incapable of controlling their intake of liquor and she felt particularly uncomfortable with alcoholics. Even at the first meeting with Hamer, she realised he was suffering from severe alcoholic degeneration. The production chief Sir Michael Balcon assured her that Hamer had promised he would lay off drinking completely if only he could direct Bette Davis. But she spent the entire length of shooting wondering anxiously whether Hamer would keep his word. And she was bothered by his evident incompetence, his attacks of shaking, and his disagreeable atmosphere of someone aching for an indulgence he dared not allow himself.

The truth was, though Bette could not have known it, that, like John Farrow, Hamer was actually dying during

316

the production. In fact, he barely outlived it. Sir Alec
Guinness says:

Bette Davis behaved throughout with impeccable
professionalism, and, of course, we were all thrilled to be working with her. But she allowed none
of us to get to know her. I invited her to dinner
several times, and she never responded. It would
have been a much more enjoyable movie if we had
got along better.
    She acted admirably, of course: concentrated,
forceful and formidable, with a fine sardonic wit.
But I feel she was affected by being overdressed;
and the settings in which she played were dizzy
with distractions: hundreds of roses, eye-catching
bric-à-brac, rococo serendipity of every description. Not only did she not trust the director, she
was suspicious of me. I don't know whether she
thought I was going to try to take scenes from her,
which wouldn't have been possible anyway, but I
was prepared happily and rightly to sit at her feet,
as it happened. I was proud to have worked with
her and sad that she didn't seem to have enjoyed
working with me.

The cameraman, Paul Beeson, recalls:

I first met Bette Davis ten days before we started
shooting the picture for the make-up tests. I was
nervous at first, very young, and she disconcerted
me because she started to tell me what make-up
she would wear and precisely how she would like to
be photographed. This was hard for me to accept
but I was polite and said, 'Will you let me do the
tests the way I see them, and if you don't like them,
tell me?' She said, 'Fine.' I realised she was a good
sport. She liked a direct honest approach. She

hated dishonesty. She went to see the tests and said simply, 'We're on the same wavelength, Mr Beeson.' And that was it. No more trouble.

Bette rather enjoyed the experience of being in bed during the entire production. She would sit cross-legged, pretending to be lying down, and smoke furiously between takes, stubbing out her cigarettes in a great pile in a large marble ashtray hidden behind the pillows. Once or twice, the pillows caught fire and a small column of smoke began to form behind her head on camera. Robert Hamer threw up his hands in despair and the scene had to be started again.

The famous director Anthony Asquith visited the stage one day. He was a fan of Bette's. He always wore a boiler-suit. Nobody told Bette he was visiting. She noticed him out of the corner of her eye and during a break said to Hamer, 'I don't want to make a fuss, but would you please ask that workman in the boiler-suit to move out of the way?' Asquith, crestfallen, nervously disappeared.

B.D. was Bette's joy during the picture. Every time a scene was finished, B.D., aged twelve, would plop herself down on the bed and give a long, serious critique which often ended in both mother and daughter bursting into laughter. Hamer became irritated by this, and also by the fact that Bette flatly refused to allow her stand-in (whom she called in this instance, a 'lie-in') to take over when the lights were being set up. She was so comfortable in her cosy position she had to be practically dragged out in order to satisfy union requirements.

Beeson grumbled constantly about her make-up. He says, 'She wore this terrible white stuff. Most black and white make-ups were yellowy pancake but this ghastly white stuff prevented me from lighting her correctly. She apparently wanted to accentuate her eyes but she looked like a kind of talking mask.'

Everyone disliked the picture. Daphne du Maurier says, 'I felt the performances of both Guinness and Bette Davis were bad. I wanted her to play the role I had devised with zest and vitality but she had neither. I was so disappointed with her I can't even remember if I met her. I've just blanked the whole thing out. It was a disaster.'

There is no need today to question Dame du Maurier's opinion. Bette returned to Hollywood for nothing more exciting than an episode of *Wagon Train*; fortunately, an unexpected opportunity came up immediately afterwards: to appear in a series of readings of the poems of Carl Sandburg with Gary Merrill arranged by the accomplished Norman Corwin.

Bette had always admired Sandburg. She had known him chiefly for his poem *Fog*.

Corwin and Sandburg sent the package including the full selection of poems under the heading of *The World of Carl Sandburg* to the Merrills in Maine. Bette and Gary saw this not only as a chance to do something worthwhile but perhaps to re-cement their shattered marriage since a long tour was called for across the country. But Bette was tortured by anxiety after her first enthusiasm that she would not be able to sustain a stage performance; that, once again, she could not have an understudy; that her old problem of laryngitis might flare up; and that standing for hours at a stretch might prove serious in view of her recently broken back.

Her first insistence was that she meet Sandburg. They hit it off immediately. At eighty, Sandburg was an irresistible, sexy old charmer, filled with a vitality equal to her own. He made her ashamed of her own fears and tensions about growing older and her inhibitions in several directions. He was like a rock: secure, decent and noble. Not for the first time, Bette realised how different the life of a literary man or woman with a solid body of achievement was from the frightened insecure life of a performer on stage or screen.

For the Merrills' convenience, Corwin and Sandburg agreed that the show should be rehearsed at Portland, the nearest city to Cape Elizabeth. Screwing up her courage, inspired by Sandburg, Bette learned the script in record time and plunged enthusiastically into work. After so many years of speaking the dialogue of hack writers, she was thrilled by the experience of working with Great Words. She said to Sandburg during a break at the theatre in Portland: 'We don't have great words anymore. *Your* words are great.' The show in which the verse was framed was exhilarating in that it called for twenty-five speaking parts in two hours. Bette said later, 'It was like playing the full range of every part I'd ever done in fragments, during one evening.'

The problem was that, despite the excellence of Bette's performance, which inspired Merrill to give the best acting of his career, the show was not quite the commercial triumph hoped for. The tour in spite of this was perhaps the most satisfying experience of Bette's career. A special pleasure was the Hollywood opening in March, 1960, with Ruthie in the front row. Bette was overjoyed to find a highly critical audience of her peers loudly delighted with her acting.

A curious episode took place in a small town. There were two spinster sisters who had spent their lives worshipping Bette Davis. The idea of seeing her in person threw them into a state of extreme excitement. They arrived, chattering and laughing, and sat transfixed when Bette made her appearance on the stage. Suddenly, one of the sisters put her to hand to her chest. Moments later, she died of a heart attack. She was taken out of the theatre. But her sister refused to leave, stood up and insisted that the Merrills continued the performance. At the end, there was an ovation and the old lady was asked to come on stage. She said, 'I adored this performance. And my sister would have too if she hadn't died two hours ago!'

Undermining the pleasure the tour gave her, there was the unhappy fact that Bette's marriage to Merrill finally foundered. One would have hoped that, bound together in a mutual professional success, working on the most worthwhile show they had done in years, the unhappy couple would at last have found a new lease of life in the relationship. But it was not so.

In the spring of 1960, Bette filed suit for divorce. The divorce documents, followed by records of the subsequent custody battle, have a raw, disturbing quality. Merrill agreed to pay B.D. and Michael $250 a month each for child support and one half of Margot's special school fees; Bette got the station wagon and Merrill the Mercedes; Bette waived all alimony except for a token of $1.00 per year. The reason for this was that the matter could be kept open and renegotiated if Merrill's earnings suddenly increased. He agreed to keep up the insurance policies on the family and home in return for Bette agreeing to release all interest in Merrill's property other than their co-tenancy in Witch Way at Cape Elizabeth.

It was a calm beginning to a fight over Michael Merrill that would drag on for years and which was resolutely kept out of the press.

Merrill left the show, thus fatally injuring it. Many people who would have come simply to see the famous couple were no longer interested. Others were dissatisfied by the replacements – Barry Sullivan and later, Leif Erickson. The opening in New York at the Henry Miller Theatre on 14 September 1960, had mixed reviews and failed quickly. The gay audience that would have rushed to see Bette in almost anything was rapidly absorbed, and many of the homosexual New York community were disinterested in view of the show's seriousness. After four weeks, *The World of Carl Sandburg* closed.

Bette blamed Merrill's absence for the failure of the production, and Sandburg worked out a series of excuses, including the occurrence of a Jewish holiday, that rivalled in complexity his most intricate verse. None of this was true: *The World of Carl Sandburg* was, quite simply, too intellectual for the commuter audience that had kept Broadway alive since the Second World War. At the end of the tour, there was a consolation prize: the show was greatly successful in North Carolina where almost a quarter of a million high-school students saw it before it finally emerged in Flat Rock where it appeared in its author's home territory.

Despite the sadness of the divorce from Merrill and the extreme strain of the trip, Bette never forgot the joy of playing to young students from one end of America to the other. There is no question that this experience represented for her one of the finest hours of a lifetime.

But she was very hard up when the tour ended. She still had to pay for Ruthie's expensive life style, with endless new clothes and new furniture, as well as a substantial allowance; Bobby's psychiatric treatments and occasional visits to the hospital when she had setbacks of mental and physical health; the rapidly increasing charges for Margot's schooling; the normal schooling of B.D. and Michael; and her own expenses as a star. She was nearly broke in her early fifties because of the financial sacrifice of paying out constantly and being paid very little for the Sandburg reading tour. Normally, given her intense dislike of discussing her private life, she would have turned down at once the offer made that year by Howard Cady of Putnam's to work on a memoir. But she couldn't afford to refuse the offer. She had just rented a house in New York and was hugely grateful for the advance against royalties.

Bette needed a good writer to work with, and asked everybody she knew whom they could recommend. A friend of hers, Kaye Ballard, recommended Sandford Dody, who combined an agreeably sophisticated personality with journalistic skill. Ballard was convinced Dody would be perfect for the task.

Ballard was appearing at the Blue Angel nightclub and it was arranged for Bette to meet Dody there. Bette arrived with the lyricist Fred Ebb, of whom she thought most highly, and she enjoyed Dody, whom she found agreeably admiring, relaxed and rather horsy. She was fascinated by his outré hats and turtleneck sweaters, toothy grins, crinkly humorous eyes, and big nose.

They lunched at her house on East 78th Street and began to sketch out plans. Dody described their working relationship in his memoirs, *Giving Up the Ghost*. He says that at first everything worked out well. But soon there were arguments over the division of profits and royalties and the credit Dody would receive. She asked to see a sample chapter and he declined saying, 'I think, Bette, it's a little unseemly for me to audition at this point in my life.' She shrugged and accepted his decision.

They met day after day, in the winter months that began 1961, starting work at ten o'clock sharp on a Monday morning, toiling in the library in chintz-covered chairs in front of a cheerful wood fire. Smoking incessantly, plucking cigarettes from pottery hens and matches from slop bowls, Bette moved about remembering everything she dared, until, Dody wrote, 'The room looked like an opium den at Walden Pond.'

Soon, Dody was calling her Bette Dervish. The story of her life became tremendously convincing as she built a matchstick castle of largely familiar information. It was difficult for her to probe into areas of her life she would have preferred to have left dark. It was harder still to include a stranger in the intimacy she had so carefully kept from reporters all of those years and at times she deliberately softened the truth, particularly about her husbands. And then, when she did become rash and bold and told the harsh and ugly truth of so much of her life, she withdrew it summarily when the manuscript was completed.

The writing continued over several months. Merrill dropped by and hit it off well with Dody; he seemed unconcerned about so much of his life being exposed. He probably knew Bette's New England sense of propriety would eliminate the more unflattering passages.

Oddly, Bette and Merrill were happier together at this time than they were to be afterwards, and than they had ever been before. Or it may simply have been that they were giving a performance worthy of *All About Eve* or *The World of Carl Sandburg* in front of an official biographer.

Dody recalls pleasant evenings with Bette, her dental surgeon Stanley Berman, and his wife, Gig Young and Elizabeth Montgomery and other friends. And yet, all along, there was the sense of discomfort any writer of talent must feel in rendering himself subservient to the ferocious egotism of a star. It was a question of flattery, cajolery, easing out secrets, playing under the great performer and never imposing one's self. Of being, in short, a courtier.

Perhaps fortunately, work was interrupted when Bette had to go to Hollywood to make *A Pocketful of Miracles* for Frank Capra. This appalling movie, which showed no trace of Capra's legendary genius, was a remake of his earlier *Lady for a Day*. It was a Damon Runyon story about a drudge called Apple Annie elevated suddenly to riches.

Once again, Bette had been last choice for the part. Shirley Booth had been offered the picture but after seeing *Lady for a Day* she cried and said through tears she could never hope to equal the great May Robinson in the original part. Helen Hayes accepted it immediately but for complicated reasons withdrew. Glenn Ford appeared with Davis and at first was pleased. But they clashed from the first day of shooting.

Bette's chief reason for taking on Apple Annie was that B.D. wanted her to. She was terrified of making her

Hollywood comeback after several years as a miserable old hag; she was convinced that comments would be rude in her old home town. They were. Several backbiters remarked that she could now play this kind of role without make-up. Glenn Ford gave an interview saying that, out of gratitude for Bette having put him into *A Stolen Life*, he had insisted she play Apple Annie in order to rescue her from obscurity. Capra said later, 'Bette read Glenn's interview. She was mad as hell! She screamed at me, "Who is that son-of-a-bitch that he should say he helped me have a *comeback*! That shitheel wouldn't have helped me out of a *sewer*! I should never have come back to Hollywood! *I hate all of you!* And Apple Annie most of all! I must have been *out of my mind* to come back!" '

Glenn Ford detested Davis for these comments. He spent the rest of the picture treating her like a supporting player. Capra suffered from severe cluster headaches because of the tension between his stars and the atrocious behaviour of everybody concerned. Bette's only friend on the picture was the very young Ann-Margret. Capra said years later, 'It was all impossible. I "lost" the picture right from the beginning. I realise now I should have understood Davis better. I didn't see that she was very sensitive, that she needed consolation and reassurance after so long away. I couldn't see that she was in fact vulnerable, living on her nerves. She'd only become a monster to take care of herself in a monstrous business. Underneath, she was a thin-skinned woman, deeply afraid and uncertain of everything except her genius. Her armour *must not* be penetrated and the fact that I tried appalled her.'

In New York after this horrible exprience, Bette plunged back into work with Sandford Dody, censoring much of what he had written in her absence but allowing some of it to be reasonably candid. Dody shrewdly observed in his autobiography: 'She was used to candour to begin with, and was shrewdly aware that admitting, for instance, that she was a bitch was the surest way of convincing the reader that she was not.'

During the months of renewed work at the house in New York, Bette was shadowed by the sudden death of Ruthie in the last days of shooting *A Pocketful of Miracles*. In recent years, Ruthie had drifted partly out of her life, but the overwhelming influence of her mother on her career remained and would never be forgotten. Indeed, the best part of the book Bette wrote with Dody, ultimately called *The Lonely Life*, dealt with Bette's extraordinary mother.

Tennessee Williams was determined, in the summer of 1961, to have Bette play the outrageous part of Maxine, the landlady in *The Night of the Iguana*. So often fascinated and puzzled by homosexuals, Bette was intrigued by Williams and loved the idea of playing a bad-tempered slut. Dody wanted her to take the arid spinster writer's daughter in the play but neither Williams nor Bette agreed. They were probably right.

In the late summer of 1961, Bette had a ferocious battle with Gary Merrill. She had been granted custody of B.D., Margot and Michael, with Gary allowed visiting rights. But suddenly she took action through her attorney Sidney Wernick against Merrill in the State of Maine Superior Court that his conduct and behaviour were detrimental to the children and he must not be allowed to see them again. She wanted the entire clause allowing such visiting rights stricken from the record of judgment of divorce.

This was a very tough action to take against a father. But Bette stated in a clear and unequivocal manner that she considered Merrill drunken and disorderly and incapable of behaving properly in front of his family. She charged that Merrill had become violently drunk in front of the children; had committed acts of physical violence against her; that his house in California was filthy and unkempt; that he was having an affair with a woman to whom he was not married; that he was irresponsible and neglectful; and that on Father's Day she had arranged a dinner for him to meet his family and he had arrived drunk and insulting and left without eating anything. She alleged harshly that Margot, who had now moved from the school at Lake Geneva to a home at Spruce Creek, Pennsylvania, would be subject to danger from Merrill. Bette and Merrill quarrelled more savagely than ever on the telephone or through their attorneys. Sandford Dody struggled on with the manuscript. At one stage, Bette cancelled it completely, throwing Dody into deep depression. He at last succeeded in finishing the book in the early autumn of 1961 just as Bette began rehearsals for *The Night of the Iguana*. He was dashed when the publishers decided not to give him joint credit as author; dashed still more when, before the book was published, Bette cut the manuscript to ribbons. He alleges she cut the best passages without Dody's permission. Dody also claims in his memoirs that Bette wrecked his prose in rewrites that at times rendered it almost ungrammatical. It is unfortunate that his contract did not allow him right of final approval. The resulting book begins excellently, falters halfway through, and declines rapidly in the last third when discretion gets the better part of common sense and the descriptions and comments on people, films and life in general become disturbingly perfunctory and predictable.

The chief merit of the book is that it is stamped with Davis's personality; that, despite the many excisions and shadings, one still gets a sense of the humour, aggression and raw vitality that propelled this great star to the top of her profession. It is Margo Channing speaking, no doubt of it.

The Night of the Iguana went into rehearsal in October, 1961. After the ordeal of *A Pocketful of Miracles,* Bette hoped for a more joyful experience, but this was not to be vouchsafed her. She was not at her best at this time. Irritated by much of Dody's manuscript and furious with Merrill over his alleged drunkenness, she was hostile and bitter from the first day of work. She disliked Margaret Leighton, the brilliantly gifted British actress who played the spinster in the production. She found Miss Leighton affected and mannered in the extreme, coldly ungrateful when Davis threw a cocktail party to welcome her to Broadway.

She also disliked Patrick O'Neal, who acted the role of the defrocked minister. And she had a terrible row with Tennessee Williams's famous agent, Audrey Wood.

Convinced that Patrick O'Neal and Margaret Leighton were ganging up on her, nervous and overwrought as always when she had to play in the theatre without an understudy, Bette opened in the play in Chicago in November. There were problems from the beginning with the writing; Tennessee Williams worked through nights to fix the more difficult speeches. Business was poor over Thanksgiving because exceptionally good weather drove many people out of town. The worst problem of all was that much of the audience was composed of Bette's loyal fans. They tended to applaud every other line, infuriating the other actors and sometimes bringing the entire play to a halt.

Worse problems arose in New York when the play opened there in December. The reviews were excellent and audiences far more substantial but the ill-feeling between the performers reached flashpoint. When Bette entered the stage at the beginning of the play she was swallowed up every night in an ovation that ruined the dramatic effect of the scene and that no persuasion on her part could stop. There was a tension-ridden backstage meeting: everyone agreed that something would have to be done at once. Tennessee Williams devised another entrance but the same thing happened. It happened night after night. Margaret Leighton was so maddened at having to come on without a single hand-clap after the storm of cheers for Bette that she didn't talk to her for the rest of the run.

At last, Tennessee solved the problem. He had Bette make her entrance as the curtain rose and go straight to the footlights to take her call. Her first words as she walked on were, 'Hiya, Shannon.' She had a cigarette in one hand and a drink in the other. She swung her hips and batted her eyelids and when the audience screamed and jumped to its feet in a state bordering on ecstasy she bowed, stepping completely out of character to do so. Only then was she allowed to give a performance without interruption.

As so often before, the bulk of her audiences were gay, or composed of women's groups from out of town. The strain of making this artificial appearance at the outset of the show, the knowledge that these audiences would accept no substitute for her and that if her laryngitis flared up the show would have to close for a night or two, cost her much sleep and wore her down. At last, confronted by particularly severe looks of dislike from Margaret Leighton both on and off the stage, she threw up her hands and walked out. She was exhausted and wanted only to rest in the country or, as an alternative, try Hollywood again.

Sixteen

As IT turned out, the producer-director Robert Aldrich had offered Bette, just before she left the play, the co-starring role in *What Ever Happened to Baby Jane?* It was a story about two former child actresses living in Hollywood in their late middle age. Aldrich, a massive, driving former football player, had hit on the gimmick of co-starring Bette and Joan Crawford in the production and making it for Warner Bros. His great flair for publicity, crude but dynamic grasp of audience taste and genuine fondness for the two stars resulted in this highly-charged, highly sensational package.

Bette was uncertain at first whether she would play in the picture. Much as she needed a change of pace, she was uneasy about acting a grotesque role that called for hideously bizarre make-up, wigs and costumes and involved serving her rival actress a dead rat on a breakfast tray. She asked Aldrich to come to New York. When he arrived at her house, she said: 'There are two questions I have to ask you. If you're honest with me and answer them correctly, I will do the picture.' She looked at him very hard, puffing at a cigarette in her best one-woman firing squad manner. 'All right. The first question is: Have you slept with Miss Crawford?' Aldrich paused before answering, and then he said, 'Not for the want of Miss Crawford trying.' 'OK. I believe you. So I'll skip the second question,' Bette said. The unspoken question, of course, was whether he would guarantee he wouldn't favour Joan.

Bette left for Hollywood in a state of nervous tension. She had to return to her old studio after thirteen years to co-star with the woman who, she knew, both envied her talent and has been secretly in love with her. On arrival, somebody told her that Crawford had suggested her for the part. Although this statement was quite incorrect, she rashly believed it. Joan got what she wanted: Joan was now appearing with the actress she most admired in the world.

Jack Warner decided to act the magnifico and gave an elaborate luncheon for Bette and Joan at the studio. Each spied on the other to see what they would be wearing. Joan was elaborately got up in a vividly coloured dress. Bette upstaged her by wearing plain black.

Warner did his best to make his two former stars feel at home. Yet it was a far cry from the old days, when Bette could rewrite most of a script and enjoy a two months' shooting schedule which would stretch to five if she wasn't feeling well. Aldrich was a bull in every imaginable china-shop. He wasn't subservient, fastidious or delicate in his dealings with the stars. He took them on like boxers. He didn't waste a minute with flattery. The entire picture was shot in twenty-one days like a B picture which, except for its baroque surface, it actually was.

But Bette, with her tough professionalism, flung herself into the part at its own level, re-working the rice-white make-up she had used in *The Little Foxes* and *The Scapegoat* and using black kohl around her eyes in an imitation of the silent stars. Her blonde ringleted wig and bizarre puffed-sleeve dresses were brilliantly thought out.

Robert Aldrich remembers:

Joan and Bette didn't fight at all on *Baby Jane*. They behaved absolutely perfectly. They never

331

allowed an abrasive word to slip out. They didn't try to upstage each other.

Bette was aggravated by the fact that Joan resumed her wooing of Bette, sending her shoes, handkerchiefs, and costume jewellery. Bette sent her a note asking her not to continue, saying that she didn't have the time to go out and choose something for Joan in order to reciprocate. As a result, Joan changed from an admiring fan to a savage enemy. She took her hate out on her unhappy adopted daughter Christina. She became a kind of monster. She constantly acted towards Bette in the manner of a cold *nouveau riche* society woman towards a fallen aristocrat turned ladies' maid. Bette became infuriated with Joan's pretentious posturings and empty, meaningless politeness. She longed for a quarrel with words and fur flying. But Joan brushed off her occasional rude remarks with saintly condescension.

As it turned out, both Bette's and Joan's performances were in every way admirable. They created touching and convincing characters instead of mere grotesques. The last scenes, in which Bette drags a dying Joan Crawford to the beach, were exceptionally well played and directed. The film sustained an effective nightmarish mood, crude and unsentimental, that entirely suited the Hollywood setting.

Relations between Bette and Joan did not improve after the picture was finished. Bette gave interviews discussing 'we two old hags' in the picture and Joan rushed her a note, immaculately typed on baby blue stationery saying, 'Dear Miss Davis. Please do not continue to refer to me as an old hag. Sincerely, Joan Crawford.' Bette laughed and threw the letter away. It was obvious to her that Joan Crawford was utterly devoid of a sense of humour.

Perhaps as a gag to help promote the picture, perhaps because she was genuinely frantic for money, Bette had borrowed $75,000 against her ten per cent of *Baby Jane*. Bette took out a famous ad in *Variety* on 21 September 1962. It read:

SITUATION WANTED, WOMAN ARTIST
Mother of three – 10, 11 and 15 – divorcee. American. Thirty years' experience as an actress in Motion Pictures. Mobile still and more affable than rumour would have it. Wants steady employment in Hollywood. (Has had Broadway.)

Bette Davis, c/o Martin Baum, G.A.C.
REFERENCES UPON REQUEST

The general view on Hollywood was that this indicated Bette Davis was finished. It therefore backfired as a joke. Fortunately, the excellent reviews for both *Baby Jane* and her memoirs *The Lonely Life*, followed by *Baby Jane*'s huge commercial success made nonsense of her enemies' remarks. She left for New York on 2 November, to begin promotions for the picture; she was marvellous on the *Jack Paar Show* but lost her temper with Jonathan Winters when he imitated her voice. She hated imitators.

She had to fly back to Los Angeles on 15 November, because B.D., now fifteen, had gone into Cedars of Lebanon Hospital for a varicose vein operation. Bette stayed with her at the hospital each day and then took care of her at home as she was unable to move her leg out of a straight position. She taped an Andy Williams television show and a *Perry Mason* show, and in mid-December appeared in court once again demanding that Merrill not be allowed to see the children. She repeated her charges that he was drunken, physically violent, filthy, unkempt, immoral and in every way unsuitable as a parent. Gary Merrill swore that he had been denied rights of reasonable visitation quite improperly, that he was unable to reach her through his attorney, that Bette had deliberately brought influence to bear against him upon Michael and that it was shocking a son should be deprived of the company of his father when he was growing up. He stated that Michael had stayed with him over Bette's furious complaints for six weeks that summer and that Bette had been unable to prove any misbehaviour on Merrill's part during the vacation. He demanded that a court order be made enforcing Bette to allow reasonable visitations.

Bette responded in court with a series of further and damaging statements. She charged that Merrill had no suitable home in which Michael should be allowed to stay overnight. She said that his temporary home at Topanga on the beach was cold, damp and foggy and that this would be injurious to Michael's health. She asserted there was no one to take care of Michael, aged ten, and that he wasn't given proper meals, or his clothes taken care of. She added that the building was in an area filled with perverts who might molest a child, and she then proceeded to give a series of reasons why Merrill should not visit with Michael at Bette's home.

She described a call from Merrill from San Francisco that 13 December, in which she alleged Merrill drunkenly demanded Michael be put on a plane. She charged that he had a hangover when he came to see Michael unexpectedly and that he dragged Michael from a party crying to be with him all night. She insisted he took Michael to a restaurant from which he had been evicted previously and that he got drunk in front of Michael. Furthermore, he 'made Michael cancel an all-important football practice' to spend a day with him. The charges went on to mention Merrill's allegedly drunken driving and threats if she decided to take the children to her old favourite resort of La Quinta for New Year. Bette concluded that it was against Margot's interests to have Merrill visit her; that she was living with a private family in the East and that Merrill excited her to the point at

334

which she was seriously unsettled by him.

Merrill responded again. He claimed that the house at Topanga Beach was well-heated and that the area was often warm and sunny in winter. He revealed that he had turned down a job on *The Naked City* television programme to be with Michael. He denied that he had ever been intoxicated in the presence of Michael or ever committed an act of physical violence. He admitted he was furious when Bette prevented him from speaking to his son on the telephone from San Francisco but denied that he was drunk. He said that he did not take Michael from a football practice but instead offered to deliver him to it and in fact did so. He mentioned that on another occasion he took Michael to the Notre Dame game.

He said he did everything in his power to adjust his schedule to fit in with Michael's; that he had not been drunk with him in the restaurant; that he had never driven a car when drunk and that to be deprived of his son was damaging to his well-being.

The hearings dragged on into January, 1963. B.D., Bette's friend the director Allen Miner and others appeared for Bette to testify and Merrill's friend, the actor Lyle Bettger, and two others appeared for him. The court order was a shocking blow to Bette. The judgment was that Merrill be given far more access to Michael than hitherto. He was to have custody of Michael on alternate weekends commencing on 25 January, and he should have complete custody for the spring Easter school vacation, the first portion of the summer school vacation from 7 June through 15 July and the Christmas school vacation. Worse, if possible, from Bette's point of view was that Merrill was allowed to visit Margot with reasonable frequency providing she was not removed from her home. There was a proviso that Merrill must always be sober in the presence of the children and not remove Michael from California without Bette's consent. Bette's motion for attorney fees and costs was denied. She and Gary had to pay their own fees and costs.

In February, the first weekend of Merrill's custody arrived. But in the early evening hours of Thursday, Merrill's attorney received a wire from Bette saying she would await further ruling of the court as to Merrill's visit. Merrill was angered since the court order was clear at the moment. On Friday, at five o'clock, he arrived at Bette's home in Bel Air to take custody of Michael. Bette refused to open the door. Merrill pounded on it angrily. She pressed the intercom button and said, very loudly, 'You shall not have custody or visitation of Michael now or ever!' Merrill said, 'May I speak to Michael?' Bette replied, 'You may not see him at all. I just told you!' Merrill said, 'May I speak to him on the intercom or may I call him from a phone booth?' '*You may not*!'* Bette snapped back and the line went dead. Merrill drove in a rage down Stone Canyon Road and called his attorney. Two days later, Merrill obtained an order to show cause *in re* contempt, in which Bette was ordered to appear and show cause why she should not be adjudged guilty of contempt of the court order allowing Merrill custody. Bailiffs came to serve the order only to discover that Bette had fled to New York, leaving Michael with her friend Barbara Barry who had instructions along with the Black-Foxe Military Academy not to allow Michael ever to see his father – according to court records.

Finally Bette was forced to agree to Merrill visiting with Michael on alternate weekends.

To Joan Crawford's fury, Bette was nominated for an Academy Award for *Baby Jane* and Joan was not. On the night of the Oscars, both ladies had agreed to be presenters. Joan had solicited an agreement with all

*conversation from court files.

nominated actresses who could not be present that she would accept the award on their behalf if they won. Bette found out about this, and it disturbed her. But she was also sure that she would certainly win. Anne Bancroft's name was announced for *The Miracle Worker*. Bette, in a dressing-room backstage, flinched from the shock of the news. And Crawford, chin held high, swept past her, turned, said 'Hah!' to her face and went onstage to collect the Oscar for Anne Bancroft.

Bette took off in a high dudgeon to Europe to promote *Baby Jane* there. She constantly called Barbara Barry in an uproar over the battle with Merrill. But she had a strong reason for leaving California. Joan Crawford had been asked to promote the picture but accused Bette of grabbing the better theatres at home and overseas out of the several hundred selected for personal appearances. Bette immediately offered to appear in all of the theatres. When she heard of this, Crawford changed her mind, but it was too late. She had to sit out the entire tour while Bette did all the appearances on her own.

What Ever Happened to Baby Jane? opened in London in early May. Bette was miserable over the situation in California with Michael but she was excited by the feeling that the Warner people in England were overjoyed with the picture. There was no premiere. Ten days after the show opened, the *Evening Standard* ran a tiny box at the bottom of the entertainment page, on a Tuesday evening. The advertisement read simply: 'Warner Cinema, tomorrow, 8:30 P.M. Bette Davis.'

A remarkable thing happened. An enormous crowd rushed the theatre at 2:30 and packed it to the rafters. They saw the movie three times around so they wouldn't miss Bette's personal appearance. Another vast crowd gathered outside. At 7:30, Leicester Square had to be closed by the police.

At 8:30, *Baby Jane* finished playing. The cinema was

337

plunged in total darkness. Even the house signs were turned off so that the only lights left gleamed from the exits. Three musicians played the theme tune of the picture, 'I'm Sending a Letter to Daddy'. Bette edged her way through the crowd in the dark and began to climb the stage, feeling her way with her hands. A spotlight had been cued to flash through the darkness and concentrate on the musicians, pinpointing her as the curtain rose. Instead, it swung around and focused on her behind as she climbed the steps. The whole theatre dissolved in a turmoil of laughter. A moment later, the spotlight focused on B.D.'s behind: tall and imposing as a stretched-out Alice in Wonderland, B.D., aged fifteen, towered over her mother. The audience roared again.

It was several minutes before the manager succeeded in controlling the audience, which was beside itself with excitement and amusement. She played up magnificently. She held up a large piece of stationery and sang 'I've Written a Letter to Daddy'. When she finished the number, she threw the piece of paper into the air and the audience screamed. She chattered to the crowd and fielded questions; B.D. sang 'Whatever Happened to Baby Jane?' in unison with Bette. When they finished, somebody rushed up to the stage with a gigantic bouquet of flowers. Instead of waiting for the flowers to be given to her, she marched over and collected the bouquet and handed it to B.D. This was a *faux pas* which brought another gust of laughter because at the same moment another bouquet was being brought up on the other side of the stage for B.D. who finished with two bouquets the size of herself. Bette dismissed her from the stage with a wave of her hand.

Bette sang another number. She closed the proceedings with, 'You don't know it, but you've all got a number underneath your seat. And when I give the command, I want you to all look for that number because the winner will be presented with a Baby Jane doll. On the command of three, you will look for your number. One, two, three . . .' Everyone bent over. And Bette found herself confronted with several hundred English bottoms. She said, 'I've never seen so many fat fannies in my life.' There was another roar. And to her disgust the doll was won by a child. She had hoped to obtain a major laugh by having it won by a man.

Three thousand people shouted as she left. When she got to the lobby she was barely able to move. Her car was surrounded by a motorcycle squad, like that of the Queen. It took twenty minutes to get her out of Leicester Square, even though it was closed off to all other traffic.

Thrilled by her reception, more fond than ever of England, Bette flew to the Cannes Film Festival. She was accorded a royal reception, and accompanied Aldrich to the screening of *Baby Jane,* which she had never seen before from beginning to end. Perhaps because she had become so over-excited in London, perhaps because of her continuing fear of Merrill getting drunk and driving Michael on the freeways in Los Angeles, she was feeling exceptionally overwrought as the film unfolded. She was horrified at her appearance, which she had gone to such extraordinary lengths to attain. She burst into tears at her chalky, painted face and Aldrich turned to her in dismay along with several members of the audience. 'I look awful,' she wept. 'Do I really look that awful?'

Bette was then dealt a blow from which it took a long time to recover. Because of her fear of Merrill visiting Michael, she had overreacted by being unduly protective of B.D. She was astonished when B.D., still so very young, went on a blind date with the young Jeremy Hyman, a nephew of Elliot Hyman, owner of Seven Arts. Bette thought nothing of the incident until B.D. told her it was love at first sight. Bette was distraught. She felt that B.D. was much too young at fifteen to be in love with anybody.

Bette was at her lowest ebb. She felt she would be all alone. Michael was far too normal a boy to cling to a mother's skirts. Margot was lost in a world of her own.

Then she caught her face in a mirror, distorted with grief and despair, and her New England horse sense took over. She burst out laughing at herself. Her face laughed back at her from the mirror. She must go on.

Bette shot the bankroll to give B.D. an enormously expensive wedding reception at the Beverly Wilshire Hotel. Furious with the press because of their constant sniping at B.D.'s teenage passions, Bette forbade them to attend the occasion. She went through the ordeal bravely but it was excruciating for her to part with B.D. when B.D. was so young. She also felt B.D. should have waited until she was older before making so drastic a commitment.

As it turned out, Bette was wrong; and at least she had the good sportsmanship to admit it eventually. B.D. and Hyman made a complete success of their marriage. As late as 1981, they are still happily united.

Bette had a private detective follow Gary Merrill and Michael during their permitted weekends together. She was still trying desperately to prevent those weekends from continuing.

Detective Michael Parlow dogged Merrill's footsteps carefully. He told Bette that on 24 January, three weeks after B.D.'s wedding, Michael and Gary were staying at the Newporter Inn at Newport Beach. Parlow asserted that Merrill had left Michael alone in his room from 10:07 A.M. until the following morning at 7:18 A.M. Merrill was drinking and partying all night in bars and private homes in the area.

The following weekend, Parlow alleged, Merrill left Michael alone again. And this continued on other occasions. There were evidences, Parlow claimed, when Gary drove Michael on a public highway and ran through two stop signs and a red light signal while drunk. Parlow charged that Merrill drank from morning till night and made love to a woman in the room adjoining Michael's. He also testified that Merrill had been loud, boisterous and vulgar in Michael's presence while pretending to sell a coat to a woman from Chicago.

Parlow's statement was read in the Superior Court of Los Angeles in an effort of Bette's to prevent further access. Merrill strenuously denied everything and stated that Bette had done everything for three years to harass him and to cut off his relationship with Michael. He said that he had had to come into court repeatedly to defend himself against 'false, unsubstantiated charges against my character and reputation'.

He insisted he had been a good father to Michael, that Michael suffered acutely from his constant appearances in court when he should have been leading the life of a normal boy, and that whenever he had seen Michael he had done everything to make him happy. He explained that he had often flown back from locations in New York, Puerto Rico and San Francisco just to be with his son and that he would scarcely have gone through such sacrifice if he had not loved Michael.

He demanded that no further efforts be made to interefere with his loving relationship. Bette was almost out of her mind when, despite the detective's report, the court once again took the view that the son should not be separated from the father, and failed to censure Merrill because he had broken his promise to remain sober in Michael's presence.

To reimburse herself for B.D.'s wedding, Bette took $125,000 for the part of Susan Hayward's mother in *Where Love Has Gone,* a heavily overwrought version of the novel by Harold Robbins. It was shot in San Francisco and Los Angeles. Bette had to play a severe, haughty matriarch rather like Gladys Cooper's character in *Now, Voyager*. Almost from the first day, Bette, not always comfortable with strangers, intensely disliked Susan Hayward. She was infuriated by Hayward's haughty behaviour and at one stage screamed 'Take this stinking wig!', snatched hers off, and flung it at Hayward. The director, Edward Dmytryk says:

Actually, Susan was scared to death of Bette. Susan was a very difficult person to know. She was very reserved, nervous and withdrawn. Bette mistook that apparently for rudeness. They were exact opposites. And then, Bette upset Susan right at the beginning. Something horrible happened. It was right on the first day. I discussed with Bette an upcoming scene. What the problems were and how I intended to handle them. Bette said, 'Fine, that's great.' Then I went out, and, I was told afterwards, Bette came on the set, she was talking to the crew, and she said, in full earshot of Susan, 'Fellows, hold everything. The whole script is going to be changed. And *I'm* going to do the changing.'

Susan was horrified. She was so insecure she had to work with a script very close to its original draft that she had accepted to work with. And worse still, here Bette Davis would be rewriting Susan's lines! I don't think Bette really meant what she said. But Susan was convinced she did. She stormed up to the bosses at Paramount and said she wouldn't tolerate anybody rewriting her lines. The bosses said not a word of this script could be changed. And that was a disaster, because the script called for changes. It never really worked.

Throughout the shooting, Susan ignored Bette and everyone else and rushed off to her dressing-room immediately a scene was over, sitting alone and chain-smoking ferociously, feeling miserably frightened and appalled by the challenge of Bette's talent even without a single line altered in Bette's favour. Excellent though she was, Susan Hayward knew she wasn't in Davis's class. This made her feel even worse. She smoked and smoked, thus helping to provoke cancer in the lungs which ultimately leapt to her brain and killed her. There was a problem towards the end of shooting. Dmytryk says:

> The studio wanted Bette to do a scene where she suddenly goes mad. The picture was finished, and Bette knew the picture was complete without it, and she refused point blank. The executives tried to get me to talk her into it, and I said, 'I don't know how I can talk anybody into going mad for one minute on the screen.' They were insistent. They were thinking of the censorship at the time, in which somebody who was guilty of anything had to suffer and pay the price either by dying or going insane. Bette refused, and I respected her for it. The studio started legal proceedings but finally gave up. Because of Bette's steadfast refusal to do it.

Her performance in *Where Love Has Gone* was simply a static repetition of well-worn mannerisms: technique operating in a vacuum. But the money made life easier for Bette, the comfortable life she had become used to was constantly expensive to maintain. For a time, Bobby came to work for her, but help was costly and the rental in Bel Air painfully steep.

Money was again the motive that forced Bette to an astonishing decision in the summer of 1964. Incredibly, she agreed to co-star with Joan Crawford in another Robert Aldrich melodrama, *Hush, Hush Sweet Charlotte*. The script cast her as a suspected former murderess driven to the point of madness by her relentless relatives. Wholesale borrowings from several other pictures, unbridled confrontations and a hotch potch of Grand Guignol elements scarcely supplied the basis of a worthy sequel to the entertaining *What Ever Happened to Baby Jane?*

Shooting took place in part in Louisiana. When Bette arrived at the hotel, Joan Crawford was sitting regally in the lobby with twenty-five pieces of luggage around her. Bette said, 'What *on earth* do you think you're doing?' And she added, '*Why* didn't you come down on the chartered flight with the rest of us?' Joan said, 'I'm waiting for my rooms. I *preferred* to come separately'. She spoke these words with an air of such insufferable haughtiness that Bette wanted to strike her.

Bette swept on to her suite. A few minutes after she had sat down and lit up a much needed cigarette, Joan was heard shouting and banging on the door. In a bad mood, Bette pulled it open abruptly. Joan almost fell in. She said, 'Bette, something terrible has happened!' Bette, in no mood to be sympathetic, coldly asked her to sit down. '*What is it?*' she asked, through a cloud of smoke. 'It's horrible!' Joan sobbed. 'They've put me next to a garbage disposal!' Bette resisted the obvious comment and Joan, finding no sympathy from her, fled from the suite.

Bette announced right at the beginning that she wouldn't play a single scene with Crawford. This was virtually impossible since many of their scenes together were crucial to the drama. She said that the director would have to use over-the-shoulder shots using doubles whenever dialogue was involved.

This was out of the question and Aldrich refused. The tension between the two women was so extreme that Crawford developed a psychosomatic illness that was described officially as 'an upper respiratory infection'. After only three scenes, she disappeared into a hospital and wouldn't come out. When she finally did return, she was so fretful and nervous about Bette she would only film for three hours a day. She went back into hospital again.

Bette was delighted. Miss Crawford's attacks of the vapours entirely made her day. Now she plunged enthusiastically into casting suggestions. Her first idea was to have Vivien Leigh. An S.O.S was sent to Miss Leigh in London. She didn't respond. Finally, a representative of the studio, Twentieth Century-Fox, called Miss Leigh who said, icily, 'I could just about look at Joan Crawford's face on a Southern plantation at seven o'clock in the morning, but I couldn't possibly look at Bette Davis's.'

Unfortunately, Bette was told this remark and was not amused. She then decided to hedge her bets by casting her old friend Olivia de Havilland. Aldrich flew to Switzerland to persuade Olivia, who had played murderesses before, but who preferred herself in saintly impersonations. He had considerable difficulty persuading her, but the thought of working with Bette again overrode her doubts. She flew to America in September. The production had been closed down for three months.

Only one person did not know Olivia had been hired: Joan Crawford. Miss Crawford, still in the hospital, heard the news on the radio that she had been replaced. There was little or nothing she could do about it except throw a vase of flowers across the room in the direction of the nearest nurse.

Bette and Olivia enjoyed working together. They often met after work, exchanging reminiscences of the old days. The days of *It's Love I'm After, Elizabeth and Essex,* and *In This Our Life.* Their biggest scene together was in a car in which Olivia had to strike Bette hard across the face. Bette called Aldrich the night before the shooting and said, in her little-girl voice, *'Of course,* you're going to use my double aren't you?'

Aldrich said, 'Shit, what are you talking about, Bette? You'll play the scene!' Bette said, 'Nothing in the world will make me do it. Anymore than I would with Crawford.' Aldrich said, 'This is *insane,* Bette!' But Bette was adamant. Aldrich had to accept a stand-in. Olivia arrived on the set, only to be told that Bette would not be there that morning because she wasn't needed.

Bette's performance in the picture was remarkable. She created a convincing figure of pathetic degeneration; of Southern nobility in ruins. She was at her best in the scenes with Olivia and her old friend, Joseph Cotten, and in one sequence she reached an extraordinary degree of intensity. Seeing Cotten seemingly risen from a watery grave (a direct steal from *Les Diaboliques*) she is reduced to gibbering on a staircase. Always at her best in staircase scenes, Bette turned into a kind of Kabuki lion, writhing around on the floor with a great mane of grey hair, moaning and growling.

The writer Gavin Lambert accompanied Bette and Olivia de Havilland to a first preview of *Charlotte*. At the end of the screening, Bette turned to Olivia with terrifying sweetness and said, 'Olivia! You were so good! Even when I was off the screen you somehow managed to hold the audience's attention!' Perhaps fortunately, Miss de Havilland's reply has not been recorded.

There was no shortage of work. Bette was experiencing the pleasures of a comeback. She flew to England to make *The Nanny*, a pleasantly unsettling melodrama in which her cosmic rage was contained in starched white uniforms. She liked the script and looked forward to returning to London, where perhaps her largest audience of fans existed.

The picture was directed by the late Seth Holt, who died three years later of an attack of hiccups during the shooting of the picture *Blood from the Mummy's Tomb*. He was a big, cuddly, plump man with great talent who suffered from poor health. She liked him immensely from the first day she met him.

She was accompanied by a companion and friend, Violla Rubber, who had formerly been the manager of Marlene Dietrich and a producer of *Night of the Iguana*. She made friends with the actress Jill Bennett, who had an important part in the picture; one night, Jill took Bette to a club where the famous female impersonator Danny La Rue performed. She hated him and his performance, especially when he imitated her. Often, in the evenings, she told Jill that despite the bitter fight over Michael, she still felt a leap of affection when she thought of her first days with Merrill. Somehow, the hatred fell away and she remembered their good times together. But these feelings soon disappeared when, in the middle of production, she heard that Merrill had finally won the long struggle for full weekend access to their adopted son.

Enjoying vodkas in her dressing-room after work each evening with Jill Bennett, Bette gave her much useful advice. Jill Bennett says:

Bette told me, never see your rushes. You'll get depressed about how you look and you won't be able to do a thing about it. I always hated the way I looked on the screen. Bette did, too. I didn't need any encouragement not to see the rushes. I loved Bette. She was real, gutsy, and very dangerous. Dangerous the way a star should be. And she told me something wonderful. She told me, 'Always make love to your props. To the furniture.' I told her I remembered that wonderful moment in *The Little Foxes* when she leaned against the door as though she wanted to kiss it. I often found myself making love to tea trays in pictures after that.

One weekend, I had lunch with her at Grosvenor House. I bought her some yellow roses. She was waiting for me outside the elevator. No other star would do that. One night, we went to the greyhound races. She was got up tremendously for the occasion. She looked at me and said, 'You look awful. Why are you dressed like that?' I had a plain linen dress on. It was summer. I think a Mary Quant. She said, 'You won't be a star if you don't look like one.' She was in sequins and she said, 'I can't go into the races with you looking like this. You'll have to walk behind me as if you're my secretary.' And I did. It didn't bother me at all.

The Nanny was a modestly successful picture. Bette gave an intelligent, carefully controlled performance based on various nannies she had observed. She even bought her own nanny's uniform in order to give the part authenticity, dissatisfied with the uniform that had been offered to her.

Bette was entering a period calmer than any she had known. In her late fifties, she had no romantic entanglements except for a pleasant, undemanding, occasional romance with a wealthy publisher. She had sufficient money to live on and moved to a delightful house in Westport, Connecticut where she felt far more at home than in the imitation New England house in Bel Air. Although she wasn't particularly happy, she wasn't particularly miserable either. In her house, Twin Bridges, Number One, Crooked Mile, she knew a measure of peace. The house was called Twin Bridges because it adjoined a stream that was crossed by two small bridges. She brought back the traditional furnishings that had crossed the country so many times – sixteen in all, by rough count. She had the round dining-room table, the dining-room chairs that (she liked to laugh about it) were actually commodes. The many books and records, the antique chairs, the albums and scores from her pictures, the piano. Her favourite room, a tiny, cosy den, looked over the flashing stream.

She became more jealous than ever of her privacy. A black lady called Ivory kept house for her; Michael came home for school holidays; B.D. and Jeremy were often there; and Margot would visit on birthdays and anniversaries and holidays. Bette, in jeans and denim shirt, with a crazy hat usually perched on her thin reddish hair, took great pleasure in keeping everything spick and span for these arrivals. She seldom saw Bobby, who once again was suffering from severe nervous problems. She corresponded energetically with her cousins the Favors in Laguna.

She worked sporadically through 1966, co-hosting the *Mike Douglas Show,* appearing in *Gunsmoke* on television and the *Milton Berle Show*. Then, in mid-1967, she embarked on one of the worst pictures of her career.

Seventeen

The Anniversary was the story of a terrifying mother, one of whose sons was a transvestite, another a miserable husband, the third a promiscuous character. The action was crass and preposterous in the extreme: a study of manic possessiveness. Bette had to wear an eye patch over her left eye, which proved to be a constant irritation.

The picture was made for Hammer Productions, which specialised in low-grade horror films. Bette arrived in London determined to do what she could with the script. She quickly ran into drastic problems.

She intensely disliked the director, Alvin Rakoff. She felt that he was incapable of directing her; he had no ability to treat her with the kind of skill (and, perhaps deference) she felt she deserved. Bette failed to have much rapport with her fellow actress, the excellent Sheila Hancock. Miss Hancock says:

> I acted in the play of *The Anniversary* on the stage. I was acutely aware that Miss Davis wanted to replace me with Jill Bennett for the picture, and was annoyed because Jill wasn't available. I was terrified of what would happen when we started work. I was a working-class actor from the Royal Court Theatre and had no interest in the so-called star system. I wasn't used to venerating a star. I wasn't prepared for Miss Davis's great entourage

350

and for the fawning attitude it had towards her. I was shocked when the producer, Mr Sangster, gave us a lecture saying that Miss Davis liked to be treated with great adulation.

In the very first scene, Miss Davis came down a staircase. It was quite uncalled for by the scene, everybody in the studio, technicians, the lot, was present, all those not working on *The Anniversary* as well as those who were. And, as she made her descent, everyone clapped on cue. And she went back and did the scene again for the cameras. I was dumbfounded. I thought, 'This is rather silly.' It took me a while to realise this was the way Bette Davis was used to operating. She was a queen, after all.

Following the ridiculous beginning, Bette kept insisting the director be removed. She also wanted the camera operator fired. She summoned producer Sangster to her dressing-room. Sangster says:

I asked Bette, 'What's the problem?' She said, 'I don't like all this whispering. I'm working with an eye patch. At the end of a take, it's very dark and I hear the operator whispering to the rest of the crew. I want to know what's going on. I ask, haven't I hit my mark? I ask, haven't I hit a light? Have I covered somebody in a shot? Nobody answers me. Neither Rakoff nor the operator. I just hear this terrible whispering, and a voice shouts, "Let's have another take." I ask, "Why?" And the answer is, "Just let's have another take!" '

Sangster promised that all discussions would take place with her. Soon afterwards, Alvin Rakoff was fired by Sangster.

Immediately, Bette approved the hiring of Roy Ward

Baker, whom she had known before because he had directed Gary Merrill in *Night Without Sleep,* a picture which sounded like the story of her life. They had met at the premiere of *All About Eve* in New York and had travelled together to Los Angeles on the train.

Once more, Bette and Baker hit it off. She admired his professional polish and in turn he saw to it that she was expertly handled in her movements, handicapped as she was by the eye patch. He found her enormously interested in making the best picture possible. But the tensions with the camera operator and other members of the crew continued. Sheila Hancock says:

Bette Davis often had rows off set. I heard a lot of shouting from the dressing-room next door. People kept getting sacked; there was an awful atmosphere. I heard her say once, very loudly, from next door: 'I *hate* a good atmosphere on a picture. Every picture I've done where everybody had been hail-fellow-well-met had been a total disaster and any film that had been miserable to make was a success.' *The Anniversary* proved her wrong.

Sheila Hancock had to screw up her courage to even speak to Bette. She watched her doing a take and said, afterwards, with typical British reticence, 'That was pretty good.' Bette puffed at a cigarette and glowered. '*Pretty* good?' she snapped. 'Well, at least, thank God, somebody has said something. The highest compliment I've had on this picture is "Cut! Print it!" '

This bitterness persisted despite the change of director. Bette went home to her house in Elstree every night on the verge of tears from irritation, exhaustion, and the ever-maddening eye patch. Fortunately, Violla Rubber proved to be supportive, checking the rushes, taking care of problems as much as she could. Bette even quarrelled with her and, not long after, they completely fell out.

The picture was a pathetic affair; but Bette, so often faulty in her critical judgment, was clearly influenced by the fact that she was in every scene, that the movie was a showcase for her and that Roy Baker, unlike Alvin Rakoff, was all-out in his devotion to her talents; she promoted *The Anniversary* wherever she could. But it did not emerge as a critical or commercial success.

She plunged into even choppier waters when, after a brief break at Twin Bridges, she returned to Britain once more to make *Connecting Rooms* in 1969. It was the story of a middle-aged lady cellist in a lodging house in London, who shares a life of poverty with a gay professor and a hustling pop singer. If this sounded like a recipe for disaster, it was.

The director was an unknown called Franklin Gollings, a friend of Irving Rapper who specialised in Americana. He had managed to snare Sir Michael Redgrave to play the professor on the basis that Bette would play the cellist; and Bette on the promise of Michael Redgrave as her co-star. Neither Redgrave nor Davis liked the script, but they wanted to appear with each other.

Bette had approved the casting of the young Alexis Kanner as the pop singer. He was strong, vigorous and very masculine, with a slightly sinister undercurrent, and she felt he was ideal.

But she had to face the ordeal of getting Kanner up to her standards. She and Redgrave abandoned their caravan, shared due to the restricted conditions at the studio, so that Gollings could rehearse Kanner in there before every scene. Kanner was so inexperienced that complete privacy was necessary. It was a common scene at Pinewood to see Bette walking around and around the set, smoking furiously, because she didn't want to interrupt these crucial rehearsals.

She also had her problems with Gollings. He was

suffering from a bad case of influenza and was taking antibiotics. One day, he was driven to taking a scotch because of his problems with Bette. The scotch and antibiotics resulted in his appearing groggy through the morning's work. Suddenly, in a scene between Bette and the actress Kay Walsh, Gollings passed out and lay on the floor in front of them. Some men arrived with a stretcher and carried Gollings out. Bette immediately took over and directed the rest of the scene.

Later, when the scene was finished, Bette said loudly to everyone who would listen, 'Never in all my career of many years have I heard of such a thing as a director being carried off in the middle of the day.' And someone else said, 'That's a tall story, with Bette Davis around.'

There was a night location scene in a square in Bayswater. Bette had to appear in a first-floor room of an actual flophouse. She was about to start her acting when a drunken woman, a hag who had somehow found her way back into the building, yelled at her obscenely. Bette instantly responded in kind. Then she remembered her royal position and delivered a dainty speech in her little-girl voice: 'Ladies and gentlemen. Will you kindly accept my apologies for my terrible lapse in manners, and for using such awful words in front of you. I do apologise to you. That person who spoke so rudely got to me and I lost my usual self-control. I'm so pleased you're here, and I do hope you'll stay.' The pronouncement over, Bette went on with the scene.

Wherever she went, she drew crowds. In one scene, she played the cello for a line of people outside a theatre waiting to go into the gallery. When she arrived, in a Rolls Royce, shooting was held up for three-quarters of an hour as an immense crowd swooped down on her. She had to shake hands for forty-five minutes. She stepped out of the Rolls Royce dressed in clothes suited to a life of poverty. She made her way through a mob shouting endearments to her. Often, stars came by to pay court;

they had to fight to reach her, and almost got trampled in the process. She filmed until 5:30 A.M. and the crowds still had not gone away.

A problem was that Sir Michael Redgrave was ill during the shooting, and, like the director, made the mistake of taking a drink. In one sequence, he nearly fainted, and Bette had to 'carry' him in her arms through the scene. Another night, at a tube station she waited all night long with the unit and he didn't show up. He had been unable to find the telephone number where the director could be reached.

Connecting Rooms was so bad it was barely even released. Incredibly, it won the Diana Award, a Belgian honour. The award was presented to Redgrave at a club in Mayfair, London. He was so amazed at receiving it he forgot to mention Miss Davis in his acceptance speech. And then, to add insult to Bette's injury, Gollings failed to mention her in his acceptance speech as well.

Back in Hollywood, Bette appeared in Robert Wagner's series, *It Takes a Thief*. Wagner was one of her favourite people: an extroverted handsome tennis player with a fierce desire to improve the standards of television. She liked his toughness, aggression, charm and energetic momentum through life.

She attended a tribute to Jack Warner in which two thousand members of the world's press enjoyed soup, squab and ice cream on Soundstage Six. She gave a generous speech, burying the misery of her departure from the studio some eleven years earlier in carefully honeyed phrases. In a gesture at once theatrical and touching, she asked for the audience to stand and give silent tribute to all those Warner Brothers actors who had died.

She must have been painfully conscious of how much had been lost with the demise of a great studio when she became involved in a picture even worse than *The Anniversary* and *Connecting Rooms*: *Bunny O'Hare,*

355

about a bank-robbing woman who steals to support her children.

Once more, her serious misjudgment got the better of her. She thought that the script would allow her an agreeable change of pace.

She liked the director, Gerd Oswald, who had directed her in *It Takes a Thief*. He wasn't afraid of her and she liked his tough approach. When she said to him, 'If I make mistakes, tell me. Don't get scared of me,' he had replied, 'Don't worry. You bet your sweet life I'll tell you!' And she respected him from that moment on.

Oswald flew from Hollywood to Connecticut several times to discuss the screenplay with her. She made many intelligent suggestions. She was pleased that Ernest Borgnine would once again co-star with her; she had liked working with him in *The Catered Affair*. But when she went on location in New Mexico her happiness, her always limited optimism, rapidly dissolved.

She had to get up at 4:30 every morning and sit for hours in the savage sun that as always before seriously affected her delicate skin. She was bothered by freezing nights with rain, snow, and sleet, followed by more suffocating days. Oddly, she told Gerd Oswald that she would rather pictures were made in the studio, like *The Petrified Forest*. She had quite forgotten that that movie was shot partly on location in an even worse area, and that she had suffered even more drastically in it from exposure and heat.

Some scenes she had to shoot on the back of a motorcycle driving on dangerous mountain roads. She hated the ordeal of this, and many times felt like breaking her professional code and flying back to New England. But her will drove her on and on. Gerd Oswald remembers:

Bette and Borgnine didn't get on very well. I wouldn't want to say they were jealous of each

356

other, but they were both wanting to be on top of the situation. There was competition between them. It never reached the boiling point or anything like that. It was funny, in a way. One night, Ernie would come to me and sit with me and ask if a particular scene to be shot the next day could be steered in his direction. Next night, Bette would do exactly the same thing. Of course, I'm calling her Bette now, but none of us would have dared to do so then. She was 'Miss Davis' at all times. Even the cable boys who were still in their teens behaved as if they'd been in awe of her from the day she was born.

The harsh sun, the freezing nights, the competition with Borgnine, the impossible script, left Bette totally exhausted. And whatever merit the picture had was destroyed when it was cut to ribbons by the producers. Bette sued them, but finally was forced to let the case drop. It scarcely seemed worth it.

It was pleasant to return from Albuquerque to Westport. Bette went to Britain yet again, the one place left where her stock was high, to film a new melodramatic concoction called *Madame Sin* with Robert Wagner as her co-star. She had to play a strange half-Chinese woman who owns a large castle in Scotland: a kind of female version of Fu Manchu drawn from the bottom drawer of gothic schlockdom.

Madame Sin was intended as a pilot for a television series. Much of it was filmed on the island of Mull, off the coast of Scotland. No sooner had production begun, than Bette had one of her inevitable accidents. She was at the local hotel when a large bumblebee flew up the sleeve of her robe and stung her twice. She was allergic to stings and blacked out. When she came to, she found that her arm and mouth were severely swollen. The doctor scarcely cheered her up by telling her that she was lucky to be alive at all, since the bee had stung her in an artery.

Some scenes were shot at Pinewood Studios. She stayed briefly at a hotel called The Compleat Angler, and later at a house in Ascot facing the race course. A Mrs Bottoms, an Englishwoman who had worked for the Royal Family, kept house for her, as she had often done before.

Liv Ullman stayed in a cottage in the grounds of the Ascot house. Liv sat by her window for hours on weekends, hoping to catch a glimpse of Bette. One day, Bette's phone was out of order; she went to the cottage and rang Liv Ullman's doorbell. Miss Ullman was overwhelmed. They became friends at once.

The shooting was reasonably comfortable despite the fact that Bette had little rapport with the director, David Greene. But once again the results were barely tolerable, and *Madame Sin* was, perhaps fortunately, never developed into a series.

In Connecticut again, Bette was asked to appear in a television special called *The Killer Bees* for ABC. She was approached by ABC's Barry Diller; she insisted on discussing the show with the director, Curtis Harrington, whom she had met and enjoyed two years earlier. She told Harrington she liked the script, about yet another matriarch who runs a clan in the Napa Valley and has a mysterious command over swarms of bees. But she admitted she was terrified of having bees settle on her face. Harrington assured her the bees would be deprived of their stings. But she was fearful of a recurrence of the episode in the island of Mull and withdrew.

She was distracted, in the early 1970s, by helping a fan of hers, Whitney Stine, put together *Mother Goddam*: a record of names, dates and places, covering her career but omitting her private life and starting, rather oddly, in 1930. To enliven the book, she filled it with rude remarks or corrections, attacking her critics, dispensing praise and blame, and underlining or altering some of Stine's statements with acid good humour. This was perhaps the only biography ever published in which the subject contributed a running commentary on the material. Her remarks were in every way outrageous, and much more entertaining than the flat mechanical text with its endless recitation of information and its failure to come to grips with her personality.

It was a bad period; but it was followed by an extraordinary and exciting new development. In 1974, Bette embarked on her most ambitious venture in the theatre. This was *Miss Moffat*, a musical version of Emlyn Williams' *The Corn Is Green*, in which she had been so admirable under Irving Rapper's direction almost thirty years earlier. The director was Joshua Logan, about whom Bette had heard much from his former wife Barbara O'Neil when she made *All This and Heaven, Too*. She had never actually met Logan.

Logan had come to her after failing to attract Mary Martin for the project. He went out to Twin Bridges with her agent, Robert Lantz, and the musical's composer, Albert Hague. Hague sat at her living-room piano and played the score. She listened, plucking cigarettes from porcelain hens, striking wooden matches under the table, and nodding vigorous approval through clouds of smoke. She liked Logan rather well. But she was nervous of him. She, with Margot and Bobby and their suffering constantly present in her mind, was terrified of nervous sickness in her presence, and she knew, as most people in show business did, that Logan was subject to severe nervous and emotional breakdowns. She was impressed by his portly charm, his keen intelligence, his brilliant reputation in the theatre.

Back in New York after meeting, Logan wrote Bette the most impassioned letter of his life. He stated in it that it would be the thrill of his lifetime if she would star in his production. He promised her she would not have one worrying moment; that he would look after her in every possible way. Logan knew her fear of failure, that she could not have an understudy, that the audience was paying to see her and nobody else. He also knew her physical problems, her weak throat, aggravated by years of smoking, her attacks of laryngitis, her back never completely recovered from the fall down stairs.

Bette was deeply touched by the note and had twelve xeroxes made of it. She put the xeroxes in her handbag, her holdall, her make-up case, her travelling luggage and her pockets so that she would never be in a position where she couldn't read it. She wrote back to say that the letter would be close to hand at any given moment; she knew that if there were any trouble she would simply pull the letter out and say, 'Josh, read the letter you wrote me.' The letter gave her great reassurance; it made her decide to do the show; it allayed her fears of the theatre, of facing a live audience. And her fear of Logan.

She had met and liked Emlyn Williams, who had appeared in an important part in *Another Man's Poison*. She was delighted to renew their friendship and told him how much she admired his changing of the location of the story from Wales to the South. She was full of compliments for his portrait of the young would-be writer, who had now become a black.

Supported by Logan's admiration, in complete accord with Williams, Bette started preparing *Miss Moffat* with huge determination. It is possible she wanted to outmatch the great Katharine Hepburn who had made such a brilliant splash in *Coco* on Broadway shortly before.

At first, Bette didn't approve the choice of the excellent Dorian Harewood as the juvenile lead. But she began to waver after she had seen him in a reading, and rather uncertainly changed her mind.

She worked desperately at rehearsals, giving all of her talent to the rich and intelligently written central role.

Gradually, she grew used to Harewood, who belonged to a different world, and who had a belligerent modern uptightness along with his great skill that she found a little difficult to handle. Above all, despite her enthusiasm, she was terrified; as terrified as she had been when appearing in *Two's Company* and *The Night of the Iguana*. And she had the new painful realisation that she really couldn't sing. This hadn't mattered so much in *Two's Company,* in which she had only been a parodist, a *farceuse*; but on this occasion she would have to convey deep emotion in her songs. And there was no protection from the secure, comforting world of the old studio system. The new world of location shooting and stage appearances was more and more terrifying.

To judge by his memoirs, Logan was troubled by Bette's insecurities, and perhaps not entirely sympathetic to them. He was used to working with hardcore theatrical professionals who would take on anything at its own level. He was upset by the fact that instead of half singing, half speaking the numbers, she wanted to sing them straight out.

Her psychosomatic fear and tension combined with her old spinal problem to cause a severe pain in her back that made working day by day excruciating. There is no doubt that the fear intensely aggravated the problem and that forced her into traction after working for only a few weeks. Logan was impatient, and Bette was more painfully aware than ever what a disaster it would be for him, for Emlyn Williams and the producers if she could not appear. She forced herself against her nerves and nightmares to come back to work just before the opening in Philadelphia.

The show was sold out for six months. Bette's audience of middle-aged and older women and gays had rushed in droves to buy tickets. The whole tour was sold out. The show was excellent despite some technical mishaps on the first night, but Bette was not quite at her best. She had a bad attack of stage fright and her voice was giving out as it so often had done before. She fluffed some lines and transposed others. Logan recalled in his memoirs that to his horror Bette turned to the audience at one stage and said, 'How can I play this scene?' She was complaining because Dorian Harewood, who was not yet ready to follow the cue, wasn't on stage. When Bette realised she had made a mistake, she turned to the audience and said, 'I was wrong. I want you to know that. It wasn't his fault. Go back, Dorian, and we'll start over.' Dorian Harewood, embarrassed and sweating, made a second entrance.

Logan says that at another occasion in the production, a child in the show thought she was drying up and whispered her line to her. She snapped loudly in front of the audience, 'Don't tell me my line! I know it! You're a naughty little boy!' The child started to cry.

Logan, watching in the wings, and from the back of the house, was desperate. He felt he wanted to take a cruise to the end of the world. But the audience gave Bette a standing ovation.

The reviews were not good. According to Dorian Harewood, everyone panicked including Bette and Logan. Emlyn Williams began rewriting the show. Bette found she was rehearsing one version of the show in the morning, playing another version in the afternoon twice a week, and at night, and was constantly being fitted for new costumes between performances. Songs were put in, others were dropped. Logan was trying to sharpen the show in response to the critics' comments. Broadway loomed ahead. But Bette felt this panic was unnecessary. The show was sold out for six months. She had had six weeks of gruelling rehearsals and surely minor changes would be enough.

Bette was used to the control she had over motion picture scripts and shooting. In all the bad pictures she had made, mostly in England, during the past few years, she had obtained complete command of everything. The results had been disastrous, but at least nothing had been changed in the writing without her permission. Now, she realised she had no control. She was being asked to read lines prepared in haste and entirely over her head. She began to go to pieces. Logan indicates in his book that he found her behaviour intolerable; that her breakdown was inexplicable to him. But he didn't realise the full story of her long imperial progress through trash over most of a decade. Or how easily she could be scared by supreme professionals like him, when she had worked only with mediocrities who were subservient to her will.

Inevitably, she broke down completely. Whether psychologically or physically, or perhaps both, her nature cracked and she took to her bed in severe agony and misery, deciding she could no longer continue. One morning, after she had given a perfect performance, the pain became unendurable. Logan called an independent doctor who said point blank that if she continued she would die. She was over sixty-eight years old and, unlike Hepburn, who followed a health regime and was possessed of iron nerves, she was not in the best of health and her perilously weak nervous system was once again in disarray.

She was genuinely distraught that she would have to give up. Logan clearly felt she had behaved mischievously and irresponsibly. But he was mistaken. He simply hadn't understood her tortured psyche; that this attack of cowardice and desperation had a hundred previous exemplars in her behaviour over the years. It was part of her pattern. It was neither unusual nor capricious.

It is unfortunate that *Miss Moffat*, which might have been the crowning triumph of Bette Davis's career, instead put the nail in the coffin of any hopes she might have had of returning permanently to the stage. Just as she swore she would never shoot on location again after *Bunny O'Hare,* so she swore she would never work in the theatre again as long as she lived.

Miss Moffat was an ordeal of ordeals – and an equally severe one for Bette was reading Logan's account of it years later. She threatened a libel suit against Logan, then abandoned it. Evidently, she dreaded the prospect of having to relive the whole experience on the witness stand.

There were consolations. Despite his miserable childhood, torn between his adopted father and mother, Michael Merrill grew up to be a well-balanced, healthy, athletic, normal American youth. He followed in Bette's father's footsteps, showing a keen interest in law, and went to law school, from which he graduated with high honours. Tall and solidly built, he was the apple of Bette's eye. He married, happily, a girl called Chou-chou Rains, the marriage worked out successfully, and soon Bette was a grandmother again. B.D.'s marriage to Jeremy Hyman continued, despite all of Bette's fears, to be a great success. Bette's marital agonies, the long history of emotional conflict in the Davises and the Favors had at last, it seemed, worked themselves out in this newest generation. And in her children, and her grandchildren, Bette found cause for rejoicing. She would look up at big, imposing B.D. like a child looking up at its own mother. B.D. had a strong will of her own without her mother's emotional fragility. She had an imposing strength that seemed to hark back to Grandmother Favor. She was born of Plymouth Rock.

B.D. and Jeremy settled down on a farm in New England where they raised cattle and chickens. Perhaps because of the many storms of her childhood, B.D. wanted peace and safe harbour. Certainly, after an early fascination, she had no interest in following the tormented puzzle of Bette's film and theatrical career in her own life. And Jeremy had no desire to emulate his successful family in the picture industry, with the constant strain, fears and tensions that lay behind the supposedly glamorous front of a movie executive's life. He was well aware how quickly a Mercedes or a Rolls Royce could change into a tumbril.

Michael joined a law firm and quickly emerged as a successful young attorney. He inherited his adopted mother's quick wit and sharp intelligence without her neuroses and her recurrent sense of guilt.

Bette followed a current fashion in the mid-1970s by making a series of personal appearances both at home and on tour. Her first appearance was at the National Film Theatre in London, under the direction of her friend Roy Moseley. It was a sell out; thousands of people were left out and hundreds lined the streets to see Bette arrive. It was a Sunday afternoon; Max Factor's opened specially for her so that she could be made up before she faced the audience. As she drove from Max Factor on Bond Street across Piccadilly Circus, down the Haymarket, along the Strand to Waterloo Bridge and across to the National Film Theatre on the South Bank, with Moseley at her side, people ran at the car. They recognised her all the way along. She was cheered as she stepped out of the Rolls and the crowd carried her a foot off the ground. She entered at the back of the auditorium; it took her eight minutes to reach the stage. People were touching her, holding her back, they wouldn't let her reach the stage. At last they released her and she walked on to a standing ovation. She was overjoyed when her frantic 'They're Either Too Young or Too Old', from *Thank Your Lucky Stars* was flashed on the screen. Too often, she had watched the picture on American television, only to discover to her disappointment that the sequence was missing.

She gave a brilliant lecture which triumphantly sustained her self-made image of brisk, no-nonsense, down-to-earth, salty New England horse sense. It was one of her most sustained performances: not a hint of nerves, insecurity, guilt, ego fragility, self-dislike or physical torment: all those things which had driven her to great performances. By seeming to be the public's image of her, she in fact became somebody else. This public Bette Davis was as much a *doppelgänger* as the good twin in *A Stolen Life*; she was 'done with mirrors' like the performance of a great magician. She was that same alter ego on the stage, humorous, pulled-together, playing with even-handed skill to the gays and the straights, that she had delivered in a bright blue ribbon package to journalists for fifty years. Just as she had always given the same interview, worked out from first word to last to disguise herself, so she had always given the same off-screen performance. And that night's was the performance of her lifetime.

After the lecture, Bette went up the staircase into the Green Room for a champagne reception. Roy Moseley had specified (he knew what he was doing) that no film stars or celebrities of any kind would be present. She had the floor, and if anyone had tried to upstage her she would still have triumphed. She immediately occupied centre stage. With her old theatrical knowledge, she gained maximum attention by seemingly being minimal. She sat on the floor cross-legged, surrounded by people who had to bend double over their drinks to talk to her. She announced, cleverly, in her little-girl voice, that she would only stay for half an hour, while firmly intending to stay for an hour and a half. The organisers begged her not to sign autographs before she left. She compromised by only signing copies of *The Lonely Life* and *The Films of Bette Davis*. Moseley carried her out bodily through the crowd; her feet hardly touched the floor. Out on Waterloo Bridge, crowds were gathered to get a glimpse of her. People had to be pushed off the Rolls; they were crawling on the roof. The chauffeur could barely get the door open, and when he did, it was almost pulled off its hinges. So many people crushed against Bette as she finally entered the car, that her legs were bruised all the way to the thighs.

Later, John Springer, a well-known publicity man, organised 'Bette Davis at Town Hall' in New York. He asked her questions and more came from the floor. The audience, plentifully filled out with her gay admirers, enjoyed her hugely. Once more, she acted up a storm as her other self.

She toured with Springer – even going all the way to Australia to appear at the Sydney Opera House. She was astonished when out of the cavernous darkness of the concert hall a voice she hadn't heard in a quarter of a century asked her a question. It was Casey Robinson, author of several of her best vehicles at Warners, who had settled in Australia with his wife Joan.

The Australian tour was as much a triumph as Mary Astor's in *The Great Lie*. Bette reconquered England on a tour for the impresario Billy Marsh. A sour note was struck when Marsh came to see her at Grosvenor House in London and told her she would be at the London Palladium but that the upper circle would be closed. Bette took this as a personal insult. How dare Marsh bring Bette Davis back to England, and then not have enough faith in her that 3,000 seats of the Palladium would be completely filled? She said that she positively wouldn't even enter a theatre unless every single seat in it all the way to the rafters was sold. Marsh quailed before her wrath; he soon found that every seat was indeed quickly disposed of on her name. She made three appearances at the Palladium and could easily have appeared there twice nightly for a month.

One night, somebody in the audience who knew a thing or two shouted out of the darkness, 'Miss Davis, I'd like to have a wager with you that I can name the mystery man, the mystery romance in your life that you wrote about in your autobiography.' She paused for a minute and looked up at the gallery. Thoughts of Wyler must have flooded into her mind: her refusal to name the one man who could have mastered her, who could have matched her in a marriage in terms of income and professional importance, who could have pitted his strength against hers, whose ego was if possible as colossal as her own. But she would still keep faith with her long-held secret. She paused, and said: 'No, I won't risk the wager. You just *could* be right.'

She brought the house down several times. This imitation Davis could emphatically laugh at herself in public. Somebody called out, rudely, 'Is that your real hair, Miss Davis?' And she lied expertly (she was wearing a wig that day), 'Yes, it is. And these are my real eyes, my real teeth and my real tits!' The gay crowd went completely mad and gave her a standing ovation on the spot.

From that moment on, Bette eschewed wearing a wig in public. She didn't need to, as it happened: her ash blonde hair was always pretty, and looked fine when dyed auburn or even a reddish-gold. The only problem was it was rather thin and lacked body; it gave hairdressers a hard time, but the results of their labours were often strikingly attractive.

Bette realised she needed a personal hairdresser. In 1974 she hired, oddly enough, Joan Crawford's. Peggy Shannon had been fired by Joan for talking too much about Joan's miserable private life. Peggy spent hours fussing over Bette's wigs, one of which was striped and made her look like a tiger. Peggy was a strange, rangy presence: six foot tall, with a mouth full of very large teeth, given to wearing Bermuda shorts over skinny legs or trousers with boots up to her knees. Today, after seven years of employment, Miss Shannon still refers to Bette as 'Miss Davis'.

Always, Bette quarrelled and made up with successive members of her personal entourage, which included at various times, a pleasant, intelligent young English male secretary, Vic Greenfield, the antique dealer Chuck Pollock, Robert Wagner, the devoted Roy Moseley, her lawyer (the expert Harold Schiff) and her agent, Robbie Lantz. But Peggy Shannon, angular and resolute, was her most constant companion, succeeding such earlier female acolytes as her maids Adele and Ivory and the remarkable Violla Rubber. The test of staying with Bette was a capacity to determine her ever-shifting moods.

The late 1970s were years of almost constant work. Television occupied most of Bette's time. She appeared in a four-hour version of Thomas Tryon's *Harvest Home,* as an elderly dowager with supernatural powers, in long black dresses and a small starched white cap like an Amish farmer's wife. On location in Ohio, a local witch coven took exception to her performance, pelted her caravan with stones, and threatened to set fire to it. She had to have police protection.

Harvest Home was done in a rush, partly because of the gruelling schedules of television, partly because she had to hurry off to Egypt to make *Death on the Nile.* The situation was so extreme that when some of her lines had to be 'looped', while Bette was in Egypt, the female impersonator Michael Greer matched her voice in the dubbing sessions.

Always fond of exotic locations, Bette had much enjoyed Australia and now responded vibrantly to Egypt. She revelled in her part of a haughty rich woman suspected of murder on a Nile cruise. She was paid an enormous amount of money and behaved like a dream, challenged by the formidable all-star cast. She was especially fond of Angela Lansbury and David Niven and Maggie Smith. She was generous with advice to the young, handsome but inexperienced Simon MacCorkindale. She was entirely in accord with the director, the stern disciplinarian John Guillermin.

Bette's behaviour on *Death on the Nile,* co-operating, doing everything consummately, indicated that at the age of seventy her fires might at last be banked, that she was finally achieving a degree of balance and calm. Yet at the same time, expert though her performance was, it lacked the nervous edge, the brilliance she conveyed at her best. She was in stronger form in two intriguing television specials: *Strangers* and *White Momma.* In *Strangers,* she was for once cast with an actress of comparable power: the extraordinary Gena Rowlands. She played a reclusive mother in a small town whose daughter returns after twenty years of absence. At first, there is a terrific antagonism; the daughter is determined to win the mother for a purpose that we don't know about. Finally, the daughter succeeds. There is a scene in a restaurant in which both actresses are at their best. The daughter tells her mother that the reason she needs sympathy and warmth is that she is dying of cancer. Here, the writing had a daring seldom found in television. Instead of bursting into tears and embracing the child, the mother reacts with bitter anger and revulsion. It was a scene that only an actress in full command of her powers could have carried off. It was one of Bette's finest moments on the screen.

White Momma, directed by the former child-star Jackie Cooper, was less satisfactory: a rather too anaemic study of a difficult, edgy but sympathetic black boy and an old woman he befriends when she is threatened with eviction. But in one scene, Davis is admirable. She returns home to her apartment of many years to find all of her furniture gone. The director cleverly shoots her from the back, so that her face cannot be seen. But the actress doesn't need a close-up. The body seems suddenly to be broken in front of us. It doesn't merely sag with disappointment and hopelessness; it is as though every bone has been shattered and splintered. It is a sequence that proves, once and for all, that Bette Davis today is as great an actress as she has ever been.

And as so often in her life before, reality disturbingly matched a screen invention. There was a strange, disturbing parallel with *Strangers* in the year of its making, 1979, when Bobby came to see Bette from her home in Phoenix, Arizona. At first, Bobby seemed better than she had in years and Bette hugged her tightly, delighted by her appearance and the absence of any drastic sign of nervous stress. But, that evening, Bobby told her the truth: she had been stricken with cancer, and had only a few months to live. The shock was grievous and Bobby's death horribly distressing. Without exaggeration, one can say that Bette did everything in her power to make Bobby's life a decent and happy one. But it was a battle lost from the beginning.

And along with the anguish of seeing Bobby ill, there was the perennial unhappiness of seeing Margot, who was now over forty, still with the intelligence of a child of six, still confined in a home in the East, still talking to Bette with the same harrowing repetitions and about the same things she had recited blankly in 1951. Time had stopped for Margot; she was trapped in a kind of hell which the constant attentiveness of her successive teachers could only partly penetrate. Sometimes Bette would leave her feeling desperately weary in spirit; but at least she knew that unlike so many mentally retarded patients, Margot didn't have to live her life out in brutal establishments with dangerous and violent inmates. Because of Bette's loving concern and great fame Margot was assured of the best possible care. And that had to be Bette's consolation in her anguish.

Gary Merrill occupied a converted lighthouse on the coast of Maine. He occasionally visited Bette, B.D. and Michael. He mellowed in late middle age and stopped drinking; after years, he returned to the stage in an excellent performance in the Broadway hit, *Morning's at Seven*.

Family ties remained. Bette spent as much time as she

371

could with her cousins, the Favors, in Laguna. Interestingly, she was very close to William Wyler and his wife Margaret Tallichet to whom she had lost that great love of her life. She was still very fond of her childhood friend Robin Brown, who lived in Connecticut, and of Betty Lynn, the diminutive former ingénue she had known since *June Bride*. Today, Bette's life is perhaps happier than it has been since her mid-thirties. She seldom goes to the theatre or to movies. When she went to a motion picture theatre in Weston, Connecticut, to which she moved from Westport in 1978, she arranged for herself and friends to see the movie in the projection booth. Always embarrassed by attention when she was not on show, she had now become virtually a recluse.

Much of the time she spends at home, which at time of writing is a large apartment in the Colonial House, on leafy Havenhurst Avenue in West Hollywood. It is almost opposite an apartment building where she lived briefly before moving to the DeMille cottage she shared with Ham on Franklin Avenue in the first years of their marriage. Sometimes, her old sense of humour flares up: she greeted her closest friends on her seventieth birthday in blackface, carrying a banjo.

In 1977, she received the American Film Institute life achievement award. Looking youthful and attractive, she made a tremendous impression; Geraldine Fitzgerald, Henry and Jane Fonda, Celeste Holm and an insufferably garrulous Joseph L. Mankiewicz joined in tribute to her career.

She was, in 1981, an angel on the set of her pictures. Punctual and disciplined, she is in constant demand on TV and was memorable in black hat, veil, and puffing a cigarette on *Good Morning, America*, laughing uproariously at jokes made at her expense, including Brian Aherne's in his memoirs: 'At the height of her career, nobody loved her but her mother!' She is alive and well and emphatically Bette Davis. Could one ask for more?

BETTE DAVIS'S PERFORMANCES

Stage

Cukor-Kondolf Repertory Theatre   Rochester   1928
The Earth Between   Virgil Geddes   1929
The Wild Duck   Henrik Ibsen   1929
The Lady from the Sea   Henrik Ibsen   1929
Broken Dishes   Martin Flavin   1929
Mr. Pim Passes By   A. A. Milne   1930
Solid South   Lawton Campbell   1930
Two's Company   Charles Sherman   1952
The World of Carl Sandburg
Carl Sandburg   1959-1960
The Night of the Iguana
Tennessee Williams   1961-1962
Miss Moffat   Emlyn Williams   1974

Films

Bad Sister   Director, Hobart Henley   1931
Seed   Director, John M. Stahl   1931
Waterloo Bridge   Director, James Whale   1931
Way Back Home   Director, William A. Seiter   1931
The Menace   Director, Roy William Neill   1932
Hell's House   Director, Howard Higgins   1932
The Man Who Played God
Director, John Adolfi   1932
So Big   Director, William A. Wellman   1932
The Rich Are Always With Us
Director, Alfred E. Green   1932
The Dark Horse   Director, Alfred E. Green   1932

Cabin in the Cotton Director, Michael Curtiz 1932
Three on a Match Director, Mervyn LeRoy 1932
20,000 Years in Sing Sing
Director, Michael Curtiz 1933
Parachute Jumper Director, Alfred E. Green 1933
The Working Man Director, John Adolfi 1933
Ex-Lady Director, Robert Florey 1933
Bureau of Missing Persons
Director, Roy Del Ruth 1933
Fashions of 1934 Director, William Dieterle 1934
The Big Shakedown
Director, John Francis Dillon 1934
Jimmy the Gent Director, Michael Curtiz 1934
Fog over Frisco Director, William Dieterle 1934
Of Human Bondage Director, John Cromwell 1934
Housewife Director, Alfred E. Green 1934
Bordertown Director, Archie Mayo 1935
The Girl from Tenth Avenue
Director, Alfred E. Green 1935
Front Page Woman Director, Michael Curtiz 1935
Special Agent Director, William Keighley 1935
Dangerous Director, Alfred E. Green 1935
The Petrified Forest Director, Archie Mayo 1936
The Golden Arrow Director, Alfred E. Green 1936
Satan Met a Lady Director, William Dieterle 1936
Marked Woman Director, Lloyd Bacon 1937
Kid Galahad Director, Michael Curtiz 1937
That Certain Woman
Director, Edmund Goulding 1937
It's Love I'm After Director, Archie Mayo 1937
Jezebel Director, William Wyler 1938
The Sisters Director, Anatole Litvak 1938
Dark Victory Director, Edmund Goulding 1939
Juarez Director, William Dieterle 1939
The Old Maid Director, Edmund Goulding 1939
The Private Lives of Elizabeth and Essex
Director, Michael Curtiz 1939

All This and Heaven, Too
Director, Anatole Litvak   1940
The Letter   Director, William Wyler   1940
The Great Lie   Director, Edmund Goulding   1941
The Bride Came C.O.D.
Director, William Keighley   1941
The Little Foxes   Director, William Wyler   1941
The Man Who Came to Dinner
Director, William Keighley   1942
In This Our Life   Director, John Huston   1942
Now, Voyager   Director, Irving Rapper   1942
Watch on the Rhine   Director, Herman Shumlin   1943
Thank Your Lucky Stars   Director, David Butler   1943
Old Acquaintance   Director, Vincent Sherman   1943
Mr. Skeffington   Director, Vincent Sherman   1944
Hollywood Canteen   Director, Delmer Daves   1944
The Corn Is Green   Director, Irving Rapper   1945
A Stolen Life   Director, Curtis Bernhardt   1946
Deception   Director, Irving Rapper   1946
Winter Meeting   Director, Bretaigne Windust   1948
June Bride   Director, Bretaigne Windust   1948
Beyond the Forest   Director, King Vidor   1949
All About Eve   Director, Joseph L. Mankiewicz   1950
Payment on Demand
Director, Curtis Bernhardt   1951
Another Man's Poison   Director, Irving Rapper   1952
Phone Call from a Stranger
Director, Jean Negulesco   1952
The Star   Director, Stuart Heisler   1953
The Virgin Queen   Director, Henry Koster   1955
The Catered Affair   Director, Richard Brooks   1956
Storm Center   Director, Daniel Taradash   1956
John Paul Jones   Director, John Farrow   1959
The Scapegoat   Director, Robert Hamer   1959
Pocketful of Miracles   Director, Frank Capra   1961
What Ever Happened to Baby Jane?
Director, Robert Aldrich   1962

Dead Ringer   Director, Paul Henreid   1964
The Empty Canvas   Director, Damiano Damiani   1964
Where Love Has Gone
Director, Edward Dmytryk   1964
Hush, Hush, Sweet Charlotte
Director, Robert Aldrich   1964
The Nanny   Director, Seth Holt   1965
The Anniversary   Director, Roy Ward Baker   1968
Connecting Rooms   Director, Franklin Gollings   1969
(Released 1972)
Bunny O'Hare   Director, Gerd Oswald   1971
Lo Scopone Scientifico (The Scientific Card
Player)   Director, Luigi Comencini   1972
Burnt Offerings   Director, Dan Curtis   1976
Death on the Nile   Director, John Guillermin   1978
Return from Witch Mountain
Director, John Hough   1978
Watcher in the Woods   Director, John Hough   1980

(Since 1970, Bette Davis has appeared in television
movies)

INDEX

380

384

386

NEL BESTSELLERS

Even Chance	*Elizabeth Bennett*	£1.50
The Marriage Bed	*Constance Beresford Howe*	£1.75
Lights, Laughter and a Lady	*Barbara Cartland*	£1.25
Forefathers	*Nancy Cato*	£2.50
Maura's Dream	*Joel Gross*	£2.25
Memory and Desire	*Justine Harlowe*	£2.50
Only Perfect	*Rochelle Larkin*	£1.75
Sisters	*Linda Lauren*	£1.50
Almonds and Raisins	*Maisie Mosco*	£1.95
The Enticers	*Natasha Peters*	£1.95
Believing in Giants	*Charlotte Vale Allen*	£1.75

All these books are available at your local bookshop or newsagent, or can be ordered direct from the publisher. Just tick the titles you want and fill in the form below.

NEL P.O. BOX 11, FALMOUTH TR10 9EN, CORNWALL

Postage Charge:

U.K. Customers 45p for the first book plus 20p for the second book and 14p for each additional book ordered to a maximum charge of £1.63.

B.F.P.O. & EIRE Customers 45p for the first book plus 20p for the second book and 14p for the next 7 books; thereafter 8p per book.

Overseas Customers 75p for the first book and 21p per copy for each additional book.

Please send cheque or postal order (no currency).

Name ....

Address ....

....

Title ....

While every effort is made to keep prices steady, it is sometimes necessary to increase prices at short notice. New English Library reserve the right to show on covers and charge new retail prices which may differ from those advertised in the text or elsewhere. (C)